THE
VIRTUOUS
CONSUMER

THE
VIRTUOUS
CONSUMER

YOUR ESSENTIAL SHOPPING
GUIDE FOR A BETTER, KINDER,
HEALTHIER WORLD

LESLIE GARRETT
FOREWORD BY PETER GREENBERG

New World Library
Novato, California

New World Library
14 Pamaron Way
Novato, California 94949

Cover design and illustrations by Laura Beers
Interior design by Maxine Ressler; interior illustrations by Laura Beers and Maxine Ressler

Sherman's Lagoon comic on page 10 copyright © 2006 by Jim Toomey / distributed by King
Features Syndicate. Reprinted with permission.
Fisher comics on pages 59 and 178 copyright © 2006, 2007 by Philip Street. Reprinted with
permission. *Fisher* appears in *The Globe and Mail* and at www.philipstreet.com.
Bizarro comic on page 101 copyright © 2005 by Dan Piraro. Distributed by King Features
Syndicate. Reprinted with permission.
Betty comic on page 130 copyright © 2006 by Gerry Rasmussen and Gary Delainey /
distributed by United Feature Syndicate. Reprinted with permission.

Author's Note: This book was written to provide accurate information on how to live and
shop in an environmentally and socially responsible manner. While I sought out the most
informative and informed experts available, the information is not meant to replace or
be a substitute for professional legal, medical, nutritional, engineering, or other advice.
Please always use your best judgment. And while every effort was made to ensure that the
information was accurate at the time of printing, I and the publisher accept no responsibility for errors or changes in information.

New World Library is a member of the Green Press Initiative, a nonprofit
program dedicated to supporting publishers in their efforts to reduce their use
of fiber sourced from endangered forests. We elected to print this title on 100
percent postconsumer-waste recycled paper, processed chlorine free. As a result, we have
saved the following resources: 57 trees, 3,635 pounds of solid waste, 41,204 gallons of
water, 7,983 pounds of net greenhouse gases. For more information on the Green Press
Initiative, visit www.greenpressinitiative.org.

Library of Congress
Cataloging-in-Publication Data
available on request.

First printing, July 2007
ISBN-10: 1-930722-74-5
ISBN-13: 978-1-930722-74-3

Printed in Canada on acid-free, 100% postconsumer-waste recycled paper

10 9 8 7 6 5 4 3 2 1

Contents

Foreword

It seems like there's no middle ground left in the world. We either take ourselves too seriously, or we laugh too much. We make tough rules, or we ignore them. What's missing? Common sense and responsibility. If I've learned anything, it's that you can't have one without the other. Too many of us have been irresponsible, one-dimensional, and unbalanced for far too long. And the price we can pay for that dangerous combination in our personal lives and the environment is far too high.

Leslie Garrett writes not about inflexible doctrine but about choice. She proposes not rules but thoughtful options, to make not just your life better but mine as well.

She rightfully questions buzzwords that have been either overused or manipulated to give us the false impression that we are doing the right thing. Furthermore, Garrett then points us in the right direction.

I embrace her approach—that it's not about product but about *process*. Ask children today where food comes from, and they'll tell you . . . the store. How sad. If you can't understand the process, how can you ever truly appreciate the product as it exists in a larger, global context? Who grew it? Made it? Got it to market? Have you ever considered these issues?

Garrett cuts through those questions in teaching us—without taking herself too seriously—how to be a virtuous consumer. The best part? We get to laugh. And every once in a while, we still get to break some of the rules.

This is an important book. It is a life manual that doesn't preach but *presents*. It is an essential guidebook to redefining our daily lives, whether we stay at home or, like me, travel. And for some of us, who consider ourselves intelligent but as consumers remain woefully unenlightened—myself included—it could not have been written at a better time.

PETER GREENBERG
Travel Editor, NBC *Today Show*

Acknowledgments

This book began, literally, with a dream and has become a reality—thanks in no small part to those around me who value dreams . . . and dreamers. First to Peter Greenberg, who believed in *The Virtuous Consumer* from the start. And to Amy Rennert who took a chance on a stranger with an idea for a book. To David Bennett who graciously stepped aside. To Karen Bouris and the amazing staff at Inner Ocean who "got" this book from the beginning and who, therefore, got the book into print. To my husband, Daniel Kelly, who, from the very start, told me to go for it. To my three children who only occasionally roll their eyes at me when I start ranting about fast food or tell me they're "tired of hearing about the poor people." But who then tell their own friends about what goes on at factory farms and what spews from the tailpipes of cars. I'm sorry, kids, that you'll likely spend considerable time being social pariahs before the world embraces you. It's all my fault.

To my two dogs who've kept me company in my home office these long, lonely months.

And to the wonderful people who've joined me on this journey and have been so generous with their time, their expertise, and their encouragement—some appear in these pages, others don't but are no less present:

Michelle Bain	Mark Evanoff
Dan Becker	Mandi Fields
Annie Berthold-Bond	Annette Gaffney
Carol Besler	Deborah Garcia
Allan Britnell	JoAnne Garrett
Mary Brune	Dalton Garrett
Alma Bune	Robin Grindley
Ronnie Cummins	Jane Houlihan
Sean DeVries	Ben Howe
Lisa DiMartino	Plum Johnson
Melanie Doerksen	Billie Karel

Niki Lagos
Debbie Langer
Hélène Lawler
Pete Ledwon and Marilyn Mets
Susan Linn
William Maas
Maria MacRae
Stacy Malkan
David Masters
J. B. MacKinnon and
    Alisa Smith
Elizabeth May
Diana Morgan
David Muchow
Marion Nestle
Summer Rayne Oakes
John Perry
Dan Piraro
Kim Pittaway
Michael Pollan
Jennifer Pritchett and
    Jessica Giordani at
    the Smitten Kitten
Suzanne Quinn
William Rathje

Craig Ritchie
Tiffany Roschkow, Tracy
    Robinson, and the gang at
    Green Drinks London
Gary Ruskin
Anita Rychlo
Judy Ann Sadler
Karen Seriguchi
Simone Smith and
    Ryan Kennedy
Ted Schettler
Philip Street
David Suzuki
Wendy Tremayne
Ann Vanderhoof and
    Steve Manley
Lee VanLieshout
Jason Wentworth
John Wade
Barbie Wagner
Frank Zaski
And many more who have
    shared their stories and
    cheered me on

> I still believe that peace and plenty and happiness can be worked out some way. I am a fool. Kurt Vonnegut, Jr.

Why I Wrote This Book

I've never attended a rally for the poor. Or written a letter of protest to a corporation whose policies are emasculating male sea turtles. Or gone on a hunger strike (unless you count the times I needed to lose five pounds by the weekend to fit into a size six). I hate tofu, have never chained myself to an old-growth tree, and don't drive a VW van powered by French-fry grease.

I like lipstick. And shoes.

But I think about the hole in the ozone layer as I slather sunscreen on my children. I cringe at the reports of children in third-world countries who are sold into bondage by their desperate families to factories that make *my* kids' toys. I worry about the increasing number of "smog days" our local radio station warns us about. I puzzle over food packages that list ingredients I can't pronounce. I hack away at the plastic that encases everything from CDs to tiny vials of face cream, cursing the corporations that seem to think their products are so worthy of toxic protection. I cry at *Free Willy*.

I buy cosmetics that weren't first worn by a bunny. I compost. I recycle. I buy secondhand. And organic, when I can afford it.

I'm probably a lot like you.

I am, however, a journalist—which means I enjoy badgering people and asking questions. I'm not afraid to phone David Suzuki to find out what, exactly, organic food is or ask Ronnie Cummins who founded the Organic Consumers Association whether organic food is really "organic" if it's made from the powdered milk of an organically raised cow half a world away. And contact UNICEF to find out what's up with allegations of child labor being used to make backyard fireworks. Or ask some

Five Products That Make Me Crazy
1. Hummers
2. Swiffers, Pledge wipes, and other disposables
3. Water in plastic bottles
4. Polly Pocket dolls
5. Oscar Mayer Lunchables

Five Eco-Products I Love
1. My bicycle and trailer in summer; my new hybrid in winter.
2. My clothesline.
3. My organic cotton, sweat-shop free little black dress.
4. Fair-trade organic dark chocolate from Green & Black's.
5. Bonterra organic 2001 North Coast Cabernet Sauvignon

corporate bigwig what the deal is with the way his products are manufactured. And ask again when he gives me a load of crap.

I'm also a great believer in the power of informed choice to bring about change.

Frankly, I'm ready for it. I'm not ready to move myself off the grid, grow my own vegetables, and churn my own butter. But I *am* ready for products that I can buy with a clear conscience. Or at least a clearer conscience.

They're out there—more every day—if you know what to look for.

I've also made a discovery that just might revolutionize the consumer world. If I shop armed not only with a conscience but also with the facts to act according to it, I feel better. Not just "I have a great new purse" better but "my great new purse is supporting a women's cooperative in the Philippines and recycling juice boxes at the same time" better. I feel a genuine connection to people I've never met and to this planet we share as our home. Not bad for a morning at the mall.

How Virtuous Are You?

Take this quick quiz to determine where you fall on the scale of virtuous consumption:

1. Which is the better choice: the fair-trade apple from South Africa, the organic apple from Fiji, or the apple from the farm down the road?

2. When you're cold inside, do you put on a sweater and make a pot of fair-trade green tea or crank up the heat to 76 degrees and fire up the blender for margaritas?

3. Which is the greater producer of greenhouse gas emissions: driving cars or rearing cattle?

4. Does a car fuelled by vegetable oil have zero greenhouse gas emissions?

5. Is organic food expensive?

6. Do you think public transit is for suckers who don't own cars?

7. Can meat or milk from a cloned animal be considered organic if the animal is raised to organic standards?

8. Which fabric is more earth-friendly: cotton or polyester?

9. With breast milk showing increasing levels of flame retardant chemicals, among others, should mothers turn to formula?

10. Can production of genetically modified food help solve the world hunger problem?

Answers:

1. From an environmental perspective, the local apple is the one to choose. However, from a social justice standpoint, supporting fair-trade products sends a strong message. Pick your cause then take a bite.

2. Mom was right. Snuggle up and feel virtuous. Save the hand-cranked margaritas for a hot summer day when you don't want to crank the AC.

3. Those cud-chewing cows are wicked with emissions, generating 18 percent more than transport, according to the United Nations Food and Agriculture Organization.

4. Veggie oil as fuel is considered "carbon neutral" because, though it releases greenhouse gases when it's burned, it absorbed CO_2 as a plant. In some cases (such as burning oil from winter rapeseed), the original plant absorbed more CO_2 than the fuel emits.

5. Yes, it's generally more expensive than conventional food. However, if you reduce consumption in other areas, it's easy to make up the difference. In my family, for example, we buy organic meat, but eat considerably less of it. Buy fewer processed convenience food items and more fresh food and you can usually expect a healthier grocery store bill.

6. Get yourself a bus pass, get a good book to read (like this one!), and get over yourself.

7. The Food and Drug Administration (FDA) is leaning toward "yes," but plenty of consumer groups are loudly disagreeing. As one consumer activist notes, "It's like putting artificial apples in apple pie."

8. Depends on whom you ask, but more experts are leaning toward polyester, which, though it's derived from petroleum, requires less water to wash and no ironing. And cotton is one of the most pesticide-intensive crops in the world. Of course, there are better alternatives to either.

9. No! The benefits of breastfeeding still outweigh the risks—studies show that the antibodies, enzymes, and nutrients in breastmilk can shield babies from some of the effects of pollutants. However, get involved with Make Our Milk Safer (www.safemilk.org) to help clean up women's bodies.

10. Nope again! Hunger is largely a problem of food distribution, not food production. This is an argument that proponents of genetically modified food march out to persuade detractors . . . but it's been disproven by the United Nations.

Speaking
Personally . . .

What the virtuous
consumer says about:

The flesh
- *Lotions, potions, and ugly notions*

The blood
- *Feminine hygiene that doesn't shame
  Mother Nature*

The pleasure
- *Sex toys that please the planet*

The planning
- *Earth-friendly birth control*

You don't have to signal a social conscience by looking like a frump. Lace knickers won't hasten the holocaust, you can ban the bomb in a feather boa just as well as without, and a mild interest in the length of hemlines doesn't necessarily disqualify you from reading *Das Kapital* and agreeing with every word.   Elizabeth Bibesco

Cosmetic Perjury

I strode onto the schoolyard, eyelids smeared with my mother's cast-off iridescent blue eyeshadow and my lips gleaming with Maybelline Kissing Potion (need I mention it was 1977?). I was all of 13 years old and probably looked ridiculous. But to my own eyes, I was transformed.

And so began my love affair with makeup. Cover Girl foundation hid my vexing freckles, Maybelline Great Lash made my small eyes suddenly wider, and just-the-right-shade of lipstick made those years of braces suddenly worthwhile.

I still enjoy applying makeup. Although I don't wear a lot, what I do wear feels good—I'm me, but brighter. As though I actually had a good night's sleep, which I haven't in close to a decade.

From kohl-rimmed eyes in the first century to lead paint during the Italian Renaissance, cosmetics and skin-care products have long been used to reflect not just style but status. These days it's the rare woman (or man) who doesn't use some form of cosmetic product, whether hair dye, teeth-whitening toothpaste, or a swipe of lipstick.

And while the industry as a whole is often demonized for contributing to esteem issues in girls and women, we consumers have to assume at least part of the responsibility. After all, we buy the stuff. Then, according to the Environmental Working Group (EWG), we apply an average of nine products to our bodies every day. One in four of us applies fifteen products daily. (Gulp.)

What's the Controversy?

Behind those picture-perfect models and promises of physical perfection is a frightening secret that the personal care industry would just as soon keep buried: 89 percent of cosmetics contain one or more untested ingredients. That's right, 89 percent. What this means is that the safety of the stuff we're smearing on our faces and slathering on our bodies is pretty much a crapshoot. Maybe it's OK, maybe it's not. The FDA simply doesn't assess the safety or regulate the use of chemicals in personal care products—chemicals that we put into our bodies and often wash down the drain into our wastewater.

But we're not eating them, you say, rolling your eyes at me the way my eight-year-old does, *only putting them on our bodies.* Maybe so, but Stacy Malkan, a spokesperson for the Campaign for Safe Cosmetics (and a cosmetic lover herself!) reminds us that at-the-end-of-their-rope smokers put nicotine patches *on* their bodies too. "It's a very direct path to distribute chemicals to our bloodstream," she points out.

What chemicals? you query, wondering what, exactly, might be working its way into your bloodstream at this very moment. From mercury (rare but still found in cosmetics) to formaldehyde to petroleum distillate to lead acetate, many cosmetics play hostess to a chemical orgy. And moms-to-be, listen up: Many of these harmful or untested chemicals cross the placenta, says Jane Houlihan, vice president of research at the EWG.

It can't possibly be as bad as all that, you say. *After all, this stuff couldn't be on the shelves if it was unsafe, could it?* Well, yes, it could. You've just come face-to-face with an ugly truth. Most consumers do believe these products have been safety tested, Houlihan says. Yet plenty of what we smear on our faces and bodies uses chemicals known to cause, or strongly suspected to cause, cancer, mutation, or birth defects. Kinda gives new meaning to "if looks could kill," doesn't it?

But, the cosmetics industry purrs, *the chemicals appear in these products in such teensy-weensy amounts.* Maybe they do, though Houlihan notes that some of these ingredients often make up 10 to 20 percent of the base ingredients. Furthermore, as the Campaign for Safe Cosmetics' Stacy Malkan points out, we're using a number of these products—each and every

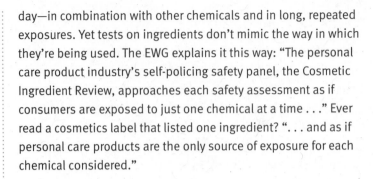

WHAT THE HELL WERE THEY THINKING?

During the Italian Renaissance, Aqua Toffana was a popular "complexion aid" named for its creator, Signora Toffana. Her rich clients were told to apply the arsenic-based makeup when their husbands were around. Roughly six hundred dead husbands later, Toffana was sent to prison and later executed.

day—in combination with other chemicals and in long, repeated exposures. Yet tests on ingredients don't mimic the way in which they're being used. The EWG explains it this way: "The personal care product industry's self-policing safety panel, the Cosmetic Ingredient Review, approaches each safety assessment as if consumers are exposed to just one chemical at a time . . ." Ever read a cosmetics label that listed one ingredient? ". . . and as if personal care products are the only source of exposure for each chemical considered."

Cosmetic Counter Intelligence

Jane Houlihan says we "can't shop our way out of all exposure, but can certainly reduce exposure," particularly to what research has revealed to be the most harmful and/or ubiquitous ingredients:

PHTHALATES. Phthalates are a family of endocrine-disrupting chemicals, which, for those without a PhD in biochemistry, means they play fast and loose with the glands secreting our hormones and can be toxic to reproduction in both men and women. They've also been implicated in liver, kidney, and lung damage. They're a commonly used solvent in nail polish, deodorant, fragrances, hair products, and lotions—look for them under such chemical code names as diethyl phthalate (DEP), dimethyl phthalate (DMP), and dibutyl phthalate (DBP).

PARABENS. These chemicals are widely used as preservatives in such cosmetics as moisturizers, shampoos and conditioners, foundations, skin creams, deodorants, even baby lotions and other products for infants. They've been found in samples of breast tumors, and they mimic estrogen—bad news, since increased exposure to estrogen over a lifetime is linked to an increased risk of breast cancer. What's more, parabens are another of the endocrine-disrupting group of chemicals. I'm closing in on menopause and, believe me, my hormones don't need any more messing with (just ask my husband). Parabens are easy to spot with monikers that sound like some bizarre quadrangle of evil: methyl-, ethyl-, butyl-, and propyl-.

COAL TAR. Yep, that's right. That gorgeous shade of chestnut hair is the result of coal tar. All together now: *Ewwww!* The European Union (EU) banned this strongly suspected carcinogen from cosmetics in 2004 but unwitting North Americans can still find it in hair dyes, shampoos, and cosmetics, generally listed as "FD&C" or "D&C" colors.

PETROLATUM. It is banned for use in cosmetics in the EU due to its link to cancer and other health problems. On this side of the pond, the stuff is still everywhere—makeup, lotions, hair removers, and more.

LEAD. While it's illegal to use lead shot to kill birds, lead acetate—banned in cosmetics in the EU—is commonly included in products used to disguise our gray hair, though it's comforting to know that our ducks and geese are safe from this carcinogen and hormone disruptor. The FDA requires a product containing lead acetate to include a warning (and I paraphrase here) that it isn't to be used near open wounds or to color mustaches. Oh yeah, and *wash hands thoroughly after use.* Now, how badly did you want to dye your hair again?

And guess what, ladies? That's only the shortlist. To see what I mean, log on to the Skin Deep website (www.ewg.org/reports/skindeep). Not for the faint of heart, this site offers up the largest existing resource for determining what we're putting on our skin, in our hair, and on our teeth. When I first checked it out, I learned that my then-favorite foundation had "areas of health concern that include cancer, penetration enhancers" (I wondered, briefly, if this meant it might boost my sex appeal—apparently not), "unstudied ingredients, harmful impurities, allergies and other concerns." Perhaps your moisturizer lists ingredients "classified as toxic; immune system toxicants; estrogenic chemicals and other endocrine disruptors, . . ." as my friend's former favorite does.

What's Up?

What the Environmental Working Group did to create its Skin Deep database is quite remarkable. Over a six-month period, the group examined more than ten thousand products available for sale. From this, it developed an online rating system that ranks the products in terms of safety (based on ingredients that are poorly studied, not studied at all, or known to pose potentially serious health risks). Ratings from zero to 10 were assigned to each product. Consumers can key in their favorite products and get their (color-coded!) rating—and more than one million people log on each month. Then, generally, comes panic and hyperventilating.

Jane Houlihan suggests that at this point you take a deep breath. The analysis is by no means definitive. While few individual ingredients pose excessive risks, most people use many products in the course of a day, so it may be that these risks are adding up. Skin Deep enables people to navigate the known concerns, explains Houlihan, who doesn't want us alarmed but does want us concerned. Concerned enough to stop using products with potentially toxic ingredients and concerned enough to demand action.

Mineral makeup is currently being hyped as the new best thing. While some do contain almost exclusively such minerals as zinc oxide, titanium dioxide and mica, others also contain the same harmful chemicals as conventional makeup. And while the minerals don't harm makeup users (and indeed can offer some UV protection), the mining and production of them can wreak environmental havoc. Mineral makeups sound another cautionary note, however. Health concerns have arisen due to the size of particles in some cosmetics, which can be inadvertently inhaled.

What Can You Do?

Start reading ingredients labels. As a general rule, if you'd lose a spelling bee upon being presented with the words you see listed, take a pass. And those claims of "natural," "hypo-allergenic," and "nontoxic"? As meaningless as claims of weapons of mass

destruction in Iraq. Experts urge mineral makeup users to stick to products that have a particle size of 7 microns or more—including such brands as i.d. bareminerals.

Avoid synthetic fragrances as well (often simply listed as "fragrance" on the label). Most contain phthalates. Even "fragrance-free" products pose a problem, as they contain a fragrance to mask the chemical fragrance of the product (see why my head is hurting these days?).

Some people give this piece of advice: If you wouldn't eat it, don't put it on your skin. While I'm not in the habit of eating makeup whatever the ingredients (though, apparently, the average lipstick wearer ingests about two pounds of the stuff in her lifetime, according to the UK's Women's Environmental Network), I now lean toward ingredients that *sound* as though I could eat them—if I wanted to. Ingredients such as witch hazel, olive oil, nutmeg powder . . . you get the idea.

And finally, at least consider this: You probably don't need much of what you invite into the bathroom. Now, now, wait a minute. I'm not suggesting you throw the baby out with the bathwater—just the bathwater, if it's full of toxic bubbles and phthalate-filled scents. Give serious thought to how much of this stuff you really need. By all means, keep what you love, but find less toxic versions. You might just find that you can pare down your beauty regimen to a level that's better for you and the planet. And think about this from Stacy Malkan: If beauty manufacturers can really create products that make us look ten years younger, why can't they take the carcinogens out? It's a good question to ask cosmetics companies, which, by the way, Jane Houlihan suggests you do. "People read those emails and letters," she says.

What you do decide to purchase, look for in containers that are recycled or recyclable and come with a minimum of packaging in order to reduce what's tossed. One estimate notes that as much as 50 percent of the cost of a bottle of perfume is accounted for in its advertising and packaging. Choose glass containers over plastic, and "better" plastics over the worst offender, polyvinyl chloride or PVC (recognizable by the number 3 in a triangle). You'll find that many organic or natural cosmetics give thought to this anyway, making your choices even easier.

Brands I Love

We are unable to control the chemicals we're exposed to in many areas of our lives. This isn't one of them. Get chemicals out of your personal care regime, and that goes double if you're pregnant or using products on an infant or young child. Find and support companies you can trust. Herewith are some recommended faves:

AUBREY ORGANICS. An old-timer in the world of healthier cosmetics, Aubrey Organics has been around since 1969. Founded by Aubrey Hampton, who still creates the formulations, Aubrey Organics is widely available and widely respected. I rely on Lumessence to keep my crow's feet in check and Aubrey Organics sunscreen to prevent any more.

AVALON. Choose from products under its Avalon Organics and Alba brands for all your beauty wants. I wake up with Alba bath and shower gel and drift off to sleep drenched in Avalon Organics CoQ10 night cream.

AVEDA. With a dedication to both eco-friendly ingredients and packaging and an insistence on fair trade principles in procuring such ingredients, Aveda is a feel-good, look-good option. The chamomile shampoo makes me salivate like some sort of Pavlovian dog, it smells so good. And it keeps my highlights (from an Aveda salon) looking fresh and natural.

BURT'S BEES. Lots of products, easy to find, and quite affordably priced. Burt's Bees Citrus Facial Scrub keeps my skin from looking dull (though it gets a finger wag from the Environmental Working Group for including fragrance). Frankly, the smell is a bit off-putting to me, but if you like nutmeg, you might not mind it. My girls and I also like the raspberry lip balm.

DR. BRONNER'S MAGIC SOAP. A friend raved so I gave it a try. Utilitarian, versatile bar and liquid soaps (choose from hemp, tea-tree, and baby, among others) for no-nonsense types. This is one company with a reputation that's squeaky clean—the soaps are certified organic, fair trade, and processed by ecological methods. Bottles are made from 100 percent consumer recycled (PET) plastic and wrappers are 10 percent hempflax/90 percent postconsumer recycled paper. And to top it all off, purchasing their soaps won't clean out your wallet.

Splitting Hares

So I'm a bleeding heart bunny-loving tree hugger. But I don't want to use products that were tested on animals. I just don't need hair spray badly enough to OK the spraying of such a product in some poor creature's eyes. Fortunately, the Leaping Bunny has leapt to my rescue. The result of cooperation among eight animal rights groups (six in the United States, one in Canada, and one in the European Union), this logo is an independently certified cruelty-free mark. It indicates to consumers that the personal care product, cosmetic, or cleaning product bearing it was free from any animal testing—from its ingredients through to the finished product. You can find out which products and companies don't use animal testing by logging on to www.leapingbunny.org.

Keep in mind, however, that the logo relates only to the animal-testing aspect of the product, not that the ingredients are in any other way free of toxins or otherwise safe.

DR. HAUSCHKA. The good doctor has a reputation for products that are not only safe, they work. They're not cheap, though they'd be comparable with some department store brands. I love the mascara—the only nonwaterproof brand I've ever tried that keeps curled lashes curled.

ECCO BELLA. Another widely available, affordable option with a wide range of products. I know someone who swears by the Organic Dark Chocolate Mask (it even contains extract of marshmallow), though I suspect I might want to sit with it in front of a roaring fire.

JASON. The granddaddy of natural skin care, this company started in 1959. Lots of skin care, bath stuff, shampoos, and deodorants. The lavender deodorant keeps my armpits smelling garden fresh even after a sweaty workout. No kidding!

KISS MY FACE. An easy-to-find and very affordable line of mostly skin-care products, though they do have some makeup and the occasional home-care product. I've discovered the oversized bar of olive oil soap cleans without drying my "maturing" (read: getting old and wrinkled) skin.

LAVERA. This German line offers 250 products, everything from baby products to a men's line. It's getting raves for its mineral-based sunscreens (which I haven't tried). I have tried the foundation—a light, moisturizing hint of color that glides on beautifully and stays put.

PEACEKEEPER CAUSE-METICS. Not only do I love the awesome colors and textures of their lip glosses, lipsticks, and nail polishes; not only do I love the fact that their products are committed to safe ingredients (no parabens, phthalates, FD&C coloring, artificial fragrance, toluene, formaldehyde, etc.); not only do I love the names (Paint Me Truthful, Paint Me Compassionate, Paint Me Strong . . .); I absolutely love that every after-tax cent raised from the sale of these products is used to support women's health advocacy and human rights issues. Anyone who says lipstick isn't powerful just hasn't found the perfect shade . . . or the perfect company to buy it from.

SUKI. If you knew Suki, like I know Suki . . . Suki Kramer has created perhaps the most luxurious natural-care products I've come across. Packaged in beautiful glass bottles (recyclable!) with labels locally printed on recycled paper with vegetable ink, Suki skin care products are a green gal's nirvana. My faves include the lemongrass exfoliating cleanser and the velvet hand and body cream. M'mmm. The products aren't cheap (about $25 for the lemongrass cleanser) but are worth saving up for.

TOM'S OF MAINE. Tom's makes a natural aluminum-free deodorant that works for me, as long as I don't work out too hard (though I've been warned that it sometimes loses its effectiveness and has to be rotated with other brands). Tom's also makes toothpaste, shaving cream, soap, and mouthwash. Indeed, it's the only natural line of dental care that has earned the American Dental Association's Seal of Acceptance. Products are free of dyes, sweeteners, and preservatives; packaging is recycled or

Give a Yogurt Container a New Career

Toothbrushes are small but ubiquitous and, as such, produce a lot of waste. With the American Dental Society recommending we replace our toothbrush two times a year, 50 million pounds of plastic makes its way to landfills. If you bristle at the prospect of tossing yet another toothbrush into the trash, help is as close as the Stonyfield yogurt in your fridge. I'm talking yogurt containers reincarnated as brand-spanking new toothbrushes. A partnership between eco-corporation Stonyfield Farm and Recycline means that Stonyfield's polypropylene (No. 5) yogurt containers get a second life as toothbrush, tongue cleaner, or razor handle. They can then be returned to be reincarnated yet again. To find a retailer selling Recycline products, visit www.recycline.com.

recyclable; nothing is tested on animals or uses animal ingredients; and 10 percent of profits and 5 percent of employees' paid time are donated to charitable organizations.

TWEEN BEAUTY. What makes this line particularly interesting is that it's aimed at "tweens"—that market of kids aged seven to thirteen. Before you get aghast and ask what seven-year-olds are wearing makeup, I'll tell you—almost all of them. My eight-year-old daughter returns from every birthday party with a loot bag full of lip gloss, nail polish, and body spray, all ripe with toxic chemicals. Even my three-year-old loves to put on lip balm and high heels—I swear it's encoded in their DNA to preen. Max Ritzenberger, brother to a ten-year-old girl, started the company together with his mom for exactly that reason. Plenty of beyond-tweens have discovered the products, too, including a friend of mine who loves their orange sherbet shampoo (my own girls squealed with delight at the scent). Might as well educate girls to choose products that don't harm them or the planet.

>>> PURCHASE POWER <<<

Avoid products that contain parabens, phthalates, coal tar, lead acetate, and petrolatum, among others. To get a printable list of twelve of the worst chemical offenders, visit www.teens4sc. org and click on Dirty Dozen. Choose products in recycled or recyclable containers with a minimum of packaging.

Clearly, there are plenty of options. Check out your local natural food and health stores or Whole Foods. Most products can also be ordered online. Even my gigantic supermarket has a good selection of organic and natural personal care products. For where to find specific brands, see Resources.

Aunt Flo? Meet Mother Nature

My own introduction to Aunt Flo, as many of we women none-too-affectionately refer to our periods, couldn't have been worse. Though I'd been anticipating her arrival for a year or more (my friends were already well acquainted with Auntie), she arrived rather conspicuously in the form of a bright-red stain on the back of my white Lee painter pants as I headed to ninth grade biology class. A tap on the shoulder and a whisper from a senior filled me in on my dilemma—and I slunk home to soak my pants in cold water and curse my now-apparent-to-all womanhood.

My hostility toward Aunt Flo has rarely abated, and I viewed three pregnancies as welcome reprieves. I eagerly anticipate menopause for the same reason. For the time being, however, I'm stuck dealing with Aunt Flo's monthly arrival in as earth friendly a manner as possible.

What's the Controversy?

Let's start by talking trash—as in each year women in the US throw over twelve billion pads and seven billion tampons into landfills and sewage systems. Nonetheless, feminine hygiene rates quite low on most lists of eco-sins. Still, if you want to reduce your footprint even further, it's worth considering all the options. And I'm not referring to menstrual huts, which—appealing as it may be to remove yourself from everyone who annoys you during that time of the month—aren't the most practical option for someone who has to hold down a job, raise children, and otherwise function as a fully present member of society.

Feminine hygiene takes its toll on the planet in other ways. Producing those lily-white pads and tampons involves the use of copious amounts of cotton (one of the most pesticide-intensive crops in the world). That cotton used to be bleached with chlorine, which had the unpleasant side effect of producing the toxic dioxin. These days, manufacturers will assure you that they've switched to elemental chlorine-free bleaching (ECF), which they claim produces no dioxin. However, the good folks at *E/The Environmental Magazine,* who wrote *Green Living,* beg to differ, noting that at least two independent studies have found detectable levels of the chemical in popular tampon brands that use ECF.

Most tampons also include rayon, warns *Green Living,* which doesn't absorb toxins the way cotton does, leaving them to roam freely in the vagina where they can be absorbed by the delicate tissue. Frankly, the idea of anything in my vagina roaming freely, like some recently escaped felon or a lost tourist, is a bit disconcerting.

Diana Morgan, Intrepid Explorer of Feminine Hygiene

Diana Morgan (full disclosure: she works for GladRags) is an enthusiastic promoter of alternative feminine hygiene products, having tried all different kinds. For example, her introduction to the menstrual cup was in Costa Rica, where she and her friend drank shots from it at a birthday party. After learning what it was, it took her a few months to get around to the notion of using it for its intended purpose. Once discovered, however, she considered the cup as "the greatest invention of all time," using it while she traveled for two years. During that time, she also purchased a cloth pad for "lighter" days or extra protection, as the cup would occasionally leak. When she settled down in Portland, Oregon, she found a job at GladRags, which seemed to her a perfect fit. These days, Morgan uses GladRags almost exclusively, noting that with them she's "more in touch with what is happening with my body. . . . I like being more aware because it causes me to take it a bit easier, get some extra sleep, and take advantage of my extra insight power during this time."

She recently, however, attended a wedding in which the dress she was wearing required her to go pantyless (who is this daring woman?). Of course, it happened to be the heaviest day of her period, so she decided to use sea sponges ("two of them, because you can . . . and I was afraid of leaking"). She says now that she "loves" them—noting that they don't make her feel dried out the way tampons do—and will use them in a pinch when GladRags won't fit the (monthly) bill.

What's Up?

Fortunately, some forward-thinking entrepreneurs have stepped up to give us some greener options:

ORGANIC TAMPONS AND PADS. I came of age at the height of toxic shock syndrome, which though rare now, still affects some women. So I tend to be leery of tampons, no matter how many smiling women in white pants astride horses on beaches try to persuade me to become a Tampax girl. I do occasionally rely on them when at the beach or wearing thong undies, which I can only be encouraged to wear when my fear of becoming a *Glamour* magazine "don't" overrides the incredible discomfort of a wedgie. But these days, if I use a plug at all, it's an organic one. The difference? One hundred percent organic cotton—no pesticides and no harmful bleaching. Also available in pads. Both options are better for the environment in terms of the manufacturing process, but do little to reduce trash.

REUSABLE PADS. Stop with the *Ewww, gross!* for just a moment and try to embrace your womanhood. (You're right. It sounds hollow even to me.) But keep in mind Mother Earth needs our help. Admittedly, reusable pads must be soaked and washed before reusing, upping the water usage of the environmental equation. But they're still a better choice than disposables. GladRags and Lunapads are two companies (though there are many others) that offer cloth reusable pads, in such fun patterns as leopard, zebra, and bright red (very practical, I can hear my mother pointing out). Roughly $30 will buy you three days' worth at which point it's time to do laundry.

THE MENSTRUAL CUP. In my pre-green days, a West Coast friend enthused during one visit east about her "cup"—a device that purported to catch her flow. Frankly, I thought it sounded weird and chalked it up to West Coast berry-eating, tree-hugging wackiness. These days, though, I'm among a number of women who swear by the little natural rubber cup that simply requires periodic emptying and is so efficient that only women with extremely heavy flow might require a just-in-case pad as well. In fact, you'd be surprised at who's using a cup: We communicate via drumbeat as it's rarely discussed in polite company.

SEA SPONGES. I know, this whole discussion is getting weirder. Sea sponges are inserted much like a tampon and absorb your flow, though they can leak when they get full. When removed, they must be soaked in a solution and left to dry before reuse. Also, they cost roughly $3 each and must be replaced every four months or so, making them not the most financially sound eco-option. However, women who've tried them (not me . . . yet) say they're just like tampons only without the scraping dryness or potential for toxins.

What Can You Do?

Start by demanding (yes, demanding!) feminine care products that aren't going to harm you. For heaven's sake—is it not enough that during my period I look like Morticia Addams and act like Roseanne Barr? Karen Houppert, author of *The Curse: Confronting the Last Unmentionable Taboo,* proposes a consumer outcry about the fact that menstrual products are considered "cosmetic," thereby leaving any testing and research to the companies that make them. What's more, she argues, medical foundations and university and government studies tend to deal with other health concerns—rarely with menstrual health. As a result, there are few independent studies of consumer risk related to menstrual products.

The answer is clear: Stick to safer, greener products.

⟩⟩⟩ PURCHASE POWER ⟨⟨⟨

Fortunately there are great options available, from the menstrual cup to reusable pads to organic tampons. Whatever your menstrual mood, there's a method to suit.

ORGANIC PADS AND TAMPONS. Look for such widely available brands as Organic Essentials and Natracare.

MENSTRUAL CUP, SEA SPONGES, REUSABLE PADS. Go to www.gladrags.com or www.lunapads.com to find a variety of women-friendly, earth-friendly options.

Mother's Naughty Nature: Sex Toys That Please the Planet Too

A woman I know discovered the "dolphin" roughly ten years into a disappointing marriage. The dolphin was a vibrator that showed this woman what she'd been missing—and became her constant companion for a few weeks after which she resurfaced with a sly smile, a knowing wink, and the name of a good divorce lawyer. Alas, the relationship was not meant to be. The dolphin, it turns out, was toxic. And I'm not speaking euphemistically here, as I might be if I were talking about her husband. I mean really toxic, as in chemicals that cause all sorts of nasty things to happen to our bodies and the planet we inhabit.

What's the Controversy?

For starters, there are no regulations governing the manufacture of sex toys. As a result, they're chock-full of all sorts of materials that most of us wouldn't want anywhere near our privates if we really stopped to think about it.

Part of the problem is that most of us don't really stop to think about it. Even if our pantry is stocked to the brim with organic pasta and locally grown zucchini, who among us goes shopping for an eco-friendly vibrator? And would we find one even if we did?

We would if we looked long and hard. Sex toys that are eco-friendly and even fair trade are out there, but they're probably not the ones you've been hearing your friends rave about. Keep in mind, though, that in order to achieve that manly-but-less-selfish feel, manufacturers generally resort to either PVC (an eco-villain from manufacture through to disposal), which uses phthalates (here they are again!) to soften things up, or polystyrene, which relies on mineral oil to make it feel real.

Jessica Giordani, co-owner of the Smitten Kitten in Minneapolis, Minnesota, advises eager beavers to steer clear of just about anything that's billed as jelly, cyberskin, or elastimer, "even products labeled latex free or phthalate free," says Giordani. "They might be, but still stay away."

Why the extreme caution? Giordani, along with co-owner Jennifer Pritchett, has been working with chemists running tests on sex toys. Says Giordani, "We knew things were bad, but it's horrifying."

She's not the only one shocked by what unwitting consumers are taking into their beds and bodies. Hans Ulrich Krieg, a German chemist, analyzed the materials used in sex toys and, in 2001, reported to the Canadian Broadcasting Corporation's *Marketplace* television show that ten dangerous chemicals gassed out of the sex toys, including phthalates, in levels many times greater than that considered tolerable for exposure. Keep in mind that phthalates have been linked to reproductive issues in men—from sperm damage to tinier penises (this from a study that noted this phenomenon in boys born to mothers exposed to levels of phthalates *lower* than those found in one-quarter of American women). Need I remind you where many of these products are being put?

What's Up?

Probably not your partner at this point. And unfortunately, not much else. Sex toys remain largely unregulated, and there are no signs of this changing anytime soon, though there are stirrings among the conscientious purveyors in this industry that something needs to be done. While the United States, Japan, Canada, and the European Union have restrictions against phthalates in some children's toys, there seems to be decidedly less concern about the toys big kids use.

What Can You Do?

Purchase adult toys that are made from safe materials. Look for silicone products from smaller companies, which often means the working conditions are fair.

Purchase dildos that can double as art when you grow weary of their climactic charms, such as those made from polished stone, glass (don't worry—it won't break), acrylic, Lucite, hard nonporous plastic, surgical stainless steel. The only safe soft material is medical-grade silicone. Look at the care instructions. If it can be boiled, then put it in your basket . . . so to speak.

Same goes for lubricants. Steer clear of lube that contains mineral oil. Silicone is what you're after—it's tasteless, free of smell, hypo-allergenic, and safe for use with latex condoms. Don't however, use a silicone lubricant with a silicone sex toy, as using silicone with silicone will create stickiness (ouch!). It's not available at most drugstores yet. More widely available are water-based lubes, but check the ingredients list and don't get any that list glycerin ("yeast infections in a tube," Giordani calls them) or parabens (remember those endocrine disruptors?).

>>> PURCHASE POWER <<<

According to the Smitten Kitten's Jennifer Pritchett, consumers can learn to shop smart wherever they are. "It is possible to buy good quality, eco-friendly toys at most sex toy stores," she says, "if you know how to wade through the piles of not-so-whole-some choices." Herewith, her suggestions for toys to make the earth move . . . in a good way:

TAKE THE SMELL TEST. Insist that a retailer open the package and let you smell the toy before you purchase it, as most stores have a no-return policy. "If you can smell a noticeable chemical odor emanating from a toy, you know without a doubt that it does contain chemical additives," warns Pritchett. While you may not know what those chemicals are, you should be very suspicious. Stick to toys that don't smell like anything.

BECOME AN EDITOR. Read the package carefully. You're looking for high-quality silicone—it might say 100 percent medical grade silicone, boilable, bleachable, hypo-allergenic. Do *not* buy anything that has misspellings such as "silicon" or "sillycone." And don't be fooled by a product billed as "hygienically superior," says Pritchett.

DON'T FALL FOR CLEVER MARKETING. If materials are listed as registered trademarks—look for a *TM* or circled *R*—they are not necessarily an actual ingredient or material. If a toy is made of solid glass, surgical steel, silicone, acrylic, polished stone, or another safe material, this will *not* be trademarked, explains Pritchett, because it's not a made-up name.

It's Getting Crowded . . .
Planet-Pleasing Birth Control

As mother of three children (and someone who wasn't sure I wanted children at all), I'm not sure I should be the one dispensing advice on birth control—earth-friendly or otherwise. As one of my more outspoken friends has pointed out, the word *no* can be effective . . . if you use it. However, if *no* isn't in your vocabulary either, then you've got some decisions to make if you also don't want to add the words *obstetrician* or *maternity*. (Note to teenage girls—and boys: Neither the rhythm nor pullout method can be relied on to keep you un-pregnant. I don't care what your friends say.)

What's the Controversy?

Consider this: In 1825, the world's population was one billion people; it was two billion a century later in 1925, when the age of oil began. Now, less than a century later, we've tripled that number to six billion. As Ronald Wright writes in *A Short History of*

Progress, "adding 200 million [people] after Rome took thirteen centuries; adding the last 200 million took only three years." The world clearly doesn't need more people. (I know, I know. I'm not exactly blameless here.)

But our earth-friendly options of controlling population aren't great. While the pill may have liberated generations of women, it hasn't been such a joyride for Mother Earth. Thanks to millions of women peeing out synthetic estrogen every day, our male water creatures are rapidly becoming . . . less male. It's the same bad scene from those on the patch, the implant, the shot, or any other form of hormonal birth control. If DC Comics published *Aquaman* today, he just might have teensy testicles and require a bra.

Condoms, while more earth friendly (depending on the material they're made from—more to come on that), are plugging our waterways, thanks to you boys who think it's OK to flush used rubbers down the toilet. What's more, those that "tie them off" create a scene in which millions of condoms float in a sea of effluent. What happens is that the contents decompose and give off gas, expanding the condom itself and making it float. Interesting in a science experiment kind of way, but not so picturesque. Fortunately, most condoms, bobbing or otherwise, are skimmed off at sewage treatment plants. But plenty more—a hundred million of them worldwide, according to one estimate—make their way into bodies of water either because of sewer system overflow or lack of sewage processing.

Latex condoms aren't a bad choice—latex comes from the sap of the rubber tree. Don't wrap anyone's privates in polyurethane-based condoms. While a less evil plastic than PVC, polyurethane nonetheless produces all kinds of nasty toxins from manufacture to disposal, and it never breaks down. On the plus side, condoms do prevent that other unpleasant surprise from intimacy, sexually transmitted diseases.

The IUD, a tiny device inserted by a doctor into a woman's uterus, messes with sperm migration or function and with fertilization, and works for years with 99 percent effectiveness. Some women have initial problems with bleeding or pelvic pain, but if you're problem free, you can be baby free for around a decade.

WHAT THE HELL WERE THEY THINKING?

Before the invention of the pill, women in the 1930s to the 1960s turned to Lysol disinfectant for birth control. Lysol was even advertised as a feminine hygiene product (though the European "doctors" who allegedly recommended it were later revealed to be fictional). Lysol was ineffective as birth control, but it sure kept the bowl clean!

The diaphragm and cervical cap methods essentially block conception. They do nothing to prevent STDs, are fairly cumbersome, and have varying rates of success.

What's Up?

Not much in the area of earth-friendly birth control. Newer options tend toward the hormonal method of controlling population, such as the patch. And the old standbys—condom, diaphragm, IUD, the pill—all have their pros and cons. Choices are based on so much more than economic and social issues—keeping in mind that preventing an unwanted child is noble in and of itself. (What's that? The pope is on the line? And he's mad?)

There is one notable eco-option: Natural methods (withdrawal or charting fertility) can work if done with diligence, care, and determination. Alas, I seem to lack all three, as do a number of surprised parents-to-be. (Dear Pope: Am I redeemed?)

What Can You Do?

Think seriously about whether to have kids. I'm not kidding. I love children, even when they have snotty noses and snottier attitudes, and if kids are what will make your life brighter, then absolutely go for it. But if you're having children to save a marriage, please your mother, or grasp at immortality, then keep your legs crossed while you think some more. Your choice is a very personal one. Just make sure you make one before you find yourself staring at a little blue line on a stick.

⟩⟩⟩ PURCHASE POWER ⟨⟨⟨

You'll need to get a prescription for a number of female options, but latex condoms are as close as your local pharmacy.

Eco-Chic

2

What the virtuous consumer says about:

The clothes
- *Sweatshops*
- *Eco-friendly fabrics*
- *Label lingo*
- *Great brands*
- *Secondhand stores and clothing swaps*

The gems
- *The fifth C in diamonds*
- *Dirty gold*
- *Gems with justice . . .*

Clothes make the man. Naked people have little
or no influence in society.   Mark Twain

I'm a clothes horse . . . and a jewelry horse (if there is such a
thing). I drool over *InStyle* and get weak in the knees at the latest
issue of *Vogue.* Still, as my conscience has awakened, I've had to
ask myself some pretty hard questions: Is that diamond bracelet
I covet untouched by conflict? Should I get my shoes repaired, or
buy a new eco-friendly pair instead? How can I tell which clothing
is made in sweatshops? Does anyone make vinyl-free rain gear
for kids? Can organic jeans make my conscience look bigger than
my butt? The questions, except for that last one, aren't always
easy to answer.

Clothing

While I've always loved clothes, my rather sad paychecks from
working as a magazine editor in a large, expensive city generally
kept my consumption in check. But then I got married, moved
to a smaller, more affordable city and began having babies. And
babies—coming as they do into the world without any clothing,
gear, or regard for mommy's sleep patterns—generally lead to
shopping. At first, I shopped at consignment stores and gratefully
received hand-me-downs. But as my husband and I started enjoying some measure of success in our careers, the shopping began.
Before you could say, "put it on my Visa," I was buying baby
sleepers, snowsuits, teensy little running shoes. . . . But one day,
as I looked at baby clothes at a store that shall remain nameless,
I held up a T-shirt that retailed for $4.99. Call it my *aha!* moment
(Oprah would!). I may not have known the actual conditions under

which that T-shirt was made, but I did know that something was wrong in the state of Bangladesh. Quite simply, I didn't want my children wearing clothes that some other child or mother had made without being paid fairly or being given safe, healthy conditions in which to work. An activist was born right then and there among the cheap T-shirts and bright yellow smiley faces.

But as I set out to determine which companies bought their clothing from manufacturers that ran fair, safe operations, I discovered that the wool is frequently pulled over our eyes.

What's the Controversy?

"You can safely assume the clothes you're wearing were made under pretty horrific conditions," says Androniki (Niki) Lagos, lead researcher for Co-op America's *Responsible Shopper* guide. (It's a great resource, by the way, for finding eco-friendly and fair trade products. Check out the site address in the Resources section.) Clearly not one to mince words, Lagos feels strongly that consumers need to understand the issues around clothing because many manufacturers are making claims that they're cleaning up their act, but, she says, "all we have are codified promises with not a lot happening on the ground."

SWEATSHOPS

Labor conditions are undeniably the most pressing issue facing the clothing industry. Garment workers—most of whom toil in third-world countries—are paid less than they need to live, and they endure crowded, often unsafe, and unsanitary conditions where they have no rights and no recourse for the abuse. In the United States, Lagos says, "chances are, the factories are better than, say, in China, but they are still largely worked by immigrants." And while US workers may not be subject to outright threats, they're vulnerable enough that they won't raise their voices against the working conditions, which are frequently conditions that US citizens wouldn't tolerate.

ENVIRONMENTAL IMPACTS

Making clothes can be an ugly business in its effect on the planet, as well. The conventional way of growing cotton, the most common fabric, requires megadoses of insecticides, herbicides, and chemical fertilizers—many of which are known carcinogens. Indeed, it takes approximately a third of a pound of chemicals to grow enough cotton to make just one T-shirt. Clothing dyes contain toxic chemicals that are released into our water systems. Some materials are certainly less than eco-friendly in both their manufacture and disposal. And speaking of disposal, only a small fraction of clothes ever get recycled. Those sent to charity often wind up in third-world countries where their availability sometimes undermines the local textile and garment industries.

OVERCONSUMPTION

Juliet Schor, the author of *Born to Buy,* reports that "between 1996 and 2002 the number of pieces of imported apparel purchased by each American consumer rose 83 percent. . . . All that acquisition has led to a culture of 'disposable clothes,' dramatic increases in consumer discard rates, and mountains of perfectly wearable but economically valueless garments piling up all over the country." A look in the closets of most North Americans shows that clearly we buy far more than we need. Part of the reason is that clothes are actually getting cheaper. Schor notes that the price of clothing between 1993 and 2003 declined by 10 percent. When t-shirts can be had for roughly the cost of a cup of coffee, we're a lot less likely to ask ourselves if we really need it.

However we look at it, what's on our backs ain't too pretty.

What's Up?

The level of dialogue, but little else. As Niki Lagos has noted, there's plenty of talk about change, but not a lot happening. That may change if a new bill introduced by a bipartisan group of senators in January 2007 becomes law. The bill would allow US companies to sue competitors that they believe are selling products imported from sweatshops. In the meantime, an optimist can see promising signs. In 2003 the United Nations Environment Programme (UNEP) kicked off an initiative to "encourage more ecologically sensitive retailing." The UNEP noted a "latent public demand for ethical and green products" and aimed to influence the $7 trillion global retail industry to "show how new lifestyles can be fashionable and cool," according to former UNEP executive director Klaus Toepfer. The initiative is designed to work both ways. By getting both the fashion industry and fashion media on board, more environmentally and socially responsible products would be created, and consumer demand for such products would get a boost. It's working in some areas, at least. For example, the nonprofit Organic Exchange reports that global retail sales of organic cotton rose from $245 million in 2001 to $583 million in 2005.

Lagos also points to a number of hopeful initiatives, including the development of a certification program through the Workers Rights Consortium (WRC) called the Designated Suppliers Program. The WRC works with colleges and universities to identify factories where workers are paid a living wage and where conditions are worker friendly. However, at this point, there isn't a uniform way to communicate to consumers that this company or store is better than that one.

Summer Rayne Oakes coproduces and hosts a television series called *Style Trek*, which takes viewers behind the fashion industry to farms, factories, and the people making change. She believes that change is imminent. "There's a realization within the industry that they have a responsibility not just to consumers," she says, pointing to an increased awareness about global warming, energy consumption, and poverty. She says changes are incremental but believes we're "going to see companies trying to . . . ask themselves how they can do better."

Green Guidance:
**Speak Out
Against Sweatshops**

Whereas there's lots of talk and not much action on the part of clothing companies concerning sweatshops, a few organizations aim to give them a kick in the right direction. Check out Organic Consumers Association's Clothes for a Change campaign at www.organic consumers.org/clothes/, Co-op America's site at www.sweatshops.org, or the Clean Clothes Campaign at www.cleanclothes.org.

What Can You Do?

While shopping for eco-couture isn't as easy as a trip to your local mall, there are trailblazers in the green fashion world. Still, most of us equipped with a Visa card and a social conscience are left bewildered. What are we supposed to be looking for? Union labels? "Sweatshop free" labels? Does country of manufacture indicate anything? What about the organic fabric movement? Is it better to buy natural fabrics or synthetics? What about dyes?

BUY CLOTHING TO LAST. Adjust your attitudes to clothing and purchase items that will see you through several seasons.

CHOOSE ECO-FRIENDLY FABRICS AND PROCESSES WHENEVER POSSIBLE. For example, organic cotton dyed with vegetable dyes produces a T-shirt that's far easier on the earth than its conventional cousin. Steer clear of clothes that require dry-cleaning (see sidebar on next page).

SHOP SECONDHAND. Back when I was a starving writer in the big city, I purchased one of the most beautiful suits I've ever owned from an upscale consignment shop. The suit was too big, so I had it tailored, and it fit like a kid glove for a fraction of what I would have paid for a new outfit. Kids' clothes are also ideal for consignment shopping. Seek out stores in more affluent areas and look for high-end labels, as better-made clothes can usually stand the test of time (and more than one wearer). I have one pair of OshKosh overalls (size 18 months) that has made it through five kids and is still going strong.

SHOP ONLINE. There are plenty of eco-friendly, fair trade offerings online, generally from smaller independent labels. I picked up a recycled sweater from Hip & Zen that was pieced together from discarded cashmere sweaters. It's definitely not your grandmother's cashmere wrap—it's hip . . . and zen, for that matter. And it can be worn with a clear conscience.

PRESSURE YOUR FAVORITE RETAILER. Ask companies what their method of production is and where they get their clothes made. "Asking questions about labor makes companies uncomfortable," says Co-op America's Niki Lagos. Tell them, "I want to shop with you, but I want to feel good about it." Ask them, "What are you doing to ensure workers are being treated according to the Fair Labor Standards Act? How do you monitor this? Have you terminated contracts in which there are violations?" Lagos says that companies take these concerns seriously, making letters and emails worth your effort. The Organic Consumers Association's Clothes for a Change campaign offers addresses, emails, and suggested comments to some of the larger manufacturers such as The Gap, Nike, and Wal-Mart. Visit www.organicconsumers.org/clothes/action.cfm.

SUPPORT THOSE GREEN-FASHION PIONEERS. Companies such as American Apparel, Cotton Ginny, Patagonia, Timberland, Levi Strauss, Loomstate, and others are setting the bar for other companies—and they're setting it relatively high. Support their

Dry-Cleaning: Soaked in Chemicals

While dry-cleaning sounds benign, it's far from it. The process uses perchloroethylene (perc), which causes a laundry list of medical problems—headaches, dizziness, nausea, reproductive problems including miscarriage and male infertility—and wreaks havoc on the central nervous system. The California Air Resources Board voted in early 2007 to ban the purchase of new perc machines as of 2008 and phase out existing ones by 2023. And the Sierra Club is currently suing the Environmental Protection Agency to phase out perc machines nationwide.

There are, however, alternatives, the best being something called "wet-cleaning," which uses water and eco-friendly detergents to clean sensitive fabrics. Another process using liquid carbon dioxide was developed under an Environmental Protection Agency contract in 1994. But while it works well, it's expensive, making it less attractive to dry-cleaning companies (which is, perhaps, why most of us have never heard of it).

Other choices, such as using hydrocarbon solvents and siloxane (known as Green Earth), are being marketed as eco-friendly because they're less toxic than perc. However, neither has passed muster with the EPA or the Coalition for Clean Air, both of which say more testing is required. The bottom line? Ask your dry cleaner if he plans on greening his cleaning, promising to support him if he does. If wet-cleaning is offered, check first that your clothing items won't be harmed by it (wool doesn't always respond favorably; silk usually does).

initiatives by purchasing their clothing with a conscience. See more under "Brands I Love."

HOST A CLOTHING SWAP. "It's like going shopping in one another's closets," says my friend Barbie, about clothes swaps. Barbie gets together with a group of women (new additions are always welcome to keep the jean pool fresh) about once a season. They cull their closets of those clothes that no longer fit their bodies or their lifestyle, or that they simply don't wear anymore. They bring the clothes to the swap, where, after enjoying wine and hors d'oeuvres, everyone picks and chooses from the items, tries things on, and, without fail, goes home with a few great new things to add to a much emptier closet. Any leftover clothes are taken to a women's shelter.

WHICH LABELS TO LOOK FOR

At this point labels don't offer us much beyond washing instructions and where the garment was made (or the pieces assembled, which is not necessarily the same place). Here's how to read between the lines:

Sweatshop free. So far, there isn't a single universal certification program that clearly shows consumers whether an article was made in sweatshop-free conditions. Some companies do business with schools, athletic teams, and other buyers that have a "sweat free" policy. Those that do, such as American Apparel, crow about it. Clothes can be ordered through companies that offer this guarantee (see the Resources section). There are also unionized companies (see "Union Labels"). In the absence of certification, it's pretty much up to consumers to do a little digging . . . or do what you're doing right now by educating yourself.

And bad news, Wal-Mart shoppers: The store has a long history of supporting sweatshops (c'mon . . . you knew there had to be some reason for those low prices). So do the Gap (which includes American Eagle, Old Navy, and Banana Republic) and Target. The problem with naming names, however, is that companies can—and even sometimes do—change. Take the Gap. Thanks in part to consistent and aggressive consumer pressure, the behemoth beacon of laid-back cool recently took the positive and widely heralded step of creating a Social Responsibility Report, in which it provided data on conditions in the 3,010 factories in more than 50 countries where the company's clothes are made. It admitted that "few companies, if any, are in full compliance all of the time" with the Gap's code of conduct. So, while the document revealed what's wrong, it also provided a blueprint for change. And change, in the case of greening our closets, is a good thing.

To keep up with corporate policy changes, check out Co-op America's website (www.coopamerica.org). It routinely runs an up-to-date retailer scorecard that tells you who to support . . . and who to avoid.

Union labels. While purchasing union products is a good step, other social or environmental concerns may be associated with a company. For more info, visit www.shopunionmade.org.

Made in . . . . This part of the label doesn't necessarily tell the whole story. For example, even labels that say "Made in the USA" could mean that the garment was assembled in the United States from components manufactured elsewhere. Besides, there are sweatshops right here in the good old US of A.

WHAT FABRICS TO LOOK FOR

It's basically a wash in terms of the environmental effects whether you buy natural or synthetic fabrics. Which means that Elvis-esque polyester jumpsuit might be a fashion crime, but it's not necessarily an eco-crime. Still, some fabrics are easier on the planet . . . and more likely to ensure that you don't become a fashion "don't" with one of those scary black bars over your eyes.

ORGANIC COTTON. Those 400-thread count sheets that you love and that baby-soft cotton T-shirt aren't as "natural" as marketers would like you to believe. Cotton is the second-most pesticide-laden crop in the world (after coffee and before tobacco). Cotton growing accounts for 25 percent of the world's pesticide use, and it requires the application of some of the most hazardous pesticides. Organic cotton is grown without chemicals or toxic pesticides. While progressive designers are offering up organic cotton options, even some of the bigger players—Levi Strauss, Victoria's Secret, and Esprit—are seeing the green light and incorporating organic cotton into their lines. For more companies that are incorporating organic cotton into their clothing lines, see

What the Hell Were They Thinking?

Tired of having to wash your underpants? Me neither. Frankly, it's not that big a chore. But tell that to the folks at OneDerWear, who think that throwing away your dirty socks and underwear is a great idea. "Just wear and toss," the company's promo material suggests, noting that disposable clothing is particularly great for travelers, college students, and hikers. Frankly, I think they should toss their marketing research person. How many hikers will think that pitching their skivvies is a great way to show respect for the environment they so love hiking in? Or travelers? OneDerWear suggests that those travelers will have plenty of luggage space left for "gifts and souvenirs." Such as black rhino parts and gorilla hand ashtrays, perhaps?

"Brands I Love" and visit www.organicexchange.org/consumer_marketplace.php.

HEMP. What do Christopher Columbus, Rembrandt, and Henry Ford have in common? They all used hemp—Columbus for sails and ropes, Rembrandt for painting canvases, and Ford for a car. Hemp bears the distinction of being the strongest natural fiber in the world—and the most eco-friendly. It produces more yield per acre than any other crop. It flourishes without pesticides or fertilizers. Thanks in part to the United States' continued refusal to allow it to be commercially grown (hemp seems to be guilty by association—it does have its counterculture cousin marijuana's reputation to consider), it's hard to find, though it's becoming increasingly available. Armani has made it famous through his "green" jeans.

TENCEL. If you haven't worn Tencel (the trade name of the generic fiber lyocell), try it. It feels like cotton . . . only better. Softer, gentler, and more elegant, Tencel is noted for its "drape," which flatters your body. It's also completely biodegradable, durable, and easily machine washed and dried. How is this possible? It's made of cellulose extracted from tree farms planted on land unsuitable for food crops or grazing. In other words, it's *almost* the perfect fabric. "Almost" because Co-op America warns that the wood used to make Tencel should be certified under the Forest Certification System. Otherwise there's no guarantee the wood came from a sustainable source. And at this point, there's no way for the consumer to know where the wood came from. Sigh . . .

BAMBOO. I bought my husband a pair of bamboo socks the other day. While they sound decidedly prickly, they feel soft and cozy. If only he didn't keep tripping on those damn panda bears nibbling at his toes! Bamboo fabric is similar to rayon and contains microbial properties that keep odor to a minimum. It's considered eco-friendly because it's a very fast-growing grass, ready to harvest within four to five years. And it's becoming a fast-growing fabric choice for everything from skirts and T-shirts to . . . socks.

MICROFIBER. A leather or suede look, but without the dead animals, tanning dyes, and need for dry-cleaning. Imagine! Long-lasting luxury without guilt.

FLEECE. Who thought a bottle of Pepsi could keep you warm! It can when you're wearing it—and twenty-four other plastic bottles—on your fleece-clad self. EcoSpun is the name of a high-quality polyester fiber made from recycled plastic pop bottles—look for such trade names Polartec, Ecopile, or E.C.O. Fleece. The process starts at your local recycling depot and ends in fleece garments—chemically and functionally nearly identical to nonrecycled fleece—without the resource depletion. Kinda makes you feel warm and fuzzy, doesn't it?

SOY. This is one magical bean—providing food, skin care . . . and clothing. Soy clothing is noted for being soft and light. And if you get hungry, you can just chew your cuff.

OTHER ALTERNATIVES. New fabrics are popping up constantly as demand for eco-clothing increases. Look for corn, seaweed, Ingeo, Lenpur, sasawashi, and more. Cotton and Lycra are *so* last year. . . .

⟩⟩⟩ PURCHASE POWER ⟨⟨⟨

- Purchase labels that support fair conditions and environmental responsibility (see "Brands I Love"; visit frequently Co-op America's *Responsible Shopper* guide).
- Stick to fabrics that are easier on the earth.
- Ask retailers to offer Fair Made and/or certified organic clothing
- Ask manufacturers for written information on the location of their factories and assurance that they will cooperate with independent verification that workers are paid a living wage and work in safe conditions.
- Buy second-hand so you're not directly supporting irresponsible companies and you're keeping more clothes out of the landfill.
- Buy less. Just because clothes are cheap doesn't mean you should buy twice as much.
- Buy from local retailers and designers.
- Swap. Clothes that is, not your spouse . . . no matter how out of style he is.

Brands I Love

I'm happy to help in your search for clothes with a conscience. Next time you buy, consider these:

AMERICAN APPAREL. Though its creator is creating controversy of his own (a few former employees are alleging a little too much familiarity on his part), the clothes at least have a conscience. The company does boast a "sustainable edition" of clothing that is not only sweatshop free like all other American Apparel clothes, but is made of USDA-certified organic cotton (available in mostly beige). The company is also taking steps to reduce the eco-impact of each stage of the production process—such as using preconsumer scrap fabric for some baby clothes and reusing cardboard boxes. Stores across the United States, Canada, Mexico, and overseas. www.americanapparel.net.

EDUN. While a bit pricey, this line looks like a million bucks. Bono, who blames himself for the resurrection of the mullet hairstyle, has promised his fashion-forward wife that he'll stay out of the design end of the business. The result is clothes that are catwalk cool . . . with a conscience. Look for jeans, jackets, and tops at various stores in the United States, Canada, and online. www.edun.ie.

LEVI'S. I used to purchase vintage Levi's jeans at a downtown market—they were already perfectly worn in and could be mine for about $10. Now Levi's, that age-old purveyor of blue-collar cool, has gone green with its organic cotton jeans. And not a moment too soon. While there are other organic cotton jeans on the market, they're not easy to find and not easy on the wallet. Levi's' organic offering, while more expensive than conventional Levi's, are still cheaper than many other organic brands. Look for them at Levi's stores under the Levi's Eco brand in both guy's and girl's styles.

MOUNTAIN EQUIPMENT CO-OP. The venerable Canadian outdoor outfitter's organic cotton line, from hoodies to capris, is clean, comfy, affordable . . . and gets better with wear. Will ship to the United States and elsewhere. www.mec.ca.

ECOGANIK. Gorgeous, sophisticated clothing made from

Wendy Tremayne, Creator of Swap-O-Rama-Rama

Take heaps of discarded clothing, a room full of shoppers, a sewing station, skilled artists and you've got the recipe for a runaway creative shopping success. Wendy Tremayne is the brains behind Swap-O-Rama-Rama (www.swaporamarama.org), an overgrown clothing swap that not only allows people to pick up some new outfits, it gives them the tools to transform them into personal, wearable art.

"I wanted to make a solution—an alternative to shopping," says Tremayne, who added in the opportunity to personalize the clothes at the sewing and silk-screen stations (among other creative offerings) to show shoppers "the many rewards offered to those who make rather than buy—such as community and the joy of being a creator."

There are currently more than thirty swaps in countries around the world. They work like this: You show up with at least one bag of your unwanted clothing and a small monetary donation to help fund the swap. Every swap begins with a pile of clothing. You dive in and find your next new clothes from the pile. Take as much or as little as you like. Then you can move on to workshops offered by local artists on how to transform your finds—sewing, embroidering, beading, silk-screening, repairing, knitting and more—including the materials you need to do it.

If you're so inclined, you can then walk the runway—adorned in just-plucked-from-the-pile. Those who see their own discards worn by someone else can offer up stories about the clothing item. You can then invite participants to vote on whether or not you should keep it. Those you do keep can be labeled with "100% Recycled" or "Modified by Me."

Tremayne still gets emotional about the whole process. "I fall to pieces and often cry watching people make things. . . . At swaps, everyone talks to everyone. They make things together, they use each other as mirrors—we have no mirrors for this very reason—and they make friends."

But there's a deeper purpose to swaps, according to Tremayne. "Once one becomes a 'maker' a knowledge comes forth . . . and people begin to ask questions: How did this garment get to me? What is it made of? So Swap-O-Rama-Rama is like a portal. Once inside there is so much to discover, and with those discoveries comes the knowledge that leads to action and change and purpose." And to one heck of a great new outfit.

eco-friendly fabrics such as organic cotton, Tencel, hemp, organic wool, and more. These California-based clothes bring the eco-friendly look from hippie to just plain hip. www.ecoganik.com.

GREEN KNICKERS. Imagine turning that horrible bridesmaid's dress into fun and funky underpants. That's exactly what a couple of UK-based eco-designers did. Green Knickers is the result—lines of lingerie that come from old dresses or organic fabrics. www.greenknickers.org.

HIP & ZEN. This website offers a wide range of eco-friendly and fair trade clothing companies, such as LovethisLife and Loyale clothing, for men, women, and kids. Plus products for your home. I'll boast once again about my recycled Deborah Lindquist sweater that I bought from Hip & Zen—which I *love* and which generates lots of compliments, allowing me to wax on about how it's made from recycled cashmere. Not only do I look fashionable, but I also earn points for being progressive. Or a braggart. I'm too hip (and zen) to care. www.hipandzen.com.

OSHKOSH B'GOSH. What's more adorable than a two-year-old in OshKosh denim overalls? The clothes are union made, wear like iron (think hand-me-downs for generations!), wash like a dream, and stand up to the toughest toddlers. There are adult clothes, too, but in the interest of not creating eye pollution, leave the overalls to the kids. Widely available at retail stores.

MAGGIE'S FUNCTIONAL ORGANICS. Eco-friendly to the tips of your toes, thanks to Maggie's socks, the cornerstone of this cooperative in Nicaragua. Though Maggie's started off marketing organic tortilla chips, the cooperative segued in some bizarre way to socks, camisoles, and T-shirts. (Read the story at www.organicconsumers.org/sponsors/maggies. It will make you feel as warm and fuzzy as wool socks.) These days, Maggie's pays a wage 40 percent higher than in the sweatshops of Central America. Look for Maggie's clothes at natural food stores or online at www.organicclothes.com, or call (800) 609-8593.

PATAGONIA. This company's synthetic fleece has diverted nearly ninety million soda bottles from the waste stream and spawned new thinking since its creation in 1993. Not only does Patagonia make indestructible clothing from recycled pop bottles, but it also pledges 1 percent of its sales to environmental causes. It also offers a variety of organic cotton clothing that's affordable and easy to find at sporting goods stores. www.patagonia.com.

NEW BALANCE AND REEBOK. Athletic shoes have taken a public relations beating over the years, thanks to exposés revealing that workers were paid pennies to produce shoes that athletes were paid millions to endorse. But these two companies make shoes that are not only awesome (I've run marathons in both brands, and if they can get me across the finish line, they're working miracles!), but are also made in factories where workers are paid fairly (although Co-op America urges both companies to stay on top of labor issues). New Balance, an acknowledged leader in social responsibility, recently phased out PVC, the poison plastic (read more about PVC in chapter 5, "Clean Living"). Reebok also has strong social impact programs, including an annual Human Rights Award for youth. Widely available at shoe and department stores.

The Greenloop. This website offers everything from clothing (men's, women's, children's) to hair products to accessories, from various companies such as Blue Canoe, Del Forte, and Stewart+Brown (you'll get to know—and love—those labels). Greenloop is a veritable green force in the eco-fashion world. Visit . . . and prepare to be transformed into an eco-shopper. www.thegreenloop.com.

Timberland. How do I love Timberland's pioneering green spirit? Let me count the shoes . . . er, ways. Timberland produces great-looking shoes (and did I mention comfy?) and clothes, but they aren't resting on their laurels, consistently creating new ways to keep us treading lightly on Mother Earth. Its code of conduct helps ensure Timberland products are being produced in workplaces that are fair, safe, and nondiscriminatory; it has made a commitment to using water-based adhesives over solvent-based ones; and it is tripling its use of organic cotton. Timberland is blazing a trail—a verdant one. Timberland products are available at many department stores and sporting goods and outdoors stores. www.timberland.com.

Vy and Elle. There are some great purses and bags being made from recycled materials (I have a Bazura Bag made out of drink wrappers by a women's cooperative in the Philippines, and Ecoist also makes cool bags from candy wrappers), but the claim to have diverted more than 12 tons of vinyl billboards from landfills belongs firmly to Vy and Elle, which has turned those billboards into funky bags. www.vyandelle.com.

All That Glitters:
The Dark Side of Gems and Gold

My engagement ring has its own history, one that precedes
the romance between my husband and me. I have diamond
earrings that sparkled on someone else's lobes long before
mine. And watches that ticked off the minutes of other lives. For
me, that's part of the magic—jewelry is so personal and long
lasting. It holds stories about other lives, other loves, and other
losses—even if I'll never know what those stories are. But jewelry
shouldn't tell stories of environmental destruction, civil war, and
human rights violations. Far too often, however, it does.

What's the Controversy?

There are different issues according to the gem or metal mined,
with some taking a greater toll on the planet and its people than
others.

DIAMONDS

The first question on a girl's mind when her boyfriend presents
her with a diamond ring is not usually, "Um, is this conflict free?"
The guy could be forgiven for thinking his girl is seeking reassur-
ance that their relationship will be free of squabbles over how
to hang the toilet paper and whose mother is more annoying.
Indeed, few consumers are aware of the fifth C of diamonds:
cut, clarity, carat, color . . . and conflict. But thanks to the 2006
release of the movie *Blood Diamond,* starring Leonardo DiCaprio,
consumers are opening their eyes to the issue.

According to the United Nations General Assembly website,
"Conflict diamonds are diamonds that originate from areas
controlled by forces or factions opposed to legitimate and inter-
nationally recognized governments, and are used to fund military
action in opposition to those governments, or in contravention of
the decisions of the Security Council." Translated into shorthand,
conflict diamonds, which primarily come from the diamond-rich
areas of Sierra Leone, Angola, and Liberia, have been used to
fund rebel groups aimed at undermining legitimate governments. While conflict diamonds account for roughly 4 percent

of the international diamond trade, the impact of that trade has devastated communities and led to the deaths of thousands and the displacement of millions of Africans.

While the conflicts in these areas have largely been settled, the situations remain fragile at best. However, many steps have been taken recently by the United Nations and the jewelry industry to ensure that conflict diamonds don't make it to market.

Rubies, Sapphires, and Emeralds

They look gorgeous—those rich red rubies, sparkling blue sapphires, and effervescent green emeralds. But so many come from such troubled places. Most of the world's rubies originate in Myanmar (formerly Burma), noted for its oppressive regime and human rights violations. Sapphires stemming from Sri Lanka, Thailand, and Madagascar carry with them the stigma of human rights violations, child labor, and sweatshop conditions. And Colombian emerald mines have long been used to launder money from the drug trade.

Gold and Silver

Metal mining is a polluting business. One gold ring that weighs one ounce requires thirty tons of rock to be dug up, then sprinkled with diluted cyanide to separate the gold from the rock. The Environmental Protection Agency notes that hard-rock mining generates more toxic waste than any other industry in the United States: 27 percent. All to feed a seemingly insatiable international consumer demand for jewelry.

What's Up?

Carol Besler, a writer on issues related to the jewelry industry, says the industry is to be applauded for its quick response to the issue of conflict diamonds. She points to the Kimberley Process, an international certification system implemented in January 2003. Its aim is to prevent trade in conflict diamonds while helping to protect the legitimate trade in rough diamonds. Participants (to date there are 46, including the United States, Canada, and the European Union) agree to certify that shipments of rough diamonds are free from conflict diamonds.

Green Guidance:
**Follow this
Golden Rule**

To find out more about the dirty practice of mining gold—and which jewelry retailers, such as Tiffany and Wal-Mart (yep, you read that right), are doing their part to clean up their showcases—search on www.nodirtygold.org.

Participants require that each export or import shipment of rough diamonds be accompanied by a Kimberley Process certificate. The certificate ensures that no shipment of rough diamonds is imported from or exported to a nonparticipant and designates an importing and exporting authority. Participants work with their governments to amend or enact appropriate laws or regulations to implement and enforce the certification scheme; and collect and maintain relevant production, import, and export data.

However, some nongovernmental organizations (NGOs), such as Amnesty International, Global Witness, and Oxfam, maintain that this isn't enough, calling on the industry to crack down on self-regulation of the process. They argue that each country sets its own standards, some too lax. And the process covers the diamonds only from mining to entry into another country. From there, each stone passes through a number of hands, increasing the chances for conflict diamonds to enter the mix.

Indeed, even while members of Sierra Leone's Revolutionary United Front were on trial in July 2004 for atrocities committed during the war, some intelligence reports indicated that smuggling still accounted for about 40 percent of the diamonds leaving Sierra Leone. And that's with the Kimberley Process certification system in place.

Less is being done at an industry level to source responsible gemstones; however, there are fair trade co-operatives—and jewellers supporting them—that offer up gemstones that haven't negatively affected those involved.

What Can You Do?

Start by seeing if you can wrestle a ring off the finger of an aging auntie or geriatric granny. She might be thrilled to know that you want a sparkling heirloom to remember her by (that is why you want it, right?). Or look for estate jewelry at jewelry stores, auction houses, even online. Read the catalog to ensure that the item is genuinely from an estate and not something new designed to look older. You can also request a condition report from a reputable auction house, which will tell you in detail about the item.

If you insist on virgin gems and gold, you need to ask your jeweler some questions:

- How can I be sure that the diamond I want to buy does not fuel conflict?
- Does the company have a policy in place to prevent selling conflict diamonds? If so, what is the policy and is it in writing?
- Has the company informed its suppliers in writing that it requires a warranty?
- Is the company keeping records of the warranties and having these records verified as part of its financial auditing process?
- Are the rubies, sapphires, and emeralds purchased directly from the mine (there are some good mines in troubled countries)? Or from a reputable dealer?

>>> PURCHASE POWER <<<

- Buy from a Canadian dealer. Canadian diamonds carry a certificate of guarantee from mine to showcase.
- Buy from reputable jewelers who can offer a paper trail to back up the provenance of their clean jewels.
- Check out retailers that offer jewelry from eco-friendly, socially responsible producers. Tiffany's is a noted carrier of conflict-free gems. Visit www.fairtradegems.com, www.brilliantearth.com, and www.greenkarat.com; or do an online search of your own.
- Buy synthetic diamonds and other gems, which are affordable as well as homegrown. Many jewelers praise their beauty.
- Open your mind to other options: citrine, topaz, marcasite, amethyst . . . the list goes on.
- Buy used jewelry. The jewelry industry, no slackers in the public relations department, generally refers to it as "estate" or "antique" jewelry. Either way, purchasing it helps reduce demand for new gems and metals. Consider redesigning what you have in your jewelry box to update it.
- Go for recycled metals—they're not ideal, as their production still requires chemicals and lots of water, but they're a better choice than virgin materials.

Food for
Thought

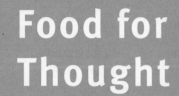

What the virtuous
consumer says about:

Groceries
- *Food, farms, fish, and more*

Food and children
- *Labels to look for*

It's bizarre that the produce manager is more important to my children's health than the pediatrician.   Meryl Streep

There was a time I thought enlightened shopping for groceries was a simple choice between organic and nonorganic produce at my local supermarket. Fast-forward three years and I'm a mostly vegetarian who will only eat meat if it's local, organic, and humanely raised. I lean strongly toward locally sourced produce—ideally from a roadside stand and, of course, in season. I make my own (mostly organic) bread. Inconvenient? A bit, although our family outing to the farmers' market is decidedly more fun than our trips to the grocery store where I had to wage war with three kids who think (really!) that Froot by the Foot is fruit. After all, they point out to me as if I'm a little slow, there are pictures of fruit right on the package. At the farmers' market my kids eat real fruit right out of the baskets (no pictures on them—none needed), urged on by the vendors. Orange raspberries? Give them a try. Thumbs up from the kids and into the reusable tote they go. Oversized blueberries? Not so much. They get a pass. They help me pick veggies and—lo and behold—feeling rather proprietorial they want to actually eat them when we get home.

So how did I get here from the canned soup eating, fast-food burger noshing university student of . . . oh . . . a while back? And is it possible to be an organic/local-purchasing, part-time vegetarian without being smug and annoying and left out of parties where people eat Doritos and French onion dip and talk about smug, annoying, organic-eating jerks?

I'll get to that. First, let's look at why there's a cleanup in aisle four. . . .

What's Eating You?

Perhaps nowhere has the environmental, social justice movement managed to grab the consciences of consumers so effectively than in the food aisles of America. Whether you buy organic or conventional, local or exotic, processed and packaged or bulk and ready for homemade, you're casting a vote. And increasingly—a 20 percent increase each year—that vote is on the side of pesticide-free, hormone-free, antibiotic-free, and genetically *un*modified food. Simply put, a trip to the grocery store has become a political act.

But anyone who has spent some time in a grocery store knows it's not that simple. Marion Nestle, a nutrition professor and author of the book *What to Eat,* states that "people are confused about everything about what to eat." The woman who spent a year in supermarkets and grocery stores poring over the shelves and trying to think like the average consumer says it's no wonder. "Just think about the range of issues," she says. "Can you believe health claims on package labels? Is it okay to eat farmed fish? When a product is 'natural,' what does that mean? Isn't everything that is vitamin-enriched, organic, and natural good for me? The questions are endless. And the answers are usually complicated."

What's the Controversy?

There are actually several controversies . . .

PICTURE-PERFECT PRODUCE, THANKS TO PESTICIDES

We all love to see produce that looks as if it sprang from the pages of gourmet cooking books. Yet that expectation has created a justification by suppliers for the increased use of pesticides and herbicides—to create these luscious-looking fruits and veggies, but also to keep them looking good and ripe for the long trip from where they're grown to where they're purchased. *Consumer Reports* recently reported on a growing body of research that shows pesticides and other contaminants are more prevalent than most of us realize in the foods we eat, in our bodies, and in our environment. And they can have serious consequences. A 2001 study by the University of North Carolina revealed that 700 women who lived close to where crops were sprayed with certain pesticides faced a 40 to 120 percent increased risk of miscarriage or having babies with birth defects.

Perfection in produce is overrated. Be aware that the misshapen green pepper might be the far better choice.

A Hot Issue: Easing Global Warming by Going Local

Michael Pollan, author of *The Omnivore's Dilemma,* is one voice urging us to go local. "I'd have to say the most serious problem with the food system is its contribution to global warming," he says, pointing to the incredible energy requirements to get food to our tables. Food travels an average of sixteen hundred miles from farm to plate, according to Richard Pirog, marketing and food systems program leader at Iowa State University. On average, for every calorie we consume, ten calories of fossil-fuel energy are used in the production, processing, transportation, and preparation. Conversely, purchasing local food creates far less pollution and generally supports smaller farmers who grow a variety of foods, thereby diminishing the need for heavy herbicides (exclusively growing one crop generally requires more pesticides). Think eating locally year-round is impossible where you live? See the sidebar on the "hundred-mile diet."

Those who support the go-local movement also believe strongly in preserving family-owned farms. However, some stores use a definition of "local" that applies to anything grown within the state. Worldwatch Institute, an independent research organization that works for an environmentally sustainable and socially just society however, offers this definition: "food raised as nearby as possible. Ideally . . . [this] means the buyer can meet the farmer or food maker and find out details about how the food was raised, and that the crops and livestock are unique to a certain area." So if you have to leave your county to meet the guy who grew your apple, it ain't local. And keep this in mind from Ronnie Cummins, national director of the Organic Consumers Association, about how we need to support our local independent businesses: "Where you buy is as important as what you buy," he says, noting that when you support a locally owned business, the money stays in the community.

FACTORY FARMING: MEATING OUR NEEDS

The stories just won't go away—though most of us have become adept at tuning them out or chalking them up to urban myths. The debeaking of chickens housed in too-confined quarters so they don't peck each other to death; the impossibly small pens in which pigs and cows can't even turn around; the aggressive overfeeding that results in animals too fat to stand up; the transport over long distances without water, food, or rest in sometimes extreme weather conditions. About the only thing one can say positively about factory farms is that the animals' lives are often blessedly short. According to Worldwatch Institute, factory farming is the fastest growing method of meat production worldwide. Millions of chickens, pigs, and cattle raised on factory farms are housed in often crowded, unsanitary, and inhumane

Words to Live By: Understanding Labels

The Consumers Union website lists 147 eco-labels, some of which are completely independent and certifiable, while others are meaningless marketing. How to tell the difference? Get to know the following labels—they're the most commonly seen. Check out others at the Consumers Union site eco-label index (www.eco-labels.org).

ORGANIC. Labels can read "100% organic" (no synthetic ingredients allowed; production processes must meet federal organic standards and must be independently verified by accredited inspectors); "organic" (at least 95 percent of ingredients are organically produced; the remainder can be nonorganic or synthetic); or "made with organic ingredients" (at least 70 percent of ingredients are organic; the remaining 30 percent must come from the USDA's approved list).

NATURAL, OR ALL-NATURAL. It sounds all homespun goodness and mother's love . . . but the term "natural" is generally meaningless and certainly is not a substitute for "organic." The USDA does require that when the term is applied to meat and poultry products that they not contain any artificial flavoring, colors, chemical preservatives, or synthetic ingredients. But this claim can be used by anyone—there is no independent agency verifying its accuracy.

FREE-RANGE. While this conjures up images of chickens clucking and pecking their way blissfully around a farmyard, the reality is considerably less storybook. Technically, free-range chickens must be offered access to the great outdoors. But bully chickens, higher up in the pecking order, often don't allow less-pushy poultry to get to the door. What's more, that opening could be open for only minutes each day and still, legally, allow a farmer to call the meat or eggs "free-range."

conditions. Factory farms contribute significantly to water pollution and air pollution, and—bird-flu and mad-cow worriers take note—factory farm conditions offer the perfect environment for the spread of disease.

Fishing for Healthy Seafood

Health-conscious consumers have been told that a diet rich in fish is a good one. However, that hardly holds water when much of the fish being eaten is high in mercury or when we're eating seafood right out of the food chain. According to the Union of Concerned Scientists, "habitat destruction and wasteful fishing practices have led to significant declines in wild fish populations." Indeed, it is estimated that some 70 percent of the world's natural fishing grounds have been overfished. So what's a fish aficionado to do? There are a couple of basic tenets for seafood lovers:

Go wild, not farmed. Among the concerns with farmed salmon is the large amount of fish waste and excess feed released into coastal waters. The crowded conditions make the fish more prone to disease, requiring antibiotics.

A Cuppa Coffee Consciousness

Fair trade, shade grown, rain forest friendly . . . even bird friendly. There seems no end to the labels stamped on such products as coffee and tea. Nor any end to the ecological ramifications related to delivering us those treats we love. Global Exchange calls them "sweatshops in fields"—plantations worked by poorly paid, badly treated people and dedicated to one crop (there are dangers inherent in monoculture including a generally greater need for pesticides). It is possible, however, to get a jolt of caffeine without jolting the planet. Problem is, there's so many darn labels that we start to wonder where the consumer-friendly label is. Herewith, your drinking dictionary (as for those Starbucks sizes where a "tall" is a small and a "grande" isn't so grand at all—it's just a medium . . . well you're on your own).

Shade grown. Grown the traditional way, under a canopy of trees, which attracts birds that act as natural pest control.

Bird friendly. Both shade grown and organic.

Rainforest Alliance Certified. Shade-grown coffee by family farmers.

Green. Means only that you roast it yourself, though you can get green beans that are shade grown and organic.

EDUCATE YOURSELF ABOUT OVERFISHING. The popularity of certain species of fish has led to a serious decline. Find out what fish are widely available and what fish are on the run. Blue fin tuna, for example, is under siege; while wild-caught Alaskan salmon is a go. The widely regarded best resource comes from Monterey Bay Aquarium, which produces a Seafood Watch Pocket Guide, conveniently divided into geographic regions so it's pertinent to your particular area: Download it at www.mbayaq.org/cr/cr_seafoodwatch/download.asp.

DONATING OUR BODIES TO SCIENCE: GENETICALLY MODIFIED FOODS

While the average consumer may not have heard about genetically modified food (also called genetically modified organisms or GMOs, genetically engineered or GE foods, biotech foods, or, by those opposed, Frankenfoods), they've likely been eating it.

Your bowl of Kellogg's Raisin Bran? It most likely contains GMOs, says The True Food Network. Skippy peanut butter? Probably. That Heinz ketchup? Uh-huh. . . . GM food is produced from crops whose genetic makeup has been altered through a process called recombinant DNA, or gene splicing, to create a desirable trait. GE foods differ from non-GE foods in that they contain one or more new genes and usually make a new protein. Cornell University, which has a Genetically Engineered Organisms Public Issues Education Project (GEO-PIE) estimates that at least 60 to 70 percent of processed foods contain at least one ingredient from a GE plant—mostly because conventional farmers have embraced GE corn and soybeans, both of which are common ingredients in so many food products. On labels, they'll appear as soy protein, soy flour, soy protein isolate, lecithin, oil, isoflavones, corn-flour, oil, syrup, starch, masa, and gluten, among such other ingredients as aspartame, dextrose, fructose, monosodium glutamate, and xanthan gum (for a full list, go to www.geo-pie.cornell.edu).

One major concern—already addressed in the EU, Japan, Hungary, Brazil, and other countries, all of which don't allow GMO crops at all or allow only limited GMO crops and insist on labeling them as such—is that this is essentially uncharted territory. With no labeling, dubious safety testing, and little regulation of GMOs in the food supply, there is certainly the potential for problems.

Green Guidance:
Fishing for Answers

It's easy to drown in the confusion surrounding seafood. Just when you think you've got the wild or farmed question down, you come across something labeled organic farmed. Besides, with the predictions that overfishing will deplete fish stocks by 2050, it's enough to make you order a burger. However, fish is still recommended by many with good eco-cred as a healthy choice. But choose carefully. A good rule is to eat lower on the food chain—think sardines. With the issue of sustainable seafood, there seems to always be a catch. One label that's working hard to clear things up is the Marine Stewardship Council. Fish with the MSC certification are the reel . . . er . . . real deal.

Mooo-ve away from rBGH

The artificially engineered growth hormone, known interchangeably as rBGH, rBST, or Posilac, produced by agri-giant Monsanto and used to boost milk production in cows, has been getting a lot of attention recently. And that's a good thing. Milk, we're told from the time we're tots, is good for us. But increased scrutiny around the use of this growth hormone, which contains elevated levels of insulin-like growth factor (IGF-1) and which some studies indicate could raise the risk of various cancers, is challenging whether that's always true. Samuel Epstein, author of What's in Your Milk, writes that "rBGH makes cows sick. . . . As a result, rBGH milk is frequently contaminated by pus from the mastitis and antibiotics used to treat the mastitis." Monsanto, not surprisingly, disagrees.

While many nations have banned rBGH, the hormone is still widely used in the United States. And dairies wanting to label their milk rBGH-free are being challenged by Monsanto, which has filed a formal complaint with the FDA to demand a label ban. My advice? Purchase organic milk, when possible, which also generally allows you to skirt the whole factory farm issue. And steer clear of companies interested only in milking profits from consumers.

On the health side, one concern is the introduction of allergens into foods that have historically not caused allergic reactions. Another is the inadvertent creation of toxins and the alteration of a food's nutritional makeup.

Proponents point to genetic engineering of food as a way to solve world hunger, and produce crops that can withstand severe weather conditions, such as storms and drought, as well as crops that require fewer pesticides, as protection can be built right in. However, even the United Nations notes that world hunger is more a problem of distribution of food than production. And Cornell University points out that there's been only a modest decline in pesticide use applied to GE crops and that "real environmental impacts [are] difficult to assess."

Opponents also fear that virulent new strains of viruses, pests, or weeds will emerge. Also, genes engineered into plants and animals can spread to other species and into wild populations, effectively altering complex ecosystems—and there would be no way of turning back. And, in a fox-guarding-the-henhouse way, the companies pioneering most biotech research are the same companies that stand to gain the most from controlling it. It all sounds very futuristic. But it's happening right now.

We've been part of a GM experiment, mostly without our knowledge or our consent. Deborah Garcia, creator of the documentary on genetically modified foods, *The Future of Food,* says that 80 to 90 percent of consumers are outraged to discover that GM food is in our supply. "We don't want it," says Garcia. "It hasn't been properly tested . . . and [most] don't want to support corporate control of food." She says consumers need to demand proper health testing and labelling of GM products. "Let the consumer decide," she says.

To avoid GM foods:

- Don't purchase packaged or processed foods.
- Buy foods that are certified organic.
- Visit www.truefoodnow.org's shopper's guide and check out which brands are free of GMOs.

What's Up?

A food revolution, that's what.

Ronnie Cummins of the Organic Consumers Association says that "consumers are on a journey of awakening," admitting that it can be confusing at first until consumers realize that with every purchase they're revealing their key values. For many that realization has kicked in, which, he believes, is exactly why organic is booming, along with fair trade and the trend toward supporting local businesses. "Driving this trend is the consumer," he states, pointing to a leap in consciousness. "If we continue mobilizing as consumers, we'll move beyond casting votes in the marketplaces to changing public policy."

Marion Nestle agrees, citing the increased focus on and criticism of the food industry and corporate agriculture as "a social movement. . . . Just by the simple act of going into a store and choosing organic, you're making a statement about the way that you want food grown, and a lot of people are willing to pay for that."

In a nutshell, organic food is free of pesticides and chemical fertilizers, which means it's much less harmful for the environment and for farm workers. And of course, it's better for us. David Suzuki, award-winning scientist and environmentalist, notes that in a taste-test, organic fruit was rated to be the sweetest of the bunch. Simple choice, right? Well, it was until big business realized

Coke: The Choice of a New Generation . . . of Farmers

You know how annoyed you get when you open a can of Coke and it sprays all over you? Well, if you were a cotton crop, you'd now be protected from bugs and pests. Really. Farmers in India have discovered a new use for soda pop—protecting their cotton and chile fields. According to a 2004 report in *The Guardian* newspaper in the UK, hundreds of Indian farmers were turning to Coke, Pepsi, and local soft drinks to deter pests. It's a much cheaper—and safer—alternative to the most common pesticides from giants Monsanto, Shell, and Dow.

that the organic market is booming—and they want a piece of the organic pie. Noting that there's green to be made (cash, not crops), corporate heavyweights such as Kraft, Heinz, ConAgra, even Pepsi and Coca-Cola, are offering organic products. Take, for example, Organic Oreos and Organic Frosted Flakes, which certainly strain the traditional definition of organic. Ronnie Cummins said in a February 2006 *Consumer Reports* article that "Consumer spending on organic has . . . attracted big players who want to bend the rules so that they can brand their products as organic without incurring the expenses involved in truly living up to organic standards." There is some concern about Wal-Mart entering the organic market—that demand exceeding supply will drive standards even lower . . . and that Wal-Mart's legendary price cuts will mean that even organic farmers will be compelled to cut corners to produce organic food more cheaply.

This means that the organic certification offering consumers a reliable shorthand they can trust to mean that the food has undergone a unified, centralized evaluation system with very clear guidelines is under siege. In October 2005, Congress weakened the organic-labeling law to include the use of synthetic ingredients in "organic" goods, over the protests of more than 325,000 consumers and 250 organic-food companies. This new law affects mostly processed products. In the meantime, organic farmers and dedicated organic food companies have been valiantly holding firm, in the hopes that an educated public will insist on food that subscribes to genuine organic principles.

What Can You Do?

Fortunately, there are plenty of options in the food aisle, from buying organic to visiting your farmers' markets to eating less meat. Find options that suit your taste.

BECOME A LOCAVORE

Try to eat foods grown close to your home, which helps to reduce greenhouse gas emissions from transport as well as supporting your neighbors. This means, of course, that you'll be eating produce only in season. Living in a colder climate, I confess I cheat occasionally and splurge on organic raspberries or cantaloupe to offset the steady diet of root vegetables and apples. I'm inevitably disappointed, though, as produce from far-flung locales just isn't as juicy or sweet. And there is still winter bounty—expect potatoes, pears, apples, onions, turnips, and more, along with preserves from summer. Farmers need our support in the winter, too. If you like to eat out, choose a spot that also uses local, seasonal ingredients. More chefs are embracing the Slow Food Movement, which focuses on savoring meals and savoring the planet together.

Buy Organic

True, the price can seem unreasonable, given that a very similar looking item is just across the aisle for less. In particular, dairy and meat can cost considerably—sometimes 100 percent—more. Is it worth it?

The short answer is yes. Organic food remains one sure way to guarantee that the food you're eating and feeding your family is free of pesticides, hormones, and antibiotics and isn't genetically modified. And eating an organic diet has almost immediate effects. Scientists at Emory University and the University of Washington, along with the Centers for Disease Control and Prevention conducted a study that measured organophosphates (pesticides) in twenty-three children aged three to eleven, all of whom had been eating a conventional (read un-organic) diet. Urine samples from all of them contained metabolites of the common pesticides malathion and chlorpyrifos. Then the children switched to an organic diet, and the pesticides in their urine almost immediately dropped to undetectable levels. When the children returned to a conventional diet, the pesticide levels went back up.

Lizzie Vann, founder of the British children's food company Organix, puts it this way: "Organic food's strength lies in what it doesn't contain. This stretches well beyond excluding agricultural chemicals such as fertilizers and pesticides, to prohibition of artificial preservatives, colors, sweeteners, residual antibiotics, hydrogenated fats, processing aids and meaningless starches. There is, in fact, only food in organic food."

And that's a good thing, especially for little people. Because children eat two to four times more food per pound of body weight compared to adults, it only makes sense to ensure that

Green Guidance:
Drink Wine and Save the Iberian Lynx

Wine with screw tops is losing its stigma as the choice of unsophisticated coeds. Fine wine is increasingly coming capped with twist offs. But all this convenience comes at a price: Indeed, no less of an eco-authority than the World Wildlife Fund pleads with us to keep drinking wine with cork stoppers. "There is a risk that the Western Mediterranean cork oak landscapes will face an economic crisis, an increase in poverty, an intensification of forest fires, a loss of irreplaceable biodiversity," says the WWF in its Cork Screwed? leaflet. Turns out these cork forests also provide homes to such endangered species as the Iberian lynx, the Iberian imperial eagle, and the barbary deer. Cork stoppers represent 70 percent of the market.

they're ingesting as few contaminants as possible, particularly when their immature systems have a harder time excreting those contaminants.

BUY DIRECT FROM FARMERS

You may not live on a farm, but that doesn't mean you can't have farm-fresh produce at your door once a week. Just ask Simone Smith and Ryan Kennedy. The couple joined a local Community Shared Agriculture (CSA) for $325 for a half share (a full share would have cost $550). From June through October, "vegetables are harvested Friday morning and delivered to our home Friday afternoon," says Smith. CSA programs help support local organic farmers by ensuring they're prepaid for a share of their annual produce. What's more, by buying local, far less greenhouse gases are emitted because the food doesn't travel as far. Farmers' markets are another great option—you can meet the folks who grow your food, get some great deals, and reconnect with the rhythms of nature. To find CSAs or farmers' markets near you, visit www.ams.usda.gov/farmersmarkets/map.htm, www.localharvest.org, or www.foodroutes.org.

EAT FAMILY MEALS

It seems that during the past few decades or so while we were busy scarfing down Big Macs in our car, wondering why the hell everybody around us was getting so damn fat—and now that you mention it, even my sweats are feeling a bit snug—a scary thing was happening to our food system. Call it the convenience

---

The Dirtiest Dozen

The Children's Health and Environmental Coalition offers this list of the most pesticide-contaminated produce:

- apples
- bell peppers
- celery
- cherries
- imported grapes
- nectarines
- peaches
- pears
- potatoes
- red raspberries
- spinach

Buy these organically when possible, or check with your local farmer in season. You can also print out a wallet guide to pesticides in produce by visiting www.foodnews.org, brought to you by the Environmental Working Group.

The Creators of the Hundred-Mile Diet

James MacKinnon and Alisa Smith are both journalists, often writing on environmental issues, who kept coming up against the troubling statistic that most food travels at least 1,500 miles from farm to plate. They decided to start, on the first day of spring 2005, eating for one year only food that came from a hundred-mile radius around their home in Vancouver, British Columbia. They insisted that every ingredient of every food item they ate was local. While MacKinnon admits it was "a fairly extreme experiment" and one that he wouldn't recommend starting on the first day of spring (late summer or fall might be better, he says with a laugh), it ultimately gave him and Smith an incredible experience.

"It's not about self-denial," he explains. "The process was challenging but the experience of reconnecting to the seasons, to the landscape . . . the rewards are instant." He points to the relationships they developed with a beekeeper and a fisherman, among others. "There's real pleasure to be had in that reconnection." He admits the experiment had its challenges—he got sick of potatoes, he notes, and at one point took a break from salmon—but he also discovered the diversity that was available. "Most people would be blown away by what's available if you look for it," he says. To those who are afraid to make such a commitment, MacKinnon advises they try what they think they can manage. It might be that instead of a banana each morning, they eat an apple or another locally grown fruit. Or they might start shopping at a farmers' market. "Do what you feel you can take on," he urges.

He believes the reason this experiment resonated with so many people—media from around the world covered it, there continues to be an active website (www.100milediet.org), and their book, *Plenty,* was published in April 2007—is that there's a sense of loss among North Americans around the issue of food. "We've forgotten just how good eating can be."

coma. We're crazy busy, the ads tell us. We nod in agreement. Far too busy to prepare a meal. But help is at hand—as close as the nearest prepared meal that requires we do little more than heat and eat. And what do we do with all that time we saved? Well, if you believe best-selling author Michael Pollan, who commented in an interview with the online environmental magazine Grist (www.grist.org), we're surfing the net, watching television, and chatting on the phone. "I think if people want to put some time into getting good food and cooking good food," he says, "they absolutely could do it."

Now before all you hardworking parents band together to create little voodoo dolls of me and stick them with tiny needles

What the Hell Were They Thinking?

Arsenic in chicken feed? Yep, that was the brainchild of those in the chicken industry—add arsenic to the feed to kill parasites and promote growth. Problem is, the arsenic then winds up in the chicken, which winds up on the plate in front of us. The Institute for Agriculture and Trade Policy conducted a study in 2006 in which among 155 samples from supermarket chicken it was found that 55 percent had detectable levels of arsenic (do I need to mention that arsenic is a highly toxic carcinogen or do you, like the average ten-year-old, already know that?). All 90 of the fast food chicken products sampled contained arsenic.

(I'm just quoting Michael Pollan—though I do think he has a point), hear me out: Plenty of other insanely busy people think that North Americans need to reconnect with the pleasure of good, fresh food and sharing a meal with family and friends. And to all you naysayers, get a load of this (I'm not making this up): A decade-long study from the National Center on Addiction and Substance Abuse revealed that teens who regularly have meals with their family are less likely to get into fights, think about suicide, smoke, drink, or use drugs, and are more likely to wait until they're older to have sex, and perform better academically than teens who do not. And when they move away from home, they always remember to call their mothers and thank them for such a blissful childhood (OK, I'm making that last bit up). The study also showed that eating with parents was associated with a higher intake of fruits, vegetables, and dairy products.

Become a Veg-head, at Least Part Time

For me, it started with those huge trucks on the highway transporting animals to their death. I'd see those woeful eyes looking at me from between the metal slats, feel the familiar pangs of guilt, and vow to stop eating meat. However, generally less than a few hours later, I'd be biting into a burger, chewing on a chicken fajita, or tucking into turkey. What's more, I wasn't really a vegetable fan. Can't stand asparagus. Think cauliflower tastes weird. Won't touch a Brussels sprout. What, exactly, was I going to eat if I cut meat out of my diet?

Quite a bit, it turns out. One night at a barbecue shortly after my fortieth birthday, I tasted my first veggie burger. It tasted good—really good. And in that instant, I decided I would not turn back. I decided, at forty years of age, that it was time to stand up for my principles—which included not being complicit in the warehousing and abuse of animals. I had to admit I viewed vegetarianism as somehow contrary to our position as top of the food chain, but frankly, the view from the top looked decidedly inhumane. I wanted no part of it. Besides, I always imagined vegetarians to be these willowy, ethereal women, though in hindsight I guess counting on a vegetarian diet to make me grow three inches and lose ten pounds was expecting a bit much.

Nonetheless, for the next two years, I discovered the delicacies of vegetarian cuisine. And I've never enjoyed food more.

©2006 Philip Street / Fisher archive at philipstreet.com

Turns out I didn't dislike vegetables at all—just vegetables cooked to within an inch of their lives.

The benefits of vegetarianism extend far beyond personal health (and emotional well-being—it feels really good to be able to look a cow straight in the eye). While a vegetarian diet is credited for providing a longer life with reduced risk of such diseases as diabetes, hypertension, coronary artery disease, and some cancers, it also makes sense from a environmental point of view to eat less or no meat:

- The world's cattle alone consume a quantity of food equal to the caloric needs of 8.7 billion people—more than the entire population of the planet.
- Eighty percent of agricultural land in the US is used to raise animals for food.
- Nearly half of all water consumed in the US is used to raise animals for food. While it takes 2,500 gallons of water to produce a pound of meat, it takes only 60 gallons of water to produce a pound of wheat.
- Raising animals for food creates more water pollution in the US than any other industry, with 87,000 pounds of excrement being produced each second (yep, you read that right), much of which enters streams and rivers.
- Each vegetarian saves an acre of trees each year. Tropical rain forests are being cleared to create grazing land for cattle with space equivalent to seven football fields being cleared every minute.
- Compared to pasta, producing red meat uses twenty times the land, causes seven times the water pollution and water use, and creates three times the greenhouse gas emissions.

I've since started eating organic, humanely raised, local meat—in large part because my family of carnivores didn't want to join me in my vegetarian world and I found it hard to cook for three meat-eating kids, a meat-loving husband, and me. We do, however, eat meat considerably less often and when we do, it makes up a much smaller part of our plates. So while the cost of organic meat is higher, because we're eating so much less our spending has remained pretty much the same.

Those more virtuous than I, who want to embrace a truly vegetarian or vegan diet, can find considerable support. Check out: www.vegetariantimes.com, www.goveg.com, www.vrg.org, or www.vegsource.com.

There are also a number of great cookbooks, books on raising vegetarian children, and more. Far from being a fringe movement, vegetarianism is growing, with an increase in restaurants, food choices, and acceptance. Just don't expect to get taller and thinner.

Shopping with Kids

You've pledged to buy local to help reduce greenhouse gas emissions from transport, and suddenly you've got a cart filled with cantaloupe from Guatemala and grapes from Costa Rica. (I ask you, what mother is going to say no to a three-year-old begging for fresh fruit, even if it was flown three thousand miles to the store? The kid isn't asking for Ding Dongs!) You're wrestling Oscar Mayer's Lunchables out of your eight-year-old's hands while she hangs on as if it's the Holy Grail and tearfully pleads that "all the other kids bring them to school." You refuse. She sulks. You both lose your appetite.

What's the Controversy?

How is it kids have such strong opinions about what cereal, cookies, or snacks to buy? It can't be that the labels are just so appealing (though Dora the Explorer seems adept at hawking everything from gummie snacks to lip balm). Marion Nestle says parents barely stand a chance against marketers who instill the message in kids that we're bumbling idiots and that the real power to make purchases is—and should be—in kids' hands. In a no-holds-barred interview, Nestle referred to the food industry's marketing to kids as "extraordinarily subversive of parental authority." She states the obvious, which had escaped me and, I suspect, countless other parents: "The purpose of marketing to kids is to put the power over food choices in kids' hands. . . . How dare they do this? How dare they target six-year-olds for eating junk food?" Damn good question, Marion. And one that raises the further question: Why are we letting kids—who think they can save the world from evil by donning a dishtowel as a cape—make decisions about how to spend the family's grocery money? These delightful but not entirely responsible little beings would consume a steady diet of Twinkies and root beer.

What's Up?

Junk food, obesity, diabetes, and other concerns are putting kids' nutrition on the front pages of many agendas. And there are plenty of organizations fighting the powerful marketing machines for kids' food and encouraging parents to think with their wallets. Here are two:

THE CENTER FOR SCIENCE IN THE PUBLIC INTEREST. This nonprofit's *Nutrition Action Healthletter* offers easy-to-read and family-friendly info on many convenience foods and dietary issues. Check it out at www.cspinet.org/nah.

THE ORGANIC CONSUMERS ASSOCIATION. This group's website (www.organicconsumers.org) is another that offers timely, pertinent info on issues of concern to parents. Check out its "Appetite for Change" section, specifically addressing children and junk food.

What Can You Do?

So what's a tired parent to do when Junior is in the cereal aisle screaming for Reese's Puffs and Mom has her eye on organic granola? Those who market to children call it pester power—the unrelenting demands of children that finally wear a parent down—and they work hard to harness it for their own benefit. But knowledge is power. Herewith, tips for combat:

- Teach kids to cook. Marion Nestle believes this is the single best thing we can do with our kids around food. Children, even little ones, love to help create a meal—and generally derive great pleasure in sharing it. If it seems daunting, try to do it on weekends, when everyone isn't so busy. Or assign each family member a different evening to take responsibility for the evening meal. Family cook-offs can also be fun—vying for the chance to dazzle each other with culinary creativity.

- Limit the amount of advertising your child is exposed to. In the United States, the average child sees 40,000 advertisements a year. And you can bet they're not for broccoli and peaches. If kids don't see it, they tend not to think about it.

- Involve kids in the planning of meals. Let them know why we make healthier choices. (My kids are getting tired of me telling them, "It's not my job to make you happy. That's your job. My job is to keep you healthy. And it's a job I take seriously . . ." But I'm convinced that someday they'll thank me.)

>>> PURCHASE POWER <<<

- **Avoid packaged and processed foods in favor of fresh.**
- **Buy local and/or organic when possible.**
- **Buy direct from farmers either through roadside stands, farmers' markets, CSAs, or food co-ops.**
- **Consider joining or starting a buying club where you get your staples in bulk, then divvy it up.**
- **Help your kids become critical consumers—teach them to understand labels (you'll have to learn first!) and what to avoid, and why.**

Curbing Pint-Sized Consumers

4

What the virtuous consumer says about:

The toys
- *Detox the toy chest*

The gear
- *The "must-haves" to the "don't-bothers" of baby gear*
- *The defining word on diapers*
- *Eco-friendly school supplies*

The marketing
- *Protecting children from commercial exploitation*

It's amazing how much a few pieces of plastic and paper will sell for if the purchasers are parents or grandparents. Lawrence Kutner

I stared at the blue line in shock. Though I'd suspected it for a week or more, the evidence was now clear. I was pregnant. I was also terrified. I didn't know how to be someone's mother. I'd never even been a particularly good babysitter, generally eager to get the kids to bed so I could get to the chips and soda pop and call my friends. As per my usual coping strategy, I began to panic and frantically searched my mind for ways out of this mess. My husband remained unruffled. From there I moved into information gathering. I read every pregnancy book and parenting manual I could lay my increasingly swollen hands on. But the worry raged on unabated. And now, three children later (I really should revisit that birth control section of this book), I, like so many other parents, continue to worry.

Studies reveal that we are probably the most diligent parents ever. Yet worry is our national pastime. We worry that our children will get some childhood disease if we don't vaccinate them. We worry that our children will get some disorder if we *do* vaccinate them. That they'll be social pariahs. That they'll be abducted. That someone will slip them crack at recess. That they'll get shot by a classmate who watched one too many violent video games. That they'll go out in the world and get hurt. Disappointed. Defeated.

I'm tempted to simply put my children under glass and keep them safe forever.

However, it seems my worry has been largely misplaced. Instead of worrying about what might threaten my children *out there,* I should have been taking a closer look inside my house. For the most part, the objects we bring into our homes pose the most pervasive threat to our children's health and well-being. (Cue ominous music here.)

The Toys

I loved Barbie. I loved her clothes, her hair, her Porsche, her bright orange camper off-gassing toxic fumes. The smell of vinyl still evokes in me strong memories of Christmas morning 1973.

Yet, despite my passion for all things Barbie—a passion I reluctantly abandoned long after my friends had deemed me a freak—I made the decision early and easily after the birth of my first daughter that I didn't want her playing with Barbie. Perhaps I should have devised a plan to execute this feminist stance of mine. Because then, on my daughter's third birthday, her beloved babysitter (who looked a lot like Barbie herself, come to think of it) offered a gift that contained no less than the updated incarnation of my beloved childhood playmate. I was almost speechless—though the realization quickly settled in that, while Barbie entered my daughter's life considerably earlier than she'd entered mine, she would have nonetheless arrived at some point, all long hair and long legs, racy cars, and flashy clothes.

As soon as our babysitter left, I sized up my daughter, still staring at the doll that looked so unlike the baby dolls she was accustomed to. Finally, I spoke. "Real women don't look like that," I said lamely. My daughter, a wise old soul since birth, looked at me, then Barbie, then back at me. "I know," she said.

Is there anywhere that our out-of-control consumerism, our gotta-get-it greediness, is more apparent than in the stuff we purchase for our offspring? I've been in playrooms that rival Toys "R" Us. Come to think of it, when I was a kid, who, except Richie Rich, even *had* a playroom? And I am, by no means, an innocent. While I headed into parenthood with the best of intentions—wooden shape sorters, Lego, a staunch refusal to allow Barbie to dominate my daughter's toy box—something went seriously awry. Three kids later, my house runneth over with Bratz, Hot Wheels, Rescue Heroes, and My Little Pony. And gender role stereotyping is the least of my worries.

What's the Controversy?

There are two areas of concern around children's toys—their impact on children's health and their influence on children's social development. Turns out toys can be toxic in more ways than one.

HEALTH EFFECTS

Most toys are still manufactured out of less-than-earth-friendly materials, including that demon PVC, a known carcinogen that keeps on leaching long after it's landfilled. Other toxins of concern are lead, phthalates, PBDEs (toxic flame retardants) and bisphenol A.

PVC. The manufacture of PVC releases toxins into the air and water called dioxins, which enter the food chain and contaminate food sources. Two additives in PVC make it so demonized in the environmental world—lead and phthalates.

LEAD. Lead, as we all know from paint and pencils, is bad stuff, and even in the teensiest amounts can impair brain development. It can also be found in the paint in older buildings and on metal toys.

PHTHALATES. These ubiquitous chemicals are used to soften hard plastic. Ernie's beloved rubber duckie? Might well be PVC. Phthalates have been linked to premature birth, early onset of puberty in girls, reduced sperm quality in males, and reproductive defects. Not exactly gifts you want to give your children.

While the EU has banned certain chemicals, including PVC and phthalates, the United States is lagging. A widely proposed ban a few years ago led many companies to at least remove PVC from infants' toys, as babies are notorious chewers and suckers. However, that still leaves the over-threes and their parents pretty much on their own in fending off toxins in the toy box. And since manufacturers aren't required to label products as containing toxic chemicals, and there's an increasing influx of toys from China and other Asian countries that have no regulations around this, parents without a PhD in biochemistry are left puzzled. What's more, in response to consumer concern, some manufacturers are labeling toys "phthalate free." But according to the US Public Interest Research Group (PIRG), the federal government doesn't regulate the use of this label or ensure its accuracy. The PIRG commissioned its own test and found that of eight toys labeled phthalate free, six tested positive for detectable levels of phthalates.

Bisphenol A. This hormone-disrupting chemical has been linked to Down's syndrome, early onset of puberty, cancers, and a host of other conditions. It leaches out of products in normal use and has been found in humans, especially in placental and fetal tissue.

PBDEs (polybrominated diphenylethers). The purpose of these is to slow the spread of fire in many consumer products. But their use in baby products poses a threat to developing bodies and brains. They've been found in the breast milk of mothers and in some fetuses at levels that are shown to impair learning.

And plastic toys aren't the only ones that threaten to poison playtime. Stuffed toys are frequently full of synthetics or pesticide-soaked cottons. PVC is often used for the eyes and noses of stuffed animals. And, as we will discuss in the next chapter, toys are routinely bound and gagged in enough packaging to make even Russian nesting dolls claustrophobic.

Social Effects

You're not imagining it—toys are cheaper than they used to be. You're also not imagining the proliferation of toys imported from Asia. As my just-learning-to-read five-year-old once asked me, "Why is everything made in China?" The answer, reported Juliet Schor, the author of *Born to Buy: The Commercialized Child and the New Consumer Culture,* is that "wages in Chinese toy factories [range] from 7 to 33 cents an hour and toy prices have declined . . . by 33 percent in the past 10 years." She estimates, conservatively, that the average American child is now acquiring sixty-nine new toys per year.

"I want my kids to have what I didn't" has become the mantra of a generation of overworked, overtired parents—and many can afford to give more to their kids. But overconsumption creates a sense of entitlement that's hard to break, long after someone else has stopped footing the bills. In other words, it could be a one-way-ticket to Debtsville as children grow into adults who simply can't be without the latest "toy." Perhaps not surprisingly, credit card debt in the past decade has doubled among those aged eighteen to twenty-four.

And more toys, at whatever age, don't bring happiness. For her book, Schor conducted a study of three hundred kids. She

Kids love to adorn them-
selves, and manufacturers
are happy to supply little
Ivanas with plenty of faux
pearls and gems. However,
the Sierra Club warns
parents to keep cheap
jewelry out of kids' hands
because of the possible
lead it may contain. Noting
that "there is no safe level
of lead for children" (indeed
a child died in Feb. 2006
from ingesting a piece of toy
jewelry), it urges parents to:
avoid purchasing toys from
vending machines; avoid
glossy fake painted pearls,
which might be painted with
lead paint; avoid toys that
have small metallic parts
(that can be swallowed);
and find out which stores,
suppliers, and manufacturers do not contain lead in
their products. Search on
www.cehca.org/jewelry.
htm#other, the site of the
Center for Environmental
Health.

discovered that kids consumed with consumption were more
likely than others to feel anxious or depressed.

Whatever they might say to you, most kids would prefer your
attention to your money. *Yeah, sure,* you scoff. But get this: A
2003 New American Dream poll revealed that more than half of
the nine- to fourteen-year-olds who responded would rather do
something fun with their mom and dad than go to the mall. They
like you. They really like you.

What's Up?

The level of pressure on the Consumer Product Safety Commission (CPSC) to ban PVC and phthalates in all children's
toys, though consumers must keep it up. According to a 2003
Greenpeace USA report, toy behemoths Mattel and Hasbro
simply skirted the issue of what chemicals are in their toys,
while Playmobil and Lego took the high road and went PVC free.
Greenpeace spokesperson Lisa Finaldi, however, warns that the
research is out of date (Greenpeace no longer issues a toxic-toy
report) and even those countries that banned the chemicals
might not necessarily be upholding the ban. Parents are left to do
the homework.

In fall of 2006, San Francisco took the radical step of
instituting a ban, modeled on the EU ban, prohibiting the sale,
distribution, and manufacture of baby products containing any
level of bisphenol A and certain levels of phthalates. The ban
was being challenged by toymakers and affected companies, and
a hearing was slated for January 2007. A spokesperson for the
EPA admitted to the *San Francisco Chronicle* that the agency's
guidelines for safe human exposure to the chemicals are decades
old and don't take into account new research. And storeowners
expressed confusion about what products they would have to
take off their shelves, as no one really knows what chemicals
go into what products. The *Chronicle*'s own tests revealed that
most toys—even those labeled "safe, nontoxic"—contained the
banned chemicals.

With regard to the volume of toys and products today's kids
have, parents are fighting an uphill battle with a clever, merciless
marketing machine aimed at children. However, an increasing
number of organizations—such as Commercial Alert (www.

The Kids on the Bus Go Cough, Cough, Cough

Anyone who has idled behind a school bus knows the toxic fumes spewing from its tailpipe. But in fact it's worse for the student riders inside, says Environmental Defense, a leading nonprofit. Indeed, 24 million kids board the big yellow buses each day for a round trip to school—breathing in a chemical cocktail that boosts asthma attacks and the risk of contracting cancer later in life. To find out more, including what you can do about this, go to www.epa.gov/cleanschoolbus.

commercialalert.org) and Campaign for a Commercial-free Childhood (www.commercialfreechildhood.org)—are working hard to legislate the amount of advertising aimed at children. Ultimately, it comes down to parents themselves to set the limits. And to endure the tantrums, which will—I promise—eventually subside.

What Can You Do?

Without appropriate labeling, it's hard for parents to know how to avoid toxic chemicals. Greenpeace's Finaldi recommends that parents simply avoid soft plastic toys unless they're clearly marked as PVC free, or call the manufacturer's customer service number and ask what is in the toys. The latter approach also sends a clear message to companies to clean up their act—and their products. You may also want to get involved in your local Public Interest Research Group (see www.uspirg.org) to put pressure on toy companies to keep chemicals out.

Parents can also test for lead in products that they suspect might contain PVC (that "vinyl" smell can also be a tip-off). Designed to test for lead in paint, these testing swabs can also indicate lead in toys.

Finally, keep in mind that young children can be happy with an attentive adult and a soft blankie. My first daughter spent hours on the floor with wooden spoons and old pots and lids. She also loved to climb in and out of a laundry basket and would do it, no kidding, for an hour or more. A tea towel over her head to play peekaboo was another big hit. And my two younger children delighted in the antics of the older kids. In other words, toys are a luxury, not a necessity, no matter what the toy companies are telling us.

>>> PURCHASE POWER <<<

- Get your child a library card (and one for yourself, while you're at it) and teach them the pleasure of borrowing and returning. Library cards can change lives. I've seen it happen—I've had it happen.
- Look for the words *PVC free* on toy labels. Or give them the sniff test—if it smells like a beach ball, toss it.
- Choose wooden toys, toys made with organic materials, or those from companies such as Brio, Chicco, Discovery Toys, Haba, and Lego.
- For the bathtub, stick to natural rubber toys if you can't find PVC-free ones.
- Purchase a Lead Check Swabs kit—either online at www.leadcheck.com or at stores like Lowe's, Home Depot, True Value. Your local hardware or paint store might carry it, too.
- Cut back. Encourage kids to favor quality over quantity—and lead by example (in other words, cut back on your own toys).
- Buy toys with long lives. For example, dollhouses, building sets, and train tables are all famously long lasting and long loved.
- Create a costume box. An old cedar chest from a garage sale filled with clothes and accessories picked up at a secondhand store (or passed down from Grandma) will give kids years of fun. Look for purses, hats, shoes, dresses, and so on.
- Get (and give as gifts) memberships to a local toy library. Kids will always have new-to-them options and you won't have a house full of forgotten toys. Visit the USA Toy Libraries Association at http://usatla.home.comcast.net for more information.
- Purchase products that keep on giving, such as items that support nonprofit organizations. World Vision, World Wildlife Fund, and UNICEF are three worthy groups.
- Avoid battery-operated toys. Batteries contribute mercury, cadmium, and lead to the landfills. Five billion of these little demons are purchased each year. If you must have them, use rechargeable batteries.

The Gear

I sometimes wonder if many newly pregnant folks begin shopping for the baby to distract themselves from the anxiety of impending parenthood. And marketers, no fools at persuading us to part with our money, tap into that anxiety, convincing parents-to-be that Baby needs everything from a stroller that can navigate the terrain in Afghanistan to a plug-in apparatus to warm up baby wipes. Truth is, most babies can easily get by with a lactating mommy and a cozy receiving blanket.

What's the Controversy?

And baby makes . . . a whole lotta stuff, much of which is toxic, unsafe, and expensive. From off-gassing crib mattresses to carcinogenic baby bottles, parents face an obstacle course of kids' products, all vying for a spot in the nursery.

I have poverty as opposed to lofty ideals to thank for the minimalist approach we took with our first baby. But how I coveted those little rattle socks I saw on other babies, convinced that my child's development would be impaired without them. My third child, born into a wealthier family, had all sorts of goodies, including rattle socks (thanks, largely, to incredible generosity on the part of friends). Yet I see little difference in terms of intellect and social adjustment, and all three of my kids began walking at

Getting to School a Greener Way

I don't think I ever got a ride to school. Didn't matter if hailstones the size of cats were coming down, it never crossed my parents' minds to drive me. This isn't an indictment of my parents (honestly, I've worked all that out with a therapist) but proof that kids can walk to school. Or hop on a bike or skateboard. Or lace up their inline skates. Honest. They probably won't be abducted. Or bullied. Or hit by a car. Instead, they'll be less likely to become obese or develop diabetes. They'll live longer. They'll be happier, with higher self-esteem. All because they walked to school. Even in the rain.

For more information about walking to school, organizing a walking school bus, ensuring a safe route for children, and more, visit www.saferoutesinfo.org.

almost exactly the same age, despite their access to (or lack of) a Jolly Jumper. So with knowledge born of experience—together with my newly acquired environmental sensibility—here's the down-and-dirty list of "must-haves" to "don't-bothers."

THE NURSERY

Let's be honest: A decorated nursery is more for the parents than the child, who would happily sleep in the garage. Still, I'm aware how powerful that nesting urge is in new parents, so decorate away. Just be careful not to compromise Junior's—or the pregnant mom's—health.

PAINT. Regular paints and varnishes release volatile organic compounds (VOCs), such as benzene, methylene chloride, formaldehyde, and biocides—all known or suspected carcinogens that pollute indoor air. Pregnant painters are another bad idea—leave the job to the nonpregnant person. In fact, the mom-to-be shouldn't even be around wet paint. Steer clear until surfaces are dry and leave windows open to air out the room. There are a number of zero- or low-VOC paints on the market—a far better choice.

FLOORING. Choose natural-fiber carpets (wool, cotton, or grasses) or a nontoxic, machine-washable rug. You can find great-looking rugs made of everything from recycled bicycle tires to Lycra swimsuit scraps (like those from ABC Carpet & Home). Look also for the Carpet and Rug Institute's new seal of approval, called Green Label Plus, based on the most stringent tests for emissions of individual VOCs. If you opt for hardwood, ensure that the wood is Forest Stewardship Council (FSC) certified, which means it comes from a sustainable source. See other flooring options in chapter 6, "Home, Sweet Home."

BABY FURNITURE

While I've heard lots of arguments for and against the family bed, my own bias is for a crib. Frankly, I'm all for a device that keeps my child safe and contained. What's more, sleep is an increasingly scarce resource at my house, so I support anything that gets me more of it. Since all three of my babies loved their cribs, I could frequently doze in bed in the morning half-listening to them sing, talk to themselves, or work on their standing skills, confident that they were safe. To maximize that safety, you should steer clear of anything made of pressboard, laminated wood, or particle board, as all of these release formaldehyde. If you must choose particle board (or if it's a hand-me-down), the Children's Health and Environmental Coalition recommends that you seal it with a water-based sealant.

A better choice, however, is to look for solid hardwood with low-VOC paints or finishes at "green" stores. Often Mennonite or Amish furniture makers will create eco-friendly baby and kids' furniture, including cribs, high chairs, and playpens. Or you can buy unfinished hardwood furniture and finish it yourself with low-VOC paints or sealers; see Resources for other options.

The mattress you put in that crib will likely, thanks to a government mandate for minimum flammability standards, be treated with a flame retardant. It seems the jury is still out on the pros and cons of the protection (which, unfortunately, comes in the form of toxic fire-retardant chemicals). Some say it's a necessary evil; others note that an organic cotton mattress with wool is naturally flame retardant (I've never seen a sheep up in flames, so maybe there's something to that theory). There are also rubber crib mattresses available, again with organic wool to act as flame retardant. Or purchase a used mattress (make sure it's firm and fits in the crib snugly), which will have likely already off-gassed much of its toxins.

Select organic sheets and blankets. Organic undyed cotton is the best bet for baby clothing, though sleepwear, again, is legislated to have flame retardants. If you eschew sleepwear with PBDEs, ensure that what you choose is snug-fitting (like long underwear).

For change tables and pads, stick with hardwood where possible, though a child spends considerably less time on a change table than in a crib. Avoid vinyl change pads.

BOTTLES

We all know that breast is best—but many moms, for many reasons, offer bottles to their babies (often with breast milk in them). Bottles, however, can contain more than milk—such as bisphenol-A, a hormone-disrupting chemical linked to Down's syndrome, early onset of puberty, cancers, and a host of other

Mary Brune, Mom with a Mission

In March 2005, Mary Brune arrived home from work, then sat down in front of the news to nurse her six-month-old daughter. Brune learned from the television reporter that researchers had examined samples of breast milk across the country. Perchlorate, a toxic component of rocket fuel, had been found in 100 percent of the samples.

Brune was outraged. "This was in my breast milk," she says, still incredulous more than a year later. "Without my consent, without my knowledge, beyond my control . . . [The information] brought something out in me that I didn't know existed."

What came out in her was the motivation to protect something she views as sacred—the ability of a mother to nurse her child without contamination.

Brune did some research and discovered there's more than perchlorate in breast milk: pesticides, lead, mercury, phthalates, flame retardants, and more have all found their way into the milk of nursing moms.

Brune is always careful to stress that, in spite of what she's learned—and passes on to other mothers—breast milk remains better for children than formula. But tackling the issue of contaminants in breast milk, she insists, means speaking out.

And that's exactly what she's been doing. Together with Genevieve Raymond, Shannon Wright, and Kristi Chester Vance, she formed MOMS—Making Our Milk Safe (their website is www.safemilk.org). The California-based group—all relatively new mothers—has been busy trying to make the issue of breast milk contamination front-page news. They succeeded in helping get a law passed that establishes a statewide program to monitor chemicals in the body. But MOMS isn't waiting for that legislation to take effect; they're too busy persuading other moms to take back their own power. "Women as a consumer base have power," Brune says. "We make a lot of buying decisions. And," she says pointedly, "we share information."

That includes information about the toxic chemicals that go into so many of the toys, shampoos, and other products that mothers and children are exposed to.

Retailers and manufacturers would do well to pay attention. "Companies need to understand that if something is hazardous to our families, we're going to talk to each other about it," Brune says. And more are talking about it all the time. The core group of four has grown to three hundred members in twenty-eight states in one short year. And there are more pissed-off moms signing on every day. "We're empowered," Brune says. "It's the job of consumers to police what's out there. Unless you know about it, you can't take action. We're demanding change. Our children deserve it."

This is one mom you don't want to argue with.

conditions. There's no label that indicates what plastic the bottle was made of—the number 7 stamped on many just refers to "other" plastic, though it's often polycarbonate. You can contact the toll-free number for the company and ask, or just stick with glass bottles. If you stick with plastic (even "safe" plastic, such as PETE or HDPE), never heat milk in the microwave and toss plastic items when they're the least bit scratched or cloudy.

NIPPLE CREAMS

Non-mothers might cringe at the thought of cracked, bleeding nipples but they were the sad truth for me. Nipple cream was the balm I needed. Since babies clearly ingest nipple creams every time they breastfeed from a mother using them, it's important to use the safest ones. Consider Natural Nipple Butter or Motherlove Nipple Cream (www.katescaringgifts.com and www.greenfeet. com).

LOTIONS, POTIONS, AND CREAMS

The same concerns apply—times about a bazillion—as laid out in the personal care products section of chapter 1. Too many chemicals are wreaking havoc on endocrine systems, kidneys, livers, and brains (for starters!). The smallest and most vulnerable people deserve—and need—special protection from the chemicals in so many products, even those designed for babies from companies we think we can trust.

Stick to organic or natural brands, such as Burt's Bees, Dr. Bronner's, Aubrey Organics, Avalon Organics, Earth Mama, and Weleda. Or check out Environmental Working Group's Skin Deep site and key in whatever baby product you want to check: www. ewg.org/reports/skindeep.

DIAPERS

There is a movement (ha!) referred to as "elimination communication," or, more to the point, "diaper free," that aims to encourage parents to let their babies bare their bottoms, free of cloth or disposables. Must you tie a poop bag to your baby's posterior? According to the folks at Diaper Free, "Parents learn to listen and respond in the present moment to the baby's needs and communication." In other words, your wee baby goes wee in the toilet. Sounds simple. The catch? Parents must be free to pay close attention to their baby and be able to respond *immediately* when the child exhibits signs of needing to pee or poop. Sound like any parents you know? I don't think so, either.

So, if you also have a life in which you must occasionally turn your attention away from your baby or, perhaps, actually leave your home for, say, bread, you have a decision to make: cloth or disposable. The debate rages on and, frankly, the true eco-winner isn't clear. In one corner, we have disposables, whose fate is to lie for hundreds of years in landfills. In the other, cloth, which requires copious quantities of water to launder.

However, advances in both cloth and disposables are rendering the debate obsolete. Those who want the convenience of disposables might want to try gDiapers, which contain a flushable insert (available at Whole Foods, Wild Oats, and other natural food stores), or Tushies, which are chlorine free and gel free. Cloth-diaper users can either buy their own to launder or use a service. Washing your own cloth diapers is a clear winner in terms of price: Cloth diapers washed at home cost an estimated three cents per use, while a disposable will put you back close to a quarter. Following the laundry tips in chapter 5 makes washing at home greener. But because of their volume, diaper services are an even greener choice.

However, with all the decisions attached to new parenthood, diapering isn't one to lose sleep over (as though you had any sleep left to lose). Choose whatever method suits you. Here are a few tips to green up either choice:

- Flush the poop out of both disposables and cloth. This keeps it out of landfills and reduces the greenhouse gases from its decomposition.
- Choose organic cotton rather than conventional cotton diapers. No pesticides from growing, no dioxins from bleaching.
- If you choose a diaper service, ask if it has any environmental accreditation. Make sure that it doesn't use detergent with phosphates and that there's no chlorine in the rinse water.

WIPES

Companies such as Seventh Generation and Tushies make flushable, eco-friendly wipes bleached by hydrogen peroxide rather than chlorine bleach. Those that are chlorine free will say so on the package. Better still, use little reusable washcloths dipped in warm water. As kids get older (and require less wiping), you can keep a damp washcloth in a zipper-lock bag for emergencies—just ensure it's routinely replaced with a fresh one.

The Marketing

I can distinctly recall the panic I felt at Mommy Group when a one-year-old, prompted by his mother, counted to three. "He learned that from *Teletubbies*," the mother informed us, bursting with pride. "It's very educational. You should turn it on each morning." Like most other parents, I want my children to have access to what they need in life to succeed. At that instant, I stared at my one-year-old, who could *not* count to three, and I wondered if what my child needed was a daily dose of *Teletubbies*. At that point in my motherhood trajectory, I think that if someone had suggested I drink the blood of a spotted gecko to boost my production of breast milk, I would have paused to consider it. Those mommy insecurities can run deep. And I can't deny I've felt it since—every time some other child proudly displays a new video game and the parents boast of the child's incredible hand-eye coordination. Or I hear that a family trip to Disney World was the stuff of their five-year-old's dreams.

What's the Controversy?

Childhood is being bought and sold—to the tune of $15 billion a year, which is what corporations spend on advertising to children. That's 150 times as much as it was in 1983, when the figure was $100 million. And that doesn't even account for the money that goes into the research into *how* to reach into kids' minds . . . and wallets.

Kids today are an easy mark. The average American child between the ages of two and eighteen spends about forty hours a week sitting in front of a television set watching mostly commercialized shows. These days you can't visit the pediatrician or sit in the back of a minivan without staring at a screen.

Susan Linn is the author of *Consuming Kids: The Hostile Takeover of Childhood* and an associate director of Campaign for a Commercial-Free Childhood (www.commercialexploitation.org). She believes that the level of marketing to children is "profoundly disturbing." Kids are easy to access, she points out, thanks to the proliferation of electronic media; they're more frequently home alone, making them increasingly susceptible; unfettered, unregulated capitalism is booming; and we no longer support public space, such as public television and public schools, so they can be free of advertising. And with BusRadio, a new company in Massachusetts, proposing to have a million students by September 2007 listening to radio advertising on the school bus, there's little refuge from the commercial onslaught.

While Linn sees it as largely a societal issue, parents aren't off the hook. Particularly the one in five parents who has put a television in a one-year-old's (or younger!) bedroom. Or the one in three parents who's installed a television in the bedroom of a kid six and under. While Linn says it's naive to think the average parent can combat a $15 billion industry, parents must do what they can to limit the commercial exposure of their children, beginning when they're babies. Indeed, only 6 percent of parents are even aware that the American Academy of Pediatrics recommends that children ages two and under watch no television at

Green Gear for Back to School

Each September, kids across the country drag their parents around malls (or are parents dragging the kids?), talking them into pencils, erasers, binders, and snow-white paper-filled notebooks. Indeed, more than 14 billion pencils are manufactured every year—enough to circle the globe 62 times. Add in highlighters, pens, crayons, and other paraphernalia that students need to go about the business of learning, and you've got a lot of stuff. But is there a greener way to stock the lockers of America? You bet there is.

A FINE POINT. Start by purchasing wood pencils certified by the Forest Stewardship Council. FSC wood comes from forests that are managed in a responsible and sustainable manner. Dixon Ticonderoga makes No. 2 (HB) pencils out of FSC-certified wood and also produces a line of colored pencils. Paper Mate makes recycled pencils called EarthWrite that are available at most office supply stores. Avoid strongly scented markers, which release VOCs.

ROCK, PAPER, SCISSORS. Look for paper that has at least 30 percent postconsumer content. Harder to find but better still is 100 percent postconsumer content. Check out your local Kinko's or visit www.conservatree.org. Kids can cut with recycled stainless-steel scissors with handles made from 30 percent postconsumer plastic—check them out at Office Depot. 3M's ubiquitous Post-It notes are also available in 100 percent recycled versions.

To hold your paper, Office Depot boasts binders made of 100 percent recycled materials. Office Max and Staples both stock notebooks made from varying percentages of postconsumer waste. Kids can even doodle in notebooks made from banana tree fibers (though they can't nibble on them). If just 1 percent of students bought notebooks made from postconsumer waste, 60,000 trees would be saved.

RUBBER BAND MAN . . . ER, COW. Cool animal-shaped rubber bands made from nontoxic silicon make securing stuff fun. A cool recycled rubber bulletin board is just the spot to post reminders, photos, and whatever else. Both are available at www.containerstore.com.

COLOR A TOUCAN—AND SAVE HIS HOME TOO. Crayola's Rainbow Riters—while they might promote poor spelling (I mean, really, "riters"?)—save tropical trees. You probably didn't know that many are made with jelutong, a tropical wood that is frequently clear-cut.

PAINT YOUR WORK GREEN. Stick to watercolors and liquid tempera paints to avoid VOCs. If your child is channeling the Group of Seven and insists on oils, make sure all colors are free of toxic metals (read the label). You can also find water-soluble oils.

GREEN-BAG IT. What can you use to carry your green gear? Look for pencil cases of unbleached cotton or hemp. Stuff everything in a backpack made from recycled rubber or hemp. Whatever pack you choose, make sure it will last so you aren't replacing it every year. And steer clear of PVC or "vinyl" (I don't really need to explain why again, do I?).

And if you've got unused rulers, erasers, or pencils lying around, check with your local Ten Thousand Villages store (www.tenthousandvillages.com). Many of the store's eighty US or forty Canadian locations collect supplies to send to needy children around the world.

all, citing their inability to differentiate between what they see on television and real life. According to Canada's Media Awareness Network, children between the ages of two and five cannot differentiate between regular TV programming and commercials. Young children are especially vulnerable to misleading advertising and, until they're eight, don't begin to understand that advertisements are not always true.

Gary Ruskin, with Commercial Alert, a nonprofit organization that aims to help parents avoid the commercialization of children's lives (www.commercialalert.org), says that many of the issues facing children today are marketing related. He points to obesity, addiction, gambling, health, and body image problems. Studies back him up: Today's kids are more anxious, depressed, overweight, and sedentary than ever. And negative feelings about self and family actually go up with the level of consumerism.

What's Up?

The level of common sense around marketing to children in countries that don't wave the red, white, and blue. Greece bans ads to kids between 7 A.M. and 10 P.M. Italy has banned advertising to children altogether. (Italy has also made organic food compulsory in its schools. One more reason to pack up and move to Tuscany.) The province of Quebec has banned print and broadcast advertising aimed at kids under thirteen. And Sweden has banned advertisements to kids under twelve.

Lice My Mother Told Me

It's a fall tradition. At least once every September, I pick up my children at school and receive a notice that a classmate has head lice. Instructions advise me to check my children's scalp for lice or nits and, if any are found, to eliminate them. Kids cannot return to school until they are lice free. That evening, I generally add a drop or two of tea tree oil to the kids' shampoo. I then toss personal hygiene to the wind for a week or so, shampooing their hair only occasionally (lice prefer clean hair). My kids have never had lice, but I'm not sure if it's luck or the tea-tree regimen (the theory is that lice don't like the smell).

If your children do get lice—and refuse to let you simply shave their heads—check out any of the eco-friendly and less toxic ways to remove the critters that are on the market. There are even folks who will nitpick for you. Check out www.licesquad.com.

Canada has also instituted the Broadcast Code for Advertising to Children, and ads on Canadian television must play by its rules, which govern how frequently an ad can be played and forbid such techniques as the exaggeration of a product. However, the code was created and is administered by the advertising and broadcast industries, which, critics point out, makes it far from objective. What's more, it can't control the flood of American ads. And unfortunately, the United States refuses to legislate advertising to children.

What Can You Do?

Take back the remote. Limit the amount of time your kids spend in front of a screen—any screen, including TV, computer, and cell phone. But not the porch screen. Let them sit there all day looking at the sky, the trees, the birds . . .

Have a frank discussion with them about advertising—what its purpose is, how it makes us feel, whether it works. Linn points out that parents must have a discussion regarding advertising from the moment children are exposed. "You can encourage skepticism, but there's not evidence that it has an impact on consumer behavior." However, I can speak anecdotally that my daughter felt completely outraged when she discovered, at the age of five, that the kids playing with toys on television were *being paid*! It was as if I'd told her there was no Santa Claus or Easter Bunny. I can only imagine her reaction when that jig is up. But she's now far more skeptical about products she sees advertised. And skepticism, in the case of marketing to kids, is a good thing.

>>> PURCHASE POWER <<<

- It's particularly important when decorating babies' and kids' rooms to stick to the least toxic options. Paint should be low- or zero-VOC. Look for rugs or carpeting that's natural-fiber or machine-washable—or is labeled Green Label Plus. Aim for solid hardwood furniture, with nontoxic finishes. Organic or rubber mattresses and undyed organic cotton sheets and blankets will ensure sweet dreams.

> ### And That's (Sorta) Final!
>
> Kids won't take no, no, no, no, no, no, no, no, no, no for an answer. Studies have shown that American children aged twelve to seventeen will ask their parents an average of nine times for products they've seen advertised. More than half of the parents eventually give in.

- Buy glass bottles when possible to avoid bisphenol A, which is in polycarbonate plastics—labeled with a #7 or PC. Evenflo offers a widely available glass baby bottle. Or stick to "safer" plastics, such as numbers 1, 2, and 4 (polyethylene), or even stainless steel. Formula in cans can also be contaminated with bisphenol A, which is in the can lining.
- Your baby doesn't need a lot of creams, lotions, and so on. What you do choose, look for in a nontoxic product. Brands such as Burt's Bees and Weleda are some of the easier-to-find labels, but there are plenty of others.
- If you want to use a diaper service, log on to www.diapernet.org, which will help you locate a service near you. Or check out Ecobaby's organic cotton offerings at www.ecobaby.com. If you opt for disposables, keep them as green as possible: gDiapers offer a biodegradable, compostable panty that's available at Whole Foods and other natural food stores, and Tushies offers both a chlorine-free diaper and wipes. Seventh Generation is another eco-friendly company that offers diapers and wipes. It even offers a specially formulated baby laundry detergent that aims to take out tough baby stains while being gentle on clothes . . . and baby. Visit www.seventhgeneration.com to find out more and to locate a store near you.
- Teach kids to shop critically. Look at the pictures on the packaging. If possible, open the product before your purchase and let kids see whether it appears different from what they expected from the advertising (it might be smaller or have fewer accessories, for example).
- Avoid buying branded products, though that's easier said than done, as just about everything bears a logo—whether Winnie the Pooh or Sean John.

Clean Living

5

And Man created the plastic bag and the tin and aluminum can and the cellophane wrapper and the paper plate, and this was good because Man could then take his automobile and buy all his food in one place and He could save that which was good to eat in the refrigerator and throw away that which had no further use. And soon the earth was covered with plastic bags and aluminum cans and paper plates and disposable bottles and there was nowhere to sit down or walk, and Man shook his head and cried: "Look at this Godawful mess."   Art Buchwald

The Dirt

I'll come clean—I come from a long line of slackers in the household scrub-and-shine department. My own mother has always had a cleaning person, as did my maternal grandmother and great-grandmother (though I believe my great-grandmother's lived with her full time and was referred to as the "maid").

While I'm not in an income bracket that can afford a maid, my husband and I decided early in our marriage that it wasn't strong enough to withstand arguments over whose turn it was to clean the grout in the shower. Back then, we found a cleaning person named Max, who charged us the price of a takeout pizza to clean our two-bedroom apartment every second week. He even cleaned under our microwave and pulled out dressers to dust behind. What's more, he was witty and kind-hearted—a pleasure to have around even if he wasn't vacuuming and dusting. I loved Max. Which is why I suffer such guilt that I unwittingly exposed him to such toxins.

What's the Controversy?

Cleaning products are, ironically, a dirty business. The detergent we use to wash our dishes (you know, the same dishes we *eat* off)? Full of chemicals such as acetone, camphor, benzaldehyde, and others that read like an eye chart and can disturb the central nervous system, damage the immune system, make it hard to breathe, and give us headaches (and not just because nobody will help with those dishes). Fabric softeners? Might eliminate static cling, but might also eliminate healthy air as they release chloroform, benzyl acetate, and pentane—all of which have been individually linked to cancer. That bright blue window cleaner? Likely contains diethylene glycol, which depresses the nervous system. Those handy disposable dusting cloths? Teeming with petroleum distillates. And they generate a *lot* of trash. Get a load of this: Each year Americans throw away 83,000 tons of these dust-laden disposables, enough to fill nine thousand 18-wheelers, according to the David Suzuki Foundation.

The Environmental Protection Agency says that the average household contains as much as twenty-five pounds of toxic cleaning products. You likely don't know that, as you won't find most toxic ingredients listed on the containers of many common household cleaning supplies. Companies aren't legally required to list ingredients on their labels or to test their products for safety—and many refuse to disclose the ingredients, calling them trade secrets.

The real secret is that many household cleaning products rely on petroleum distillates to dissolve grease and grime. Which means it's not only your car that's addicted to oil but also your oven, bathtub, and toilet bowl. And any petroleum product brings with it the same host of environmental issues—pollution from digging for it, transporting it, spilling it (which happens at an astounding average of a million gallons a month), and refining it.

Truth is, many cleaning products leave not only a sparkle, but a toxic souvenir of petrochemical volatile organic compounds and the synthetic fragrances used to give us that "just cleaned" smell. Those VOCs nestle into carpets, upholstery, wood, and bedding, and we keep breathing them in. The EPA, in a study that examined six communities in various parts of the United States, found that concentrations of many VOCs are consistently higher indoors than outdoors—up to ten times as high, according to a study by the American Lung Association, even in areas with significant outdoor pollution (such as petrochemical plants). And on cleaning day, levels of chemicals in the indoor air can be hundreds, even thousands, of times higher than the outdoor air of the most polluted cities. So now that we know that our homes have worse indoor air quality than the parking lot at Exxon Mobil, what are we going to do about it?

You could persuasively argue that it's better to give up cleaning altogether. But the mold and enormous dust bunnies (more like dust goats!) might take their emotional toll, not to mention increase the potential for germs and bacteria to take up residence. Better that you clean with good-for-you, good-for-the-planet cleaners. They're a cinch to make (not to mention cheap), though if you're lazy like me, you'd still prefer to have someone else do the whole job, from making the cleaners to using them. Luckily, everyday more folks are stepping up to do the job.

What's Up?

The number of people who say they're interested in eco-friendly cleaning products. A full 84 percent say they want greener cleaners, cites www.care2.com, an eco-living website. But, notes Annie B. Bond, a writer and part of Care2's team, only 31 percent report that they bought an eco-friendly cleaner in the previous year. So although we're waking up and smelling the chlorine, too many of us are content to live with it.

There are a few reasons for this, says Bond, who has also written a number of books on nontoxic cleaning. Some homemade cleaners, such as vinegar and water for windows, don't do a good job of cleaning initially after so much buildup from conventional cleaners. Add a drop of liquid soap or detergent, she promises, and vinegar and water will do a great job. Unfortunately, most recipes don't include this tip. What's more, some nontoxic cleaners, such as borax for the toilet bowl, have to sit overnight. Lack of proper information about how these products work, Bond believes, has led too many to abandon their detoxification efforts.

Clean Sweep: Vacuums, Sponges, Mops, and More

Don't forget to take a look at the things you use to clean—so you can green your cleaning tools too:

- Steer clear of sponges treated with a synthetic disinfectant (generally marked with "resists odors" or "kills odors" on the package). Stick with a pure cellulose sponge, which can be kept germ free by being boiled in a pot of water for three to five minutes, tossed in the top rack of the dishwasher the next time you run a load, or microwaved on high for one minute.
- Give that tattered T-shirt new life as a cleaning rag, or purchase any of the microfiber cloths on the market that can be used over and over.
- Vacuums with a HEPA filter can go a long way toward keeping indoor air cleaner. *Consumer Reports* offers its Greener Choices selections for vacuum cleaners that produce lower emissions (www.greenerchoices.org).
- A squeegee works wonders with homemade window cleaner. Use it daily in your shower, and mold won't have a chance to take up residence.

Too many consumers also assume that government agencies have run tests and deemed safe those products we see on store shelves. But, more than seventy thousand chemical compounds are in production, the vast majority of which have not been tested. We have the United Nations' Stockholm Convention to thank for taking a first step toward changing the way industry thinks of many of these household chemicals. The Stockholm Convention is a global treaty to protect human health and the environment from persistent organic pollutants (POPs), which are long-lived, widely distributed, and toxic to humans and wildlife. Treating POPs as a category—with the notion of regulating an entire group of compounds based not on chemical similarities, but on the way a chemical behaves in the environment and in our bodies—marks an important step.

Jeffrey Hollender, the president and chief executive officer of Seventh Generation, a best-selling brand of natural, nontoxic household products in the United States, thinks the industry should be forced to list ingredients on labels, noting in an article that "consumers would be horrified to find out what's in some of them." Ingredients, for example, such as ammonia, dichloro (or trichloro) isocyanurate, glycol ethers, oxalic acid, phenols, sodium carbonate, sodium hypochlorite, sodium metasilicate, tripolyphosphate, and trisodium phosphate are mildly to very irritating to skin, eyes, nose, and throat; they are corrosive or poisonous if swallowed; and they pollute the air.

What Can You Do?

Start by taking an inventory of the products you have on hand, even the crusty, rusty containers that you're hanging on to for . . . what? sentimental reasons?

Sort by toxicity, putting all the products with Danger, Warning, or Caution labels in one spot. Then put the more benign cleaners in another spot. Now go through and determine which products you want to keep. You face some decisions: Do you want to dispose of all the toxic products right away, or are you willing to simply use them up, replacing them with more healthful alternatives? If you choose the former, don't just dump all those cleaners down the drain or toss them curbside; call your Department of Public Works to find out how to properly dispose of them

Labels to Be Leery Of

Most Dangerous

Poison ------------- highly toxic

Danger ------------- extremely flammable, corrosive, or highly toxic

Warning/Caution ---- moderately hazardous

Safest

No warning --------- least hazardous

"DANGER" on a label basically means that the product can essentially kill you in small doses (one taste to one teaspoon).

"WARNING" means that you need to take only a little more for it to kill you (one teaspoon to one tablespoon).

"CAUTION" means you'll have to ingest one ounce to one pint.

Are you getting this? In various doses, anything with these labels can be lethal. As in dead. And keep in mind that these doses are rated for an average adult. Much smaller doses can be lethal to a child. Doesn't matter how clean your house is when your two-year-old is clinging to life. Tell me again why we have this stuff in our homes? Oh yeah—so we don't have fingerprints on our stainless-steel appliances or rings in the bathtub. H'mmm . . .

Do Not Try This at Home: Mixing Ammonia and Bleach

I distinctly remember in 1981 taking my brand-new stiff-as-a-board Levi's and dumping bleach all over them to give them that had-'em-for-years faded look that wasn't available in store-bought jeans. Then, to get rid of the smell, I washed them in water and vinegar. Turns out those two ingredients—chlorine bleach and vinegar—are a bad combination. Like drinking and driving. Tina and Ike. Me and home perms.

Fortunately, I did not blow myself up with chloramine gas, which is the potential byproduct of mixing bleach and vinegar or, more likely, bleach and ammonia. Chloramine gas is really bad for you—the gagging and choking you'll experience kinda tips you off. Come to think of it, strike chlorine bleach right off your list. And ammonia, too. And home perms. But keep Tina and the new organic cotton Levi's (read more in chapter 2, "Eco-chic").

in your area. Some can be taken care of at home; others will need to be taken to a hazardous materials facility. If any products do need to be taken to a household-products exchange or hazardous-waste collection site, visit Earth 911 (www.earth911.org) to find one near you.

If you choose to use them up, store them out of the reach of children (it's amazing how similar some cleaning products look to Kool-Aid). More than half of all accidental poisonings in the United States occur in children younger than five, and cleaning supplies are one of the main culprits.

When it comes time to replace a cleaning product, resolve to choose a greener one.

If you're feeling truly ambitious, you can make your own cleaning supplies. I've done it. Really. The simplest is an all-purpose cleaner made of equal parts white vinegar and water—perfect for spraying cutting boards and other kitchen surfaces to disinfect and deodorize.

If you do choose to let someone else do the job of mixing and measuring, there are some awesome alternatives. Some, such as Bon Ami or Arm & Hammer Oven Cleaner, can even be found in your grocery store, not just in specialty stores.

Look for products that do list ingredients: generally, the more they reveal, the less they have to hide. Instead of just *biodegradable,* look for something telling you the period of time in which the product will biodegrade; instead of *nontoxic,* look for a description of how a product is nontoxic (for example, "nontoxic if inhaled").

>>> PURCHASE POWER <<<

You might find some greener cleaners at your local Home Depot or supermarket, most of which will be in the natural or organic section. Or visit a natural food store and support a local business. Wherever you find more healthful products, pick them up. More specifically:

- Look for plant-based rather than petroleum-based surfactants. Not only are they better for you, but they also smell better. Less eau de hospital, more field of daisies.
- Go with chlorine-free cleaners—oxygenated is the latest buzzword—which are safer than chlorine bleach.
- Look for products in glass or easy-to-recycle plastics, such as PETE (number 1) or HDPE (number 2).

Now use (or, well, pay someone else to use) your new, better-for-you cleaning arsenal. Then sit back and enjoy the clean. Your great-smelling house will make you feel better—more organized, more together, more . . . polished.

Brands I Love

Well, OK, maybe I don't *love* them—after all, their very nature implies a chore I deplore. However, one must clean, so it might as well be as pleasant and healthy a chore as possible.

METHOD. Notorious as the organization of "people against dirty," Method is the brainchild of Adam Lowry and Eric Ryan, who combined their passion for chemistry with their passion for the environment. The result is a host of products that are good for you and your family and better for the planet. Oh yeah—and the Method products work well (and smell great). I love Wood for Good so much that I polish my furniture *by myself,* rather than waiting for Adelia, my indispensable cleaning person, to do it. For those who love disposable wipes (for shame!), Method offers biodegradable versions for cleaning leather, granite, stainless

Washday: Getting Clothes Clean and Green

I was a loser with laundry, sort of laundry challenged. My clothes inevitably came out stretched, shrunken, or creased—and with the stains exactly where they were before washing. My three children all refused bibs and ate with such gusto that their clothes offered taste tests of the day's meals. However, I recently wised up and am happy to say that my clothes are now clean, great smelling, and greener than green. Here's how I did it and how you can, too:

COOL THINGS DOWN. Using hot water for both washing and rinsing uses three and a half times the energy as washing in warm water and rinsing in cold. Even better—wash in cold, using a cold-water detergent, and always rinse in cold. Note that being phosphate free doesn't make one detergent superior to another. No laundry detergent includes phosphates anymore. But some are certainly more benign than others. Avoid bleach, perfumes, and other nasties.

LOAD IT UP. Most people underload, rather than overload, their washer. Make sure you're filling your machine to capacity (but not too full, or the clothes won't get clean). If you must wash smaller loads, use the washer's "half-load" option if it's available.

SAVE THE SUDS. Jason Wentworth, who operates the eco-minded coin laundry Washboard in Portland, Maine, advises consumers to buy a natural-brand detergent in the biggest box you can get. Then use half the recommended amount. "Most detergent manufacturers, even some of the eco-ones, recommend using much more soap than is actually needed to get clothes clean," he says. To get really dirty clothes clean, he recommends spot treating them with diluted detergent and using a longer wash cycle.

SUPERPOWER YOUR SUDS. Speaking of detergents: buy the concentrated versions when possible. The others simply have water added, which adds up to more packaging and more weight in the 18-wheelers that cart them to grocery stores around the country.

BUY A FRONT LOADER IF YOU'RE IN THE MARKET FOR A NEW WASHER. I did—and my clothes come out of it practically dry! It uses at least 40 percent less water and 65 percent less electricity, and it's easier on clothes since it relies on gravity to work the dirt out, rather than twisting. What's more, if every US household used the most efficient washers, the equivalent of up to 40 million barrels of oil a year could be saved.

LET SOLAR ENERGY DRY YOUR CLOTHES. Buy a clothesline. (Your kids will thank you! It makes a great base for a backyard baseball game and the perfect "home" for a game of tag, and it's pure delight to disappear into a maze of sunshine-scented sheets.) If you don't have a backyard or if the weather prevents outdoor drying, you can use any number of portable, removable indoor drying racks or lines. Not only will you save money on energy use, but your clothes will last longer (also saving money) and, if you hang them up while still damp, wrinkles virtually disappear upon drying. (My husband was a bit grumpy at first about his "crunchy" clothesline-dried underwear. The solution? I throw them in the dryer for mere minutes, then hang them.)

CLEAN THE DRYER FILTER AFTER EACH USE. Cleaning the lint filter on your dryer can decrease the energy used per load by up to 30 percent. Check the outside dryer exhaust vent, too. Make sure it is clean and that the flapper on the outside hood opens and closes freely.

steel, and more. It also offers microfiber cloths that promise to clean faster and better. I just like the silky feel of them—though I'll likely continue to use ripped-up old T-shirts and tattered PJs as cleaning cloths. Method products are widely available. www. methodhome.com.

SEVENTH GENERATION. Purveyor of the nation's best-selling "green" cleaning products, Seventh Generation is so-named to reflect the Native American principle that we must consider how our decisions will affect the next seven generations. Which is so poignant that it makes me want to buy their products for that reason alone. Founded in 1988, the company makes household cleaners, paper goods, and feminine hygiene products that are widely available at Whole Foods, Ralph's grocery stores, and other locations. www.seventhgeneration.com.

ECOVER. This Belgian-based company has put to rest the argument that natural products can't work as well as those with aggressive chemicals. *Consumer Reports* ranks its dishwasher detergent above most others, including Palmolive and Electrosol. The company, which sells in markets around the world, also produces laundry detergent, floor soap, limescale remover, and a tub and tile cleaner that was selected by *Organic Style* magazine in May 2005 as one of its faves. Available at Whole Foods, Wild Oats, and other natural food stores, or online at www.ecover.com.

MRS. MEYER'S. Don't you just love the idea of Mrs. Meyer cleaning your house? She sounds so efficient, so no-nonsense. And indeed, there is a real Mrs. Meyer, mother of nine and wife to Vern, who has been creating her own cleaning products for forty years from essential oils, which prompted one of her daughters to start a company so mom's products would be available to all. From countertop spray to laundry detergent to toilet bowl cleaner, Mrs. Meyer's products are reasonably priced, biodegradable, phosphate free, and never tested on animals. Find them at natural food or organic grocery stores, or online at www.mrsmeyers.com.

AND OTHERS. There are any number of other less toxic products, such as Earth Friendly Products (www.ecos.com), Mountain Green (www.mtngreen.com) and Bi-O-Kleen (www. naturallysafecleaning.com). Get in the habit of reading labels and trying out the ones that appeal to you.

The Clutter

It's ironic that our unchecked accumulation of goods has spawned an entire cottage industry of uncluttering. There are experts who are paid a pretty penny (is there an ugly penny?) to tell us where to stick our stuff. There are stores dedicated to selling us more stuff to store our stuff. And you can't pick up a women's or home magazine that doesn't offer advice on how to organize clutter. Funny thing is, none of these "experts" are really telling us what we need to hear: Stop buying so much stuff!

Well, I am telling you. Forget for a second that I have to maneuver through an obstacle course of toys, books, and dogs to reach my own computer. (I'm working on it!) It's time that we step off the consumer grid and simply stop bringing more things into our homes, especially when many of us are already straining at the bricks. Oprah once commented that, before she brought a new item of clothing home, she made herself get rid of something she already had. Whether she has stuck to that policy, I don't know. I do know that it's a policy worth considering because I've adopted it. And while it doesn't stop consumerism in its tracks, it does force me to decide how badly I want that something new. The result? I've curbed my consumerism considerably. What's more, what I do have in my home, I love. No more "mistakes" stuffed into drawers or stashed in the basement or garage. I've walked away from more things than I've bought. And I've kept my clutter in check, except for that damn drawer stuffed full of reusable food containers. Which brings me to . . .

Plastics: Cracking the Code

They're like something out of *The Da Vinci Code*—those tiny little triangles on the bottom of all things plastic that are trying to tell us something, but what?

It's hard to believe, but plastic has been around less than a century. It's so ubiquitous that we can hardly imagine our lives without it. But while plastic has taken a great many forms and filled many functions, from car bumpers to baby bottles, it has taken a toll on our planet.

Perhaps you know, in an abstract way, that the plastic water bottle you drink from started out as petroleum (another reason to just reach for a glass or reusable stainless steel bottle). Put simply, plastic is created by linking small molecules (monomers) into chains (polymers). Ethylene monomers are the basic building blocks of plastic—added chemicals give it different qualities, such as stretchiness, hardness, and strength.

But we probably spend more time thinking about how to dispose of plastics than how they were created. Or, perhaps less altruistically, we wonder what they're doing to us, surrounded as we are on all sides by these chemical compounds.

The answers are as varied as the types of plastics.

What's the Controversy?

Plastics pose a threat to us, both personally and environmentally (which becomes personal when we have to breathe, eat, or drink), because producing plastic resin is a highly polluting business. In 1996, the Berkeley (California) Plastics Task Force reported that the manufacture of plastics contributed 14 percent of the most toxic industrial releases—including styrene, benzene, and trichloroethane—into the air. It also emits sulfur oxides, nitrous oxides (no laughing matter!), methanol, ethylene oxide, and volatile organic compounds.

Plastics are also just plain gross. Take the mass of plastic the size of Texas floating halfway between San Francisco and Hawaii, brought together by ocean currents from our trash. It's estimated that albatross, who spend their chicks' first six months scouring the ocean for food to feed them, offer them about five tons of plastic a year. Of course, plenty of these birds are found dead with bellies full of plastic. And they're not the only ones. Whales, turtles, and dolphins frequently confuse plastic with food. The plastic sometimes blocks their digestive tracts, and the marine animals essentially starve to death.

The UN Environment Programme estimates that for every square mile of ocean, there are forty-six thousand pieces of plastic junk—of which close to three-quarters will eventually sink, forming some kind of Lost City of Atlantis garbage dump.

Here's what's lurking in your plastics—and what you don't want lurking in your body.

DIOXINS. We met them in the personal care chapter, and—look!—here they are again, as toxic as ever. These are produced when plastics are manufactured and incinerated. Dioxins are actually a *family* of chemicals, but they're all highly toxic, even in small amounts. They also break down slowly, meaning they're the nasty gift that keeps on giving such adverse health effects as disrupting the endocrine system, damaging the immune system, and potentially affecting reproduction and childhood development.

PHTHALATES. Another fave of the cosmetics industry and beloved of the food industry, for use in polyvinyl chloride (PVC, or vinyl). We all know by now—unless you haven't been paying attention!—that vinyl is the most vile of plastics. Why? Let me reiterate: Both the production and disposal of vinyl create some of the planet's most damaging industrial pollutants in the form of dioxins. What's more, vinyl releases toxins at every stage of its life cycle. And to make it so flexible, manufacturers add plasticizers during production—such as phthalates—which can then leach into the food that's wrapped in it. As Nancy Reagan advised us about drugs: Just say no!

BISPHENOL A, OR BPA. Created in the 1930s as a synthetic estrogen. So it shouldn't come as a surprise that this polycarbonate plastic (signified by a 7 and frequently used in baby bottles, microwave ovenware, and eating utensils, among other things) simulates the action of estrogen in our bodies—thereby disrupting the production of hormones. Recent studies suggest that male rats exposed to low levels of BPA had lower testosterone levels. What's more, they spoke in voices that reminded researchers of Alvin and the Chipmunks. So while the rats had a good shot at a recording career, their chances of scoring with girl rats were significantly reduced. (Sorry, guys. Lowered testosterone levels are nothing to joke about.)

ANTIMONY. It might sound like something you pay your toxic ex-spouse, but it refers to a suspected cancer-causing compound that is a "priority pollutant" in the EU, an oddly benign way of referring to something you don't want in your body. You may

recall the scare in 2006 when University of Heidelberg researcher Bill Shotyk (from my hometown of London, Ontario—Go Bill!) released study results that indicated antimony levels in PET water bottles were higher than in regular tap water or in natural springs or wells. While the antimony levels in PET plastic bottles are considered below concern for "safe drinking standards," there is some fear that more chemicals leach into water allowed to sit in these bottles for a prolonged period of time. In an interview, Shotyk himself said he no longer drinks bottled water but reaches for a glass of tap water to quench his thirst.

What's Up?

Unfortunately, our use of plastic. According to a *Los Angeles Times* article by Kenneth R. Weiss, "the average American used 223 pounds of plastic in 2001. The plastics industry expects per-capita usage to increase to 326 pounds by the end of the decade." Plastic is just so darned useful—from the Velcro closures on your preschooler's sneakers to the lunch carefully packed in plastic containers to the plastic toothbrush we use at day's end to scrub that grunge off our teeth.

While many of us complain about plastic—there's a general sense of invasiveness about it, as though it's winding its way into the crevices of our lives—we're grateful for its convenience, not to mention its affordability. But that affordability comes at a price. And, increasingly that price is clean water, breathable air, and a toxin-free body.

Biodegradable and compostable alternatives have become more widely available. Many, however, are made by the same agribusinesses we try to avoid by buying local, organic food. And these biodegradable or compostable plastics are made largely from corn—the genetically modified monocrop that's eating up America's heartland. There's more controversy surrounding these plastics, too: Until a large number of facilities can deal with these greener plastics, they'll likely wind up in landfills where they'll sit with the rest of the trash—there's frequently too little moisture for them to biodegrade effectively. Or they'll get mixed in with plastics being recycled and potentially contaminate the load.

What Can You Do?

The Green Guide (www.thegreenguide.com) offers a handy clip-and-save chart to plastics. (Search for "Plastic Products at a Glance.") While no plastic is "good," some are less polluting to make and easier to recycle—generally 1 PETE and 2 HDPE. Here are some other steps you can take:

- Go through your drawer of breeding plastic containers and toss any that are scratched, discolored, or cracked. If they can be recycled, put them in the bin. Then eschew plastic in favor of glass, stainless steel, and clay. Store and reheat food in Pyrex.
- Avoid purchasing drinks that come with those plastic six-pack rings: animals, birds, and fish often get caught in the rings. If you do have them, cut the rings apart before throwing them away.
- Look for products in nonplastic containers—aluminum, glass, tin.
- Carry reusable drink containers—hot and cold—so that you don't need disposables. According to Daniel Imhoff, the author (with Roberto Carra) of *Paper or Plastic: Searching for Solutions to an Overpackaged World,* our daily java jolt generates roughly 100 million throwaway cups, sleeves, and lids in a single day in the United States alone. Using a glass or ceramic cup (even accounting for manufacture and washing) reduces energy and water use, air emissions, water pollution, and solid waste by between 85 and 99 percent. Similarly, says Imhoff, bottled water generates mountains of plastic—some 1.5 million tons per year in the United States. Funny thing is, 25 percent of bottled water is tap water. If you're worried about water quality, install a filter on your tap and pour your own into a stainless steel bottle.
- Pack your kids' lunches or your own in wax paper or aluminum foil (which can be recycled: just wipe it clean and either reuse it or toss it in the bin). Or wrap food in linen napkins! My friend Plum swears by them. "I haven't bought paper towels or napkins or plastic wrap for twenty years," she says. "Instead, I buy old linen napkins from church rummage sales and we use them for everything—wiping spills, covering food in the microwave, wrapping baked goods. What we've discovered

is that linen even keeps bread as fresh as does a plastic bag! Sometimes we spy linen ones with pretty lace or crocheted edges so we save those for giveaways. We just wrap up the cookies or cake in the cloth and tie it with ribbon—pretty!"

>>> PURCHASE POWER <<<

Plastic can be a risky choice. Know which ones are better, or go for an alternative:

- Pyrex and other heatable glass containers are as good a choice today as they were when our mothers used them.
- Choose "good" plastics before "bad." Look for number 1 PETE and number 2 HDPE and avoid number 3 PVC, number 6 PS, and number 7 polycarbonate.
- Stop buying water in plastic bottles: 1.26 billion plastic bottles are discarded every three weeks. Buy a filter for your tap—see chapter 6, "Home, Sweet Home" for details—and pour your own.

The Trash

You know those people—the ones who think it's hilarious to give you a big wrapped box, inside of which is a smaller box, inside of which is another smaller box and so on and so on, until you get to the teensy-weensy box that contains your gift (which had better be good, at this point!)? Well, those people work in the packaging departments of major companies that make CDs, cosmetics, printer cartridges, electronics, and a zillion other things we purchase and bring home, then take out our chain saw and hatchet to unwrap.

Overpackaging is more than simply annoying—it's harmful, and I'm not just referring to the thumb you sliced with your X-acto blade as you tried to dislodge your three-year-old's doll from its plastic-and-wire Alcatraz. Each year, every American disposes of more than three hundred pounds of packaging materials. Indeed, packaging makes up close to a third of the trash in the world's total municipal waste stream.

There's even a term—"wrap rage"—to refer to the frustration consumers experience as they try to open protective plastic packaging. I've witnessed it, and it's a bit scary and funny at the same time. Like the times you and your brother would be fighting in the back seat over who was on whose side of the invisible line, and your dad would try to keep the car from swerving off the road, while simultaneously swinging at you and uttering futile threats that "You'll be sorry," if he had to pull over the car. See what I mean? Scary and funny. But back to trash, which isn't funny at all. Just scary.

What's the Controversy?

Landfills aren't pretty places, not even from space, where astronauts could more easily spot the Fresh Kills Landfill in New York (before it was closed) than the Great Wall of China. Landfills serve as visual reminders that we throw out tons of garbage. Their toxins leach into the soil and groundwater. As a result, most of us don't want them anywhere near our homes. Yet we continue to consume and discard at such a rate that many cities are forced to truck their trash to far-off destinations, belching greenhouse gases the entire trip. Landfills theoretically release methane, another greenhouse gas, though landfill proponents argue that most landfill refuse never gets enough sunlight, air, or moisture, necessary ingredients for decomposition, and therefore methane production is low to nil.

What's in our trash bins and landfills? A lot of packaging, of course. There's also a lot of food (that can—and should—be composted. More about that later). Most of us are shocked to realize that an average of 15 percent of our food spoils and gets tossed before it's eaten. There's also a lot of paper that can and should be recycled: newspapers, magazines, and junk mail make up as much as half of what's in landfills. Indeed, William Rathje, a garbologist (yep, that's his title) who spent more than thirty years digging into people's garbage, reveals that as many recyclables are in the garbage can as in the recycling bin. And even though we're recycling twice as much as we did twenty years ago, our levels of consumption have grown greater still, meaning we're throwing more away than ever before.

"And with everyone having their own computers and printers," says Rathje, "it's like they have their own printing presses." Add to that the incredible volume of junk mail and magazines, and there's plenty to read at your local landfill. There's also hazardous waste, such as batteries, paint, old electronics, and other items that should not have been sent to a landfill. Indeed, e-waste, as it's called, is increasingly a problem. I'll get to that later.

Daniel Imhoff, the co-author of *Paper or Plastic,* remains an optimist in the shadow of the mountain of garbage we produce. He points out that there's much the consumer can do to control waste. And with that knowledge comes the power to do things differently.

What Can You Do?

Plenty. And there are plenty of people to help you along the road toward a trashless future.

Just Say No to Packaging

Imhoff says 300 million hot and cold beverage containers are used every day in the United States. Every day! And the solution is so simple. Either eat (or drink) in, instead of going to the takeout counter or "drive thru"—assuming of course that eating in means using reusable cups and dishes. If takeout is your only option, take your own reusable coffee mug or other beverage container. (I'm convinced that Styrofoam is the devil's own coffee cup.)

At the checkout, tell the cashier that you want neither paper nor plastic bags for your purchases. Then whip out your canvas or other reusable bag (these days you can choose from bags that fold up tiny enough to fit into a change purse to funky ones that make a fashion statement). Simply by saying no to plastic bags, one consumer can help keep anywhere from three hundred to nine hundred bags out of landfills, the branches of trees, and the bellies of sea turtles.

Compost

Call me crazy, but composting is a whole heap of fun. There's something magical about putting all your apple cores, moldy

Each computer or television display contains an average of four to eight pounds of lead, according to the Computer Take Back Campaign. Consumer electronics already constitute 40 percent of the lead found in landfills, which also includes cellular phones. About 70 percent of the heavy metals (including mercury and cadmium) found in landfills come from electronic equipment discards. Instead, try to find a good home for your unwanted television set, assuming it's still working. (For computers, check out "How to Recycle or Reuse (Almost) Anything" in this chapter.) If your set is truly dead, visit earth911.org to find out how to dispose of it or how to recycle it. I once donated a TV set on the blink to my local television repairman, who wanted it for parts. In exchange, he offered me a year's worth of free cleaning for my VCR.

bread, tea bags, and eggshells into a bin then—*abracadabra*—producing incredibly rich soil a few months later that can help transform a ho-hum garden into Eden. Composting is so easy, and it diverts literally tons of organic waste from landfills. What's more, you may never need to purchase topsoil again.

You can find composters at almost any hardware or garden store, or you can build your own. Beware what materials you use, however. Case in point: Craig, an editor I know, had a "rustic" composter built out of split logs to blend into his cottage surroundings. Turns out a fox snake took up residence. "Anything that eats rabbits for a living draws one hell of a lot of blood when it clamps down on your hand," he notes.

My family has three compost locations—two bins and a fenced-in heap, which we use for leaves and grass clippings—and we're working on our fourth, an indoor composter for use throughout our long, cold winter. Sad story: Last year's indoor vermicomposter met with an untimely end. I should have known from the start that my red wiggler worms were on borrowed time. They arrived—ordered over the Internet—through our mail slot and were enthusiastically welcomed by one of our dogs, who promptly ripped open the package, scattering wigglers far and wide in our kitchen. I gathered them up and introduced them

As the Worm Turns—How to Create Dirt that Nourishes Your Soul . . . and Your Plants

Worm expert (and my composting therapist) Anita Rychlo at Annelid Cycle offers this advice:

BIN SHOPPING. While you can purchase a bin—they usually come with a ventilated lid, vent holes along the sides, several draining holes in the bottom, and a tray to catch excess liquid— Anita notes that almost any plastic container (think Rubbermaid) can be converted into a worm bin by adding vent holes in the lid and sides. She feels that bottom draining holes aren't necessary; even though liquid can build up over time from food waste with a high water content, this can be remedied simply by drawing back the bedding (see below) once a month and adding more fresh bedding to soak up any excess. You can even keep your vermicomposter under the kitchen sink for convenience—or in a laundry room, basement, or heated garage.

MAKE YOUR BEDDING. Composting worms, or red wigglers (the noted stars of the compost world), need a moist environment to live in so they can breathe through their skin, explains Anita. For bedding materials, she recommends pre-soaked (at least 24 hours) peat moss, damp paper, or newsprint (shredded); brown leaves; and cardboard strips. The moisture level should be that of a damp, wrung-out sponge. Martha Stewart-types can layer the bedding (like making a lasagna) by alternating layers of shredded paper with layers of leaves or cardboard strips until the bin is three-quarters full. Mix in a cup of soil, sand, or pulverized egg shells. "Because worms have no teeth," explains Anita, "this grit is necessary for them to grind up the food inside their gizzards." This woman clearly speaks for the worms. . . .

WORM PSYCHOLOGY 101. For the first week, feed your worms only some coffee grounds or spent tea bags (they tend to sulk at their new environment and need time to settle in before they begin their task). In the second week, you can begin adding small amounts of finely shredded veggie food waste—veggie/fruit peelings, cooked pasta, crushed eggshells . . . even citrus peels in small amounts (see the "Bin There, Done That" sidebar in chapter 8 for tips on what you can—and can't—compost). Gradually increase the amount of food waste, burying the food scraps under the bedding and covering them with new, damp bedding. Because the worms also eat the bedding, don't feel obliged to "feed" them everyday.

TAKING THE TEMPERATURE. These hard-working worms expect temperatures between 13 and 25 degrees Celsius, or room temperature.

THE WORMFUL BOUNTY. After three or four months, the original bedding will be no longer recognizable as such—instead it will be rich compost. Working in bright light with a large plastic sheet, take the vermicompost (fancy name for worm-created compost) and divide it into several small piles. Every ten minutes or so, remove the compost from the top of the piles a bit at a time until you discover the worms all huddled together at the bottom like terrified hostages in an armed robbery. Gather the worms and place them in new bedding and begin the cycle all over again. Then put your beautiful compost to work for you in your garden. . . .

to their new home in our garage. Two days later, however, rather than burrowing in and beginning their task of eating through the organic waste, they were staging an escape. Frantic calls to my composting contact revealed that the temperature was likely too cold. Or the compost heap was too wet. Anita Rychlo at Annelid Cycle, another vermicomposting expert, later pointed out that wigglers dislike light and vibration. "As a result of the move to their new home," she explained, "it's not uncommon to have a few rebels who will set out to explore the world." She also said that these little warm-blooded employees will frequently go on a hunger strike for the first two weeks and should not be fed anything except coffee grounds and a spent tea bag or two until the "pouting" is over. What's more, when wigglers become cold, they become lethargic and don't do their job, leaving food to spoil and stink. Which mine did. Which convinced my husband that the roof of his convertible, which he parked in the garage, would absorb the stink. *Pshaw,* I scoffed, determined not to face the truth about my mutinous little organic technicians. My husband shot me dirty looks over the dinner table. When I finally had to hold my breath to enter our garage and the wigglers lost all signs of life, I admitted defeat. But only for a time. Now, with days getting shorter and a chill setting in, I'm ready to start again, armed with my newfound worm wisdom and an insulated container.

There are lots of places to get instructions on making your own vermicomposter. Rychlo recommends one change: She finds that the holes generally recommended for the bottoms of containers can create problems with anaerobic germs and odor. Instead, she suggests putting a good dry layer of shredded paper or cardboard at the bottom, then checking once a month to see if water has pooled. If it has, draw back this bedding one side at a time, adding more dry shredded paper to soak up the moisture.

ELIMINATE JUNK MAIL

Forty-one pounds of junk mail is delivered each year to the average American adult. One hundred million trees are ground up every year to produce it. Close to half of that goes to landfill unopened, according to the Center for Development of Recycling (CDR) in Santa Clara County, California. While recycling this junk mail would be better than tossing it, better still is stopping it from coming through the mail slot. But that's easier said than done. The CDR says only one method really works: contacting each organization individually and requesting that your name be taken off its list. You can find a list here: www.recyclestuff.org/JunkMail.asp.

The DeVries brothers in Ferndale, Michigan, however, will do the job for you. Fed up with junk mail themselves, they put together a list of things people can do to get off junk mail lists. Then they emailed that list to friends and family. No one did a thing other than continue to complain about the volume of junk mail they received. The three brothers decided to create a service to take care of junk mail for people: www.41pounds.org. They estimate it takes four to five hours to contact every catalog company, publisher, or other organization that has you on its hit list. They promise that, for $41, they'll get and keep you junk mail free for five years. If you get any junk mail within that time, you simply forward it to 41pounds.org, and they'll take care of the rest.

New American Dream also offers advice on avoiding junk mail, including a letter you can send to Congress to enact legislation to set up an opt-out list. Follow the steps offered online at www.newdream.org/junkmail.

Reduce

It's like a jingle that almost becomes meaningless when you hear it once too often. But the three Rs—reduce, reuse, recycle—might be all we really need. Nobody likes this reduce R very much. But, frankly, it's by far the most important. Buy less stuff. Period.

My garbologist friend William Rathje is a bit less snarky than I. He advises that people look for less packaging—"buy fruit juice concentrate," he says for example, instead of juice in a ready-to-drink container. By "brick packs" of coffee, he suggests, noting that the foil package is one-twentieth the volume of a coffee can.

I still say buy less stuff. Period.

Reuse

Ahhh, the second R in the pyramid of green power. If recycling is the (perhaps undeserved) star of the show, this is the oft-ignored supporting actor. The one that rarely gets the credit it deserves. Reuse often requires an imagination that seems sorely lacking in our sequel and prequel times. Ask your grandmother—she'll be

John Perry, Conspicuous Un-Consumer

It began at a dinner party where conversation had turned to the apparent uselessness of recycling. "We were feeling defeated and deflated," recalls northern California's John Perry. "We were all expending so much energy for recycling, yet there's little market for recycled goods." Perry and his dinner companions began to talk about "creative reuse"—reusing things they and others had. They devised the notion of the Compact, so-named after the Mayflower Compact, which established a social contract for the new world, and set forth their own "laws" of consumption. "It was meant to be fun," Perry points out, but also aimed at getting the group off the cycle of unnecessary consumption.

Perry says the first step is generally to borrow, then to barter (he says the group members are huge fans of Freecycle), then, only if necessary, to buy secondhand. "We try not to just shift recreational shopping habits into secondhand," he says.

What he—and others—have discovered is that by stepping out of the malls, they've found more time for friends and family, more time for experiences that enrich their lives.

He hardly considered his idea revolutionary. But Perry has suddenly found himself in the spotlight—turns out that the idea of a group of middle-class professionals deciding they have enough stuff and refusing the notion that shopping is patriotism was international news. Perry notes wryly that this simply shows that "the situation is out of control."

As the father of two young children, Perry knows it's likely going to get more complicated. Already he says his family's strict no-gift policy makes people uncomfortable, but if others insist on getting his kids something, he suggests that they go to the Heifer International website (www.heifer.org).

While the group officially pledged to adhere to the Compact for a year, Perry says that he's undergone a wholesale lifestyle change. "I will definitely not buy anything that could be had secondhand," he says. In the end, he notes, it's simple. Getting our consumerism under control comes down to one question: Do I need this? The answer, frequently, is no.

---

able to tell you a thing or two about reusing items. Or visit Cuba, where a tin can gets fashioned into a toy airplane.

Wendy is a member of Green Drinks (an international group with regional chapters in which eco-minded people get together for drinks and discussion—look it up at www.greendrinks.org—soon to be followed by Green Alcoholics Anonymous). She's also a dedicated reuser, even making produce bags from old sheer curtains (lightweight and durable!). She notes that she gets some strange reactions from the checkout clerks, but "elderly shoppers admire these bags and inquire where I got them." Leave it to the folks who lived through the Depression to appreciate creative reuse! Wendy also makes reusable bags out of old upholstery samples. And her husband, who works in home renovations, routinely brings home discarded aluminum window screens; Wendy has turned some into a cover for the kids' sandbox (keeps out cats in search of kitty litter) and is working on a fence for her garden. Wendy admits, however, that reuse has its limitations: "When we first moved into our home," she says, "our kitchen sink drained through an old vacuum cleaner hose. The previous owner was creative but not up to code."

RECYCLE

It seems so easy. If something (paper, plastic, aluminum, glass) is recyclable, into the bin it goes. Unfortunately, far too many of us don't recycle—or we recycle incorrectly. In a fit of recycling frenzy (I thought I was so virtuous!), I began tossing anything that even seemed recyclable, thinking it was better to err on the side of too much in the bin than too little. Turns out people (like me—oh the guilt!) that toss out *non*recyclables can contaminate entire batches of perfectly good recyclable material. In my own defense, those little arrows on the bottom of plastic containers are bloody confusing. They don't mean the item can be recycled; rather they indicate the resin base of the plastic, not all of which are accepted by recycling programs. In particular, that plastic axis of evil—3 PVC, 6 PS, and 7 polycarbonate—despite an appearance of benign plasticness, are culprits in contamination, not to mention that they leach toxins into landfill long after they've been tossed. Imhoff gets quite miffed at those misleading triangles. "They shouldn't even be making that stuff," he sputters. "And it shouldn't even have arrows on it unless it has recycled materials in it." Avoid them at all costs. Or face the wrath of Imhoff.

>>> PURCHASE POWER <<<

- Buy less.
- Buy in bulk, but only as much as you'll use.
- Look for items with minimal packaging. And choose packaging that is easier on the planet—recyclable, reusable, or made from postconsumer recycled content. And please . . . fruits

and veggies come in their own made-by-Mother-Nature edible or biodegradable packaging. Avoid anything else.

- Take your own bags to the store. Check out www.reusable bags.com and www.pristineplanet.com for starters (just "search" for "shopping bags"), though you can likely find great-looking and durable totes much closer to home. If your plastic bag drawer is threatening to burst, reuse or recycle them (www.earth911.com can tell you where in your area). Similarly, take your own containers to such places as salad bars, tote your mugs to coffeeshops, and so on.

- Install a home filtering system on your tap so you can stop buying bottled water (which studies have shown is often no better than tap water—indeed, it frequently *is* tap water). A reverse-osmosis filter is your most expensive option, but your water will be free of lead, copper, arsenic, cadmium, chlorine, giardia, pesticides, salt, trihalomethanes, sulfates, cysts, and nitrates, as well as some bacteria and viruses. The downside is it wastes two to four gallons of tap water for every gallon it filters. But if your water quality is an issue, it's far better than buying bottled water. Otherwise, a lower-grade filter, such as a Brita or Pur faucet filter, will ease any concerns. Look for filters that meet MSF/ANSI standard 53, and check also which contaminants the filter removes. Tote your water in Klean Kanteen or Sigg stainless steel bottles.

- Stop buying plastic wrap and instead purchase waxed paper and aluminum foil (which can be recycled).

- Buy durables over disposables. Avoid disposable dishes, cutlery, paper napkins, batteries, and so on. If you must (you've invited, say, 250 of your closest friends to a barbecue) go for biodegradable plastics. Companies such as Sinless Buying (www.sinlessbuying.com), Stalk Market (www.stalkmarket. net), Recycline's Preserve line (www.recycline.com), the Nat-Ur line (www.nat-urstore.com), Treecycle (www.treecycle. com), and ReNewable Products (www.earthshell.com) all offer some variation on biodegradable or compostable disposables. Then ensure that they are, in fact, disposed of properly to biodegrade rather than live out their days in landfill.

- Instead of plastic storage containers, look for glass, ceramic, stoneware, and stainless steel (though the last can react with some foods), such as Anchor Hocking, Pyrex, Clay Design, Libbey, Corning, Corelle, and others.

How to Recycle or Reuse (Almost) Anything

One Person's Treasure

Plenty of people will be happy to take much of what you deem garbage off your hands and out of the landfill. Here are a few such organizations that will take anything:

FREECYCLE. All sorts of bizarre rules are attached to this list for the media. For example, I'm not supposed to rework freecycle into a noun or verb, such as recommending that readers go "freecycling"—but since I've always had issues with authority, I'm going to. Go freecycling, folks!

Aside from its obsession with parts of speech, this site offers a fun and easy way to unload and pick up all sorts of stuff, from furniture to magazine collections to toys to almost anything you can think of. Think of it like a virtual garage sale in a really good neighborhood. There are umpteen Freecycle chapters all over the continent, so log on, register, and get freecycling—ha! Did it again. www.freecycle.org.

CRAIGSLIST. While this site has taken some slack for being a for-profit, it is another great spot for people—15 million of them a month—to trade, barter, and simply get rid of unwanted stuff. Craigslist doesn't make its money off you, but rather from businesses wanting to post job listings or apartments. www.craigslist.org.

THROWPLACE. This site invites you to "take what you need and throw what you don't." Similar to Freecycle and Craigslist, registration is free, and all items are available free. www.throwplace.com.

EXCESS ACCESS. For a $5 fee, this organization will email charities in your area (in the United States and Canada) to help you locate one that needs what you have. www.excessaccess.org.

EARTH 911. Find nearby locations to recycle everything from computers to batteries to cell phones to much more. This is one incredible recycling resource! www.earth911.org.

Consider also local animal shelters (towels, blankets, old furs), women's shelters (clothing, unopened toiletries, soaps, and lots more), hospices, hospitals (magazines, books), children's charities, even your dentist's or doctor's office (clean, outgrown toys). Always call first to ensure they want what you're offering.

Clothing

Clean out your closet, and donate your unwanted garments to those who'll give them a good home.

GOODWILL. www.goodwill.org.

THE SALVATION ARMY. www.salvationarmy.org.

HELPING OUR LAKOTA FAMILIES. Accepts towels, furniture, personal care products and more. Contact the organization at www.gwtc.net/—darbob.

DRESS FOR SUCCESS. Help a low-income, job-hunting woman look her best by donating your business clothing, coats, briefcases, and more. www.dressforsuccess.org.

Footwear

Let your shoes walk a mile on someone else's feet.

WILDIZE. This organization collects hiking boots for African rangers who patrol park boundaries and wilderness areas. www.wildize.org.

NIKE'S REUSE-A-SHOE PROGRAM. Old athletic shoes of any brand get new life as athletic surfaces. www.nikereuseashoe.com.

PROJECT SHOE ASSIST. This organization collects new and barely used running shoes for underprivileged kids in Brazil. www.projectshoeassist.com.

ONE WORLD RUNNING. This group of Colorado runners collects used running shoes for aspiring African athletes. www.boulderrunning.com/oneworldrunning.

SOCCER FOR LIFE. Your kids' outgrown soccer stuff (cleats, jerseys, etc.) can give poor kids in Honduras the chance to participate in soccer leagues. www.satglobal.com/sfll.htm.

Electronics

Your old equipment may not be up to your speed, but many of your electronics can illuminate someone else's world.

WILDIZE. This organization collects computers, books, and more for its conservation work in Africa. www.wildize.org.

COMPUTER TAKE-BACK CAMPAIGN. Find out which companies will take back your old computer, what services they offer, how to use them, and how to get free recycling. www.computertakeback.com.

NATIONAL CRISTINA FOUNDATION. Used technology gets a second life helping people with disabilities or economic disadvantages and at-risk students. www.cristina.org.

WORLD COMPUTER EXCHANGE. Put your computer to work in schools in developing countries. www.worldcomputerexchange.org.

ELECTRONIC INDUSTRIES ALLIANCE. Find out what recycling facilities exist in your area for computers, digital cameras, televisions, and more. www.eiae.org.

PLANET GREEN INC. This company offers fund-raising opportunities for other groups by collecting laser and inkjet cartridges and cell phones in order to recycle them. You simply collect, submit, and await your check. www.planetgreeninc.com.

PRINTER CARTRIDGES. Often the place where you bought them will accept toner cartridges back for recycling. And some companies (like HP) include a stamped, self-addressed envelope so you can mail them back. There are plenty of options, so *don't* throw them out.

ENVIRONMENTAL PROTECTION AGENCY. Find out where and how to donate or recycle electronics. www.epa.gov/epaoswer/hazwaste/recycle/hazrecyc.htm.

Luggage

SUITCASES FOR KIDS. Give foster kids a place to keep their belongings as they move from home to home. Suitcases are preferred, but the organization will accept duffel bags and backpacks. www.suitcasesforkids.org.

Glasses

LIONS CLUBS INTERNATIONAL. Donate used eyeglasses at Lenscrafters stores, Goodwill Industries, and other spots to restore vision to others. www.lionsclubs.org.

UNITE FOR SIGHT. Kids and adults in such places as Nigeria and Ghana receive your eyeglasses from this organization. www.uniteforsight.org.

Compact Fluorescent Lightbulbs

These contain a tiny amount of mercury, which means they must be disposed of properly. Earth911.org can lead you to somewhere in your area to drop them off, or check at the store where you purchased them. Some will take them back.

Packaging Materials

Check with local shipping and packing stores—they'll sometimes take your foam peanuts, bubble wrap, and other material for reuse.

Home,
Sweet Home

What the virtuous
consumer says about:

The whole house
- *Paints, wallpapers*
- *Flooring*
- *Furniture*
- *Appliances*
- *Electronics*
- *Lighting*

The kitchen
- *Fridges*
- *Countertops*

The bedroom
- *Mattresses,
  bedding*
- *Candles*

The bathroom
- *Toilets*
- *Showers and tubs*

The home office
- *Electronics*
- *Paper*

Pools and hot tubs
- *Detox your
  outdoor fun*

What is the use of a house if you haven't got a tolerable planet
to put it on?   Henry David Thoreau

Damn those Joneses—you know, the ones on TV, always
renovating, remodeling, showing off their new digs. Suddenly,
your home, which seemed just fine moments before, looks,
well, not ready for prime time. Not to worry, you think. Just zip
off to the nearest home improvement store, grab two or three
gallons of paint, perhaps some new carpeting, one of those shiny
stainless-steel appliances, and, while you're at it, some lamps,
drapes, a duvet, throw pillows, and—jackpot!—a flat-screen TV
to better view all those home shows that make your own abode
(and life!) seem so mediocre. You and all those other people you
see at those stores? Contributing to a roughly $250 billion home
remodeling and repair industry.

The Whole House

My home doesn't look the least bit green. It's a monster of a
thing—built in the days when big mattered. It has a double-car
garage, six bedrooms, and a swimming pool. None of those
things are the reason we bought it. We bought it because it's situ-
ated on a half acre that backs onto a wooded area and parkland.
We bought it because a river, complete with rowers, meanders
nearby. We bought it because I can bike twenty minutes along
trails to get downtown. Because we sometimes see deer when
we're out for a walk. And because—I'll be honest—it was a
helluva deal (and the pool didn't hurt either).

   Since then, we've been quietly greening our home. You can't
really tell from the outside, which brings me to my point: Looks

can be deceiving. It is possible to live green (or greener than you might think) in the suburbs. And it doesn't require a wholesale lifestyle change, just some better choices.

Those choices began not long after we moved in.

What's the Controversy?

A house is basically a third skin. Unfortunately, homes are frequently filled with toxic chemicals—from cleaning, decorating, and, well, living.

That fresh coat of paint on the walls? Filling the air with volatile organic compounds (VOCs), such as benzene, formaldehyde, kerosene, ammonia, toluene, and xylene, all of which are known carcinogens and neurotoxins. Exposure can worsen asthma symptoms and cause headaches, nausea, dizziness, and in some cases liver and kidney disease. Perhaps in the interest of full disclosure, new paint colors should have names like Asthma Attack Red. Or perhaps Bile Green. Migraine Gray?

There are more chemicals, however, lurking in your home. The new sofa? Off-gassing PBDEs or polybrominated diphenyl ethers, which are fire retardants (remember when we met them in kids' pajamas and mattresses?) and chemical cousins to the banned PCBs. That great-looking new shower curtain with that whiff of new plastic is likely vinyl—one of the most environmentally hazardous consumer products ever produced. So are those window blinds.

And that gorgeous new coffee table owes its good looks to exotic wood taken from an endangered Brazilian rain forest. That avocado-green fridge you picked up secondhand from your brother-in-law? Well, along with good taste and the roughly $100 a year it'll cost to keep that second fridge running, you've squandered energy by plugging in an old, inefficient fridge—and for no other purpose than to keep the Corona cool.

And speaking of energy consumption, America's has gone up dramatically: North Americans consume 2.4 times as much energy at home as those in Western Europe, according to the Worldwatch Institute. All that energy we consume comes at a price—extracting power out of coal and other fossil fuels is the leading cause of air pollution in the United States. And air pollution—sulfur dioxide, nitrogen oxide, carbon dioxide, mercury, and more—is literally choking the life out of millions of people, plants, and the planet. And nuclear energy has its own laundry list of eco problems, such as producing radioactive waste.

Sounds dire, doesn't it? The good news is that when we make our homes more energy efficient, we're making changes that add up big.

What's Up?

Fortunately, the number of options we have to toxic furnishings, chem-clad finishes, and energy-hungry appliances. But while it's getting better all the time, you'll have to look long for some eco-friendly home products. It is changing, promises Lisa DiMartino, vice president of marketing for Seattle's Environmental Home Center, who notes that the green building industry is noticing a 20 to 30 percent growth per year for the past few years. "People are thinking more about what they're putting in their homes," she says. What's more, buying green moves consumers away from the "throwaway mentality where you redo a room every four years." Instead, she sees people getting "excited about buying something substantial." People buy green for any number of reasons, but largely for style and quality, health, and environmental concerns. DiMartino believes the issue of health hits home for some people more than environmental reasons. "If people realize their home may make them or their children sick, they will make different choices." And, DiMartino says, while protecting the environment may not be some people's primary motive, it can be seen as a bonus. "They are happy to 'do good,' especially if the product is great looking and competitively priced." And, she says, energy efficiency—thereby saving money—is a big motivator for change.

Appliances have come a long way from the inefficient energy wasters of yesteryear (not to mention that we've escaped from, as someone once called them, the Four Design Colors of the Apocalypse—harvest gold, avocado green, burnt orange, and brown). It has never been easier to select an appliance based on little more than its energy requirements, thanks to large yellow-and-black EnergyGuide labels, required by federal law on most large appliances. And the Energy Star designation makes it clearer still—appliances and electronics can be rewarded Energy Star status only if they exceed the federally mandated efficiency standard in their categories.

Appliances just got a further boost in energy efficiency, thanks—finally—to the Department of Energy (DOE). The DOE recently settled a lawsuit launched by a number of environmental groups that will raise the energy-efficiency requirements of twenty-two appliances—everything from fridges to fluorescents—over the next five years. What this means for you is that any new appliances you buy will have to be at the "maximum technologically feasible and cost-effective level possible and cannot weaken established standards." Good news for you in terms of cost savings and good news for the planet as estimates put the energy savings at enough to meet the needs of 12 million households and avoid the building of dozens of power plants.

What Can You Do?

There is a lot that the average homeowner can do, says the Environmental Home Center's DiMartino, from quick and easy fixes to a full renovation. DiMartino herself recently redid two bedrooms and a home office, putting down cork flooring (more on that later) and low-VOC paint on the walls. "I completely redid the surfaces of three rooms," she says, noting that the redecorating has had an impact both on the eye and the environment.

Don't stress yourself—and your wallet—by feeling you need to completely redo your home. DiMartino suggests people simply start where it makes sense for them. But as choices arise, do your research (new products are coming onto the green market constantly) and make the most environmentally healthful decision you can afford.

Paints and Wallpapers
VOCs are the main culprits in paints, stains, and wallpapers (and wallpapers also have the eventual problem of disposal). Look for low- or no-VOC paints and stains that are green-seal certified. Brands that are eco-safe include Benjamin Moore Aura, the green-seal-approved Olympic, American Pride, and Anna Sova.

Milk paint is another good option because it's made, literally, from earth-friendly ingredients such as milk (actually, purified milk protein . . . but the same thing, practically). Wallpapers are available in cork, jute, hemp, sisal, wood, cotton, and bamboo—all sustainable materials that don't necessarily make your house look like a tiki bar (though if that's the look you're going for . . .). More traditional-looking wallpapers are available from such companies as Farrow & Ball, who offer their elegant designs in water-based paints. You can also find wallpapers that use vegetable dyes. Steer clear of vinyl-backed wallpapers (you know why—don't make me say it again!) in favor of those with fabric or acrylic backing.

Don't forget to go to www.earth911.org to find out where to recycle or donate old paint. The website also features a handy paint calculator, so you can buy only the paint you need for a job and avoid leftovers, which, let's be honest, just sit in your basement or garage for years, off-gassing their VOCs until you finally need them for a touch-up, only to discover the paint has horribly separated. Then go to www.earth911.org to find out how to dispose of it.

FLOORING

You know that compliment—the one I've never received? *Her floor was so clean you could eat off it.* Well, turns out no one should be eating off most floors, especially mine, even if you're partial to dog fur and dirt. Besides pesticides (which you would never use in your own garden, of course, but those darn neighbors of yours . . .), lead, and other chemicals that get tracked in on shoes, your flooring might also be off-gassing VOCs or leaching toxins. But if new flooring is on your wish list, you've got a whole heap of green alternatives that could make your next dinner party a feast on the floor.

WOOD. I like wood floors. I particularly like old barn-board wood floors salvaged from some gorgeous 19th century farm. I've learned, however, that beautiful salvaged wood is hard to find and that I'll pay dearly for it. However, I'll keep looking and keep my fingers crossed. If you go for new hardwood, look for the Forest Stewardship Council (FSC) label, which indicates the company met strict social and environmental standards.

CARPET. We all love carpet because it's warm and cozy and soft—like a wall-to-wall teddy bear. But carpet is one of the worst offenders for harboring unwanted contaminants—it's like the Afghanistan of microterrorists—dust mites, pesticides, mold, not to mention all of the VOCs in the adhesives (which can continue to off-gas in small amounts for five years after installation). Also, carpet is generally petroleum-based and highly resource-intensive: it takes a lot of energy to turn that petroleum into something we want to wiggle our toes in. Instead of synthetic carpets, consider materials such as hemp, jute, and ramie as well as wool and cotton. Avoid stain repellents—it's better to have a mystery stain in front of the sofa than mystery ailments in your children. Or try the recycled modular carpet tiles that you put together like a preschooler's puzzle. The eco-beauty of these is that you can simply replace a single square or two, depending on how drunk and clumsy Aunt Martha gets at your Christmas open house. Or choose a natural-fiber area rug that can be thoroughly cleaned. Ask the company you purchase from to air out any carpet in its warehouse for three days prior to delivery. Avoid synthetic under pads in favor of untreated wool. ·

CORK. Imagine lovely flooring with a nice cushion to it, sort of like walking on the floor at an aerobics studio (except that you don't have to sweat or wear spandex). It's also always warm, says my friend Ben, who has it in his bathroom. Generally coming from well-managed plantations, cork is harvested from the bark of living trees in a process that doesn't harm them (I'm getting weepy—this is all so beautiful and balanced). You can even get cork flooring from wine stopper waste (too perfect). I have been told that cork wouldn't stand up to the claws of our two big dogs—but DiMartino has convinced me that it would bounce back.

BAMBOO. Bamboo is earning a reputation as more than just the shoot de jour for panda bears. A fast-growing grass that can reach maturity in three to six years, it is being used in everything from clothing to floors. Unfortunately, it's eco-star status is leading to overharvesting in some cases—and there's no one really looking out for the humble bamboo grass. If you choose to go with bamboo, make sure that you're purchasing from a responsible company that works with sustainability, not simply profit, in mind.

LAMINATE. Get up close with laminate. Looks just like real wood, right? Well, it's not . . . not exactly. It's actually a half-inch of wood chip between two sheets of melamine-soaked paper, on which a photograph of wood (no kidding!) is on the top layer. Most laminates don't off-gas significant VOCs, and many of the adhesives used in their manufacture are water based. However, few are made with FSC certification (though they're out there—I've seen them at Home Depot). Look for laminates made with non-formaldehyde or non-urea-formaldehyde binders, and use low-VOC adhesives to install the flooring, or go for a floating floor.

STONE, CERAMIC, TILE. Their durability makes any of these a green choice, although their weight requires more energy than other materials for transport. There's some debate about the radon that exists in all earth-based products—though most experts agree these don't off-gas in significant enough amounts to warrant worry. Recycled versions of some tile (glass, in particular) boost its eco-friendliness. Ensure that all are sealed with low-VOC sealants. This flooring can be hard on feet—and cold. But I, for one, love the look of inviting the outdoors in.

LINOLEUM. It may conjure up images of your grandma's worn kitchen floor, but linoleum deserves a second look. Linoleum—not to be confused with vinyl flooring—is a great green choice, created from materials like wood, cork, pine resin, lime, and linseed oil. Bright, vibrant, and fun, it's marketed under the names Marmoleum (fun to say!) and Artoleum.

FURNITURE

Of course you want furniture that suits your style, but also consider furniture that suits your values. Much of the wood—particularly exotic woods like teak and mahogany—comes from endangered old-growth forests (forests we need, might I remind you, to keep cranking out the oxygen we breathe and to moderate the effects of climate change). Cheaper furniture is often made from particleboard, which off-gasses formaldehyde. If you must buy particleboard, seal it with a low-VOC sealant. And the foam in furniture is commonly treated with PBDEs. A few forward-thinking companies, among them IKEA and Home Depot, have promised to buy wood only from sustainably managed forests. IKEA also avoids PBDEs and other toxins in its products (see sidebar on next page).

Greenpeace has a great website feature that outlines the best types of wood to buy for various rooms in your house. Dubbed the "Forest House" it offers the best choice (FSC-certified wood always), then the second-best and worst choices. Check it out at http://archive.greenpeace.org/foresthouse. You'll also learn that only 20 percent of the world's ancient forests are left and that an area the size of a football field gets cut every two seconds.

Speaking of seconds, furniture is a great option to purchase secondhand. My house is filled with hand-me-downs (hand-me-ups, my friend Barbie calls them, because they're too nice to be called "downs") from friends and relatives. And I know a nearby antique dealer who routinely finds whatever I need: a hall tree for coats, an oval end table, a cedar trunk for the kids' dress-up box . . . .

Appliances

Two words: Energy Star. This logo is your shorthand for an appliance that exceeds EPA standards. You'll generally get an appliance that's at least 50 percent more efficient. If you want the most energy-efficient appliance among the Energy Star offerings (you keener!), check out the Energy Star website: www.energy star.gov. You may even get rebates from your utility company, municipality, or federal government (or all three!) for purchasing energy-efficient appliances. But don't keep updating your appliances as more energy-efficient models become available. An appliance needs at least five years to work off the energy debt created in its manufacture. "Better" isn't always better. Bigger isn't always better, either. Resist the urge to supersize your appliances, and instead choose those that meet your current or anticipated needs. Bigger appliances take up more space (duh!) and use more energy—and cost more to operate.

Electronics

Again, look for EnergyGuide ratings and Energy Star endorse- ments on televisions, telephones, and more. Keep a cool head. Electronics purchasing has become a competitive sport. Don't get caught up in the race to be the first on your block with the

While some stores continue to drag their feet on such issues as fair labor, phasing out PVC, and selling products with phthalates, IKEA has simply moved forward with a characteristically Swedish social conscience. The company stopped selling PVC-laden products a decade ago, which automatically reduces the level of other chemicals such as phthalates. The company went further with a phthalate ban on all children's products and a ban on carcinogens (sad, really, that this is revolutionary and not simply the status quo). IKEA does not use brominated flame retardants (BFRs) in mattresses, carpets, or furniture and is phasing them out in light fixtures.

While they are guilty of producing about a bazillion catalogs, the company does use chlorine-free pulp from certified environmental management systems suppliers. And IKEA's build-it-yourself furniture (with, perhaps, the most annoying instructions in the world) significantly reduces greenhouse gases, as so much more can be transported flat than fully assembled. For more information, go to www.ikea-usa.com.

biggest, the best, the fastest . . . It's a race that nobody, least of all Mother Earth, wins. Buy what you need and keep it for as long as possible.

LIGHTING

How many North Americans does it take to screw in a lightbulb? Who cares, as long as they're screwing in compact fluorescents (CFLs) instead of those leftovers from Edison's day, incandescents, which might have been a better source of heat than light—only about 10 percent of the electricity used by incandescents is light; the rest is released as heat. Switching one conventional lightbulb for a CFL can prevent more than 450 pounds of emissions from a power plant over the CFL's lifetime, say the folks at Energy Star. Better still, CFLs last longer (up to 10 times as long!) and use 60 percent less energy—so while they cost more upfront, they generally are a better value in the long run. To figure out how to achieve the desired light from a CFL, choose one that offers the same lumen rating as the light you are replacing. The higher the lumen rating, the greater the light output. Better still are light-emitting diodes (LEDs), which will likely become more affordable and available but at this point aren't as easy to find as CFLs (with the exception of LED Christmas lights—see chapter 11, "Celebrations that Save the Earth").

>>> PURCHASE POWER <<<

- Look for wood products certified by the Forest Stewardship Council.
- If you're sold on carpet, look for one made with low-VOC adhesives that meets the Carpet and Rug Institute's indoor air-quality standards (look for the CRI Green Label logo).
- Buy Energy Star appliances and electronics.
- Buy the best-quality furniture you can afford. You can always reupholster as necessary, but "good bones" stand the test of time, as my mother, the queen of reupholstering, always said.
- Buy secondhand. Check out Craigslist, Freecycle, or the classified ads. Or find your own antique dealer and get him to find what you need from estate sales. It's like having your own furniture broker.

Green Your Home . . . Room by Room

There are some key spots where you can make a big difference:

THE KITCHEN

Within the heart of the home beats many of the big energy suckers in your abode—mainly your fridge.

THE REFRIGERATOR. This leviathan works hard. Keeping your veggies crisp (which it never really does, come to think of it), your organic milk cold, and your Tofutti frozen is a full-time job—a job that requires five times the energy consumption of the average television set. You can make the job easier by purchasing an Energy Star fridge (I've said that, haven't I?) with the freezer on top and forgoing the water dispenser and icemaker that boost energy usage. Then locate it somewhere it's not competing with heat, away from the stove, dishwasher, or vent. Keep the condenser coils clean and free of dust—this means pulling the fridge out from the wall and cleaning. (I know, yuck.) And, finally, keep the temperature right—37 to 40 degrees Fahrenheit for the fridge and 5 degrees for the freezer.

THE STOVE. If you plan on bringing home a range, consider this general rule: gas is a better environmental choice than electric. Having used both, I also find gas a pleasure to cook with. Either way, check those EnergyGuide and Energy Star labels.

Green Guidance:
Go Small, If at All . . .

Use smaller appliances over large—a microwave or toaster oven, for example, over a full-size oven to heat up food or cook small meals.

Self-cleaning ovens will usually have more insulation than regular ones, which means energy savings every time you cook. And don't let that heat escape by opening the door to see how things are cooking inside. Turn on the interior light to take a gander.

THE FREEZER. If you want to stock up on seasonal produce (I generally buy in bulk, then chop and bag for a long winter's worth of local veggie stir-fries and stews) or have a large family, you might need a freezer. Choose chest freezers over uprights because the cold air tends to stay put when opened. And to ensure that the seal is working properly, close the door on a piece of paper. You shouldn't be able to slide the paper out easily.

COUNTERTOPS. If the time has come and gone to renovate your kitchen, you've got some great options in countertops. Pick from grass (bamboo), paper (PaperStone looks like slate), glass (IceStone is recycled glass and concrete—expensive but gorgeous), and tile (a number of recycled versions are available in various colors and textures).

THE BEDROOM
Quiet, serene, and . . . toxic?

THE BED. There's little I love more than climbing into bed with a good book (well, OK, there's one thing I love more . . . but a great book is a close second). Unfortunately, it turns out my bed is trying to kill me. The typical mattress (of which mine is one) is stuffed with polyurethane foam, treated with flame retardants, and then, in case that's not enough to render me incapacitated, covered with material treated with stain-resistant chemicals. Now I know where the expression "on my death bed" came from.

Since I'm not partial to sleeping on the floor (I've hated camping ever since I attended Girl Guide Camp in 1976, and I still have issues with authority), the answer is an organic cotton or wool mattress, or a latex one. Wool is a natural fire retardant, which is why lambs don't get in trouble for playing with matches. Add organic bedding and you've now spent your children's education fund—*but* you'll live long enough to see them graduate. There are many, including Lifekind (www.lifekind.com) and Rawganique (www.rawganique.com). I'm still sleeping on my murderous mattress but saving up my pennies for an organic version. And I've got one eye open all night long. . . .

THE COVERS. As I nestle down under my duvet, I've never really given much thought to the geese who gave up their lives that I might be toasty in bed. According to the United Poultry Concern website, ducks and geese are sometimes plucked four to five times in their lifetime (ouch, and I thought a Brazilian sounded painful!) in order to provide down for pillows, comforters, and warm-weather clothing. In addition, down is commonly gathered from factory-farmed ducks and geese that live in filthy conditions. While it's hard to ensure your down is humanely gathered, you can opt for alternatives if you want to be goose-friendly, such as wool or synthetics. Kapok, seads from the tree of the same name, is earning a reputation as a down substitute with its silky fibers. Again, check out Lifekind or visit www.gaiam.com, which has a good reputation for luxurious organic cotton bedding.

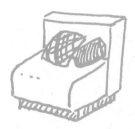

THE MOOD. To create romance (and make your stretch marks less noticeable), place candles strategically around your bedroom. Not just any candles, but soy-based or beeswax candles that add ambience without the attendant air pollution. Paraffin is a petroleum product (I confess the multitasker in me is impressed with how versatile petroleum is), which, as we're all getting tired of hearing me say, is a nonrenewable resource and causes pollution, wars, world destruction, blah blah blah. My new favorite candles are Aveda's Pure-Fume candles—safe and smelly. In a good way.

THE BATHROOM

It's where you whiz, wash, and, if you're not careful, waste an awful lot of water.

THE TOILET. With at least 3.5 gallons of water going down with every flush of a pre-1994 toilet, this is one spot that could use a makeover. Low-flush toilets use only 1.6 gallons or less. Two popular brands are the Toto Drake Toilet and American Standard's Cadet. A dual-flush toilet doesn't flush twice (bad!), but rather has two different flush buttons—one that uses 0.8 gallons for the yellow stuff and another that uses 1.6 gallons for the . . . um . . . brown stuff. Caroma was the company that introduced the dual-flush toilet and remains widely respected.

The EPA says you can create your own lower flush toilet by placing plastic containers (such as milk jugs) filled with water or pebbles in the toilet tank. More than one gallon of water can be saved per flush.

Leaking toilets can waste as much as 750 gallons of water per month, according to *Natural Life Magazine*. To find out if yours is leaking, add a few drops of food coloring into the tank. Wait about twenty minutes, then check the color of the toilet water.

THE SHOWER. Install a low-flow showerhead and a filter to remove chlorine, which is in most municipal water. Researchers at Nova Scotia's Dalhousie University found that high levels of trihalomethanes, a by-product of chlorine in tap water, were associated with a significant increase in the risk of stillborn babies. Chlorine in tap water has also been linked to an increase of certain cancers, such as bladder.

And remove that shower curtain, unless you're sure it's not PVC (most are). You can find non-PVC shower curtains, but you need to look carefully—I picked mine up at IKEA for around $6 a few years ago—or opt for organic cotton versions.

THE BATHTUB. You can buy a Bath Ball faucet filter that removes chlorine from the water for around $50. DiMartino's favorite source for the Bath Ball and other great home items is www.gaiam.com.

If you're going for a full bathroom renovation, check out the curious new material (mentioned above) called IceStone, which can act as anything from flooring to a tub surround to an actual bathtub, countertop, wall—there seems little this über-material can't do! It's created from (mostly) recycled glass and concrete and comes in about two dozen shades. The catch? It's pricey—think mid- to high-range granite.

THE HOME OFFICE

My office is located directly across the hall from my bedroom, and right now I'm typing in my pajamas and housecoat, one of the perks of working at home. It's ten o'clock on Saturday night, which is perhaps one of the disadvantages of working at home. All around me is the hum of machines—fax machine/copier, printer, computer, and phone, plus piles of paper and books. And my Far Side coffee cup featuring a dog calling Dial-A-Cat through which a voice purrs, "I'm a big fat Siamese with a broken leg and no teeth . . . " cracks me up every time.

COMPUTERS, FAX MACHINES, AND PRINTERS. Greening your home office generally starts with the equipment. Again, look for those with Energy Star status. A laptop can use up to 90 percent less energy than a desktop system. If you buy a desktop system, make sure it can be upgraded to meet future needs. Inkjet printers use up to 95 percent less energy than laser printers. Always recycle your ink cartridges or have them refilled. Be sure to turn office equipment off, or put it in sleep mode when not in use. And guess what? Screen savers do not save energy. In fact, some screen savers are so complex, they actually increase energy usage.

PAPER. As William Rathje, my garbologist friend who discovered that roughly half of landfill material is paper, put it, thanks to home office equipment—and the attendant fear of losing information that's been stored electronically—"everybody has their own printing press." Paper generally plays a big role in any office. Your best bet is FSC-certified or wholly recycled paper, made with a high percentage of postconsumer waste, that has undergone chlorine-free bleaching. Xerox and OfficeMax offer paper that's 100 percent recycled and 100 percent post consumer. Staples offers a similar product, but only online at www.staples.com. Find more brand names at www.conservatree.org.

And, of course, light your office—in addition to, ideally, natural light—with compact fluorescents.

THE POOL OR HOT TUB

My family loves our pool. Having never had one as a kid—and listening to all those neighbors doing cannonballs into their pools on hot summer nights—I confess I feel like Cinderella finally getting to the ball. However, I'm aware it is a completely over-the-top indulgence that uses enormous amounts of water. So don't for a second think I don't carry my share of middle-class guilt every time I cannonball into my own pool on a hot summer night. However, since the pool came with the house, I have no desire to have a big empty hole in my backyard, and, dammit, I love swimming with my kids on a sweltering day, we've simply resigned ourselves to making it greener.

Green Guidance:
Don't Just Toss Your Eco-Bulbs!

CFLs remain a great eco-choice but don't just toss them in the trash when they eventually burn out. Because they contain mercury, spent bulbs must be handled with care. Look for local recycling options when possible—some retailers, such as IKEA, offer a take-back program. Or check out lamprecycle.com and click on "State Lamp Recycling Regulations & Contacts" to find out local options for disposal of CFLs.

THE HEATING. Depending on where you live, you can likely get by without a heater, though I watched my young, skinny kids' lips turn blue for two colder-than-usual summers before caving in and agreeing to heat the thing. We didn't go for the most popular but least efficient choice—a gas-fired pool heater—opting instead for a heat pump, which is expensive but energy efficient. More efficient still is a solar heater.

THE CHEMICALS. Pools and hot tubs use a lot of chlorine, which has been implicated in a number of health issues, including miscarriage and stillbirth in pregnant women, asthma, and bladder cancer—though most studies focus on *drinking* chlorinated water. Still, there are options for your pool, the most common being replacing the chlorination with sea or table salt. No kidding! Just like the stuff you use to season your spaghetti sauce. We had watched with interest as friends switched to saltwater pools—mostly because of kids' allergies manifesting themselves in rashes. But my own concerns about chlorine prompted us to make the switch. According to my husband Daniel, who pays attention to these things, you dump a designated amount of salt into your pool (depending on its size and volume) and install a device that works something like a chlorinator but regulates the amount of sodium chloride (salt) that the pool requires. Daniel says that, while it costs more upfront, you save money in chemicals and have far fewer hassles. (You might need to use some chlorine when you open the pool, but rarely.) The experience is nothing like swimming in a saltwater ocean—the pH is closer to that of your tears. Your skin and hair feel soft, and you've eliminated much of the concern about chlorine. While there aren't "officially" available saltwater spa systems, some handy spa owners have retrofit theirs. Be warned, however, that this will likely void your warranty.

Power to
the People

What the virtuous
consumer says about:

Practical alternative power sources
- *The renewables: wind, solar, and
  other possibilities*
- *Greening the grid*
- *Reducing your home's energy needs*

The use of solar energy has not been opened up because the oil industry does not own the sun. Ralph Nader

This past summer, my husband and I were driving along the shore of Lake Huron when we saw dozens of huge wind turbines turning hypnotically. Whether they're inherently beautiful or we see their beauty as a renewable energy source, I'm not sure. I do know they took our breath away.

I now have a fantasy of running my entire home on wind energy. I get giddy at the majesty of the idea. Then the thought of bird carcasses raining down from the sky interrupts my reverie. Thankfully, the American Wind Energy Association (AWEA) rescues me from the myth that zillions of birds are killed by turbines, a persistent untruth with no basis in reality. Well, OK, a bit of basis in reality. Older-style turbines that were thought-lessly located in the paths of migrating birds led to some rather unfortunate feathers flying; today, however, the AWEA says that "commercial wind turbines cause the direct deaths of only 0.01% to 0.02% of all of the birds killed by collisions with man-made structures and activities in the US." In other words, I'd do better to bring my enormous avian-hunting cat Arnie indoors than abandon my dream of a wind-powered home.

However, for the time being, I'm stuck eking energy out of our recently replaced furnaces. (Full disclosure: We moved into a rather large, older home a few years ago that has not one furnace, but two—one for each floor. We said the requisite Hail Marys for eco-penance, then proceeded to replace the older inefficient models with new high-efficiency ones. And, Catholic guilt still gnawing away at my husband, we replaced every drafty window in our home—thirty-two of them, plus four doors.) We furthered our eco-cred by switching to a provider of "green" energy. Now the equivalent amount of our energy use is purchased from renewable sources, such as wind and low-impact hydro generators. So while I might not have a turbine in my yard, the wind still turns my crank.

I'll confess upfront my ignorance about wires and energy and the other mysterious workings of my home. As far as I'm concerned AC/DC is a band and solar energy is the great feeling I get after a nap in the sun. When my classmates had their noses buried in their chemistry and physics books, I was immersed in *Wuthering Heights*. (Well, OK, it was *Looking for Mr. Goodbar*. Same thing, practically.) So frankly I wouldn't blame you if you skipped this whole chapter and went straight to someone who actually understood this stuff, a step I would recommend in any case (there are plenty—see Resources). However, I have had a few chats with smart and energy-savvy people who patiently walked me through much of this stuff. So I'm encouraged to at least pass along my hard-won rudimentary knowledge.

Along with what we drive (and how far!), our homes account for the greatest amount of energy use. So more efficiently using energy there can have a major impact on the planet. Making a change in a less consequential part of your life is like planting a tree. Greening your home is like planting a forest.

Why don't more people do it? For the most part, many of us simply don't think about it, accustomed as we are to our lives of convenience. Most of us can remember a childhood in which a vigilant parent constantly took us to task for leaving lights on or doors open. ("Do you kids think I'm paying to heat the outside too?") But our homes are filled with so many gadgets and gizmos, all plugged in to the power grid, that we pay little heed to how much energy is being wasted—until the lights go out, as they did for 50 million people in the northeastern United States and Canada during the summer of 2003. And those of us left sitting in the dark—literally and figuratively—wondered what the heck could have happened.

What's the Controversy?

There are two main problems here: where we obtain our energy and how much of it we use.

Sorry if I sound like a stern priest from your childhood, but I need you to remember something that will probably fill you with shame and possibly drive you to therapy, if not action: While the United States accounts for only 4 percent of the world's population, it is responsible for 25 percent of the world's greenhouse gas emissions. It's largely our fault that Africans will be experiencing more severe droughts and floods, that South Pacific islanders will be going to sleep in life-jackets, and that polar bears need to train in long-distance swimming. Our lifestyles are hurting the world's most vulnerable and desperate people (and animals), those least responsible for the problem. Simply put, we need to decrease our emissions. The upside? Our homes are the perfect place to do it.

Most of us are aware that to meet our massive energy needs, we burn fossil fuels, natural gas, oil, and, especially, coal. Tim Flannery, who wrote the bestselling *The Weather Makers,* believes that the bulk of our efforts to combat climate change must be toward "decarbonising the power grid," which is cool science-speak for "use renewable energy sources"—wind, solar, and so on—instead. (Flannery's book will scare the crap out of you, by the way. This man does not mince words: No friendly "let's go shopping for green products" guide for this guy!)

Nuclear power has been getting plenty of play lately. It seems our memories of Three Mile Island and Chernobyl are receding as quickly as the polar ice caps. While it has plenty of supporters, among them James Lovelock, the brilliant and widely respected creator of the Gaia hypothesis (read more at www.ecolo.org/love lock/lovebioen.htm), nuclear power has plenty of detractors, leaving someone like me turning my head from side to side like I'm watching a tennis game. And I'm still not sure who's winning. While nuclear energy is touted as a "clean" source, there remain

The Statue of Liberty (and Ellis Island) are now lit via wind energy. The US National Parks Service has agreed to purchase 27 million kilowatt-hours of wind power to cover the electricity needs of Lady Liberty and Ellis Island Museum over three years. Not to be blown off the tourism map, the West Coast will be offering trips to Alcatraz Island on hybrid ferries—powered by wind and sun. How strangely appropriate that the symbol of liberty and a former prison both represent freedom from fossil fuels.

unsettling questions about how safely reactors can operate and how (and where) radioactive waste from so many reactors will be stored. So, while it may be *a* solution, it certainly isn't *the* solution—at least not at this point.

Renewable energy, a phrase on everyone's lips these days, is generally defined as solar (sun), wind (wind), geothermal (produced from heat deep in the earth's core), biomass (derived from once-living materials such as grass, grains, wood, and animal waste), tidal (waves), and hydro (falling water).

So, while we wait for the brainiacs (and governments) to make up their minds about where and how to obtain energy, we should at least be doing our part to lessen our load.

What's Up?

Temperatures around the globe, which only threaten to increase the amount of energy we use to make our homes comfortable. Almost half of the energy we use in our homes goes to heating and cooling. We can't continue to burn fossil fuels without its associated costs—pollution, the depletion of resources, and climate change, for starters. As noted, there are alternatives, and each has its proponents and its detractors. Let's examine them briefly.

WIND

Free, easy to find, poetic in its beauty. Much has been made of the noise of turbines—though more recent versions are much quieter, and many people (like me) don't object to the hum. The problem with wind, according to George Monbiot, the author of

For David Masters, the decision was simple. He was living in a big city, working at a corporate job that left him dissatisfied. When his father was diagnosed with cancer, he knew he needed to follow his own path—one that would see him setting up a business that fed his passion for nature, moving back to the family farm . . . and living sustainably in a yurt.

The company, Lunatic Adventures, is a wilderness guiding operation. It was already up and running shortly after his father's diagnosis. "I wanted him to see me happy," Masters explains of his decision to abandon a good job. But it wasn't until he moved back to the family farm that his future—and that of the company—came into focus.

It started with the yurt, an odd hybrid between tent and cabin that Masters describes as like "the underside of an open umbrella." He had seen one years earlier in his travels and loved it. So when he set up his own home on the farm, a yurt seemed the perfect choice.

He had one shipped from a company in Oregon and constructed it together with friends, adding a deck.

To supply his power needs, Masters looked to the sun and wind. For water, he counts on the rain. He found living off the grid "not that difficult," though he admits some friends thought he'd gone crazy. "They didn't understand," he says. Until they visited. Then "everybody realized it was livable and cozy." And, he adds with a laugh, now they call him "one lucky bastard" because he doesn't pay any bills.

Masters himself gets giddy at the thought that "my beer is cold because of the sun—how great is that!"

He considers his yurt very much a home and points out that it operates like any other—there are plugs for his lights, fridge and freezer, computer, TV, and more. He has a composting toilet, water heated by the sun, a woodstove to heat the yurt, and a two-burner propane stove and barbecue for cooking. He admits he's gone the bachelor route but notes that living off the grid can be "as lavish or as minimal as you want," depending on imagination and financial means. While the setup might be expensive at the outset, a yurt dweller doesn't have ongoing expenses for power.

Masters notes that his company has taken off since he's moved to the yurt. There's a connection now, he explains, between his business and his life that has "pushed business forward. It's made my vision that much clearer." Part of that vision is the pleasure of showing others how to "unplug from the world," he says. "It has spawned this whole existence of how to teach others to live a sustainable life."

Heat: How to Stop the Planet from Burning (another who doesn't mince words!), is that "you can produce reasonable amounts of electricity from wind only when it is blowing strongly and fairly consistently. If winds are weak or gusty or turbulent, wind turbines are a waste of time. In built-up areas, winds tend to be weak, gusty and turbulent." Monbiot goes on to point out that wind turbines might work in remote areas of the countryside (indeed, my friend David, who lives far from office towers and suburban sprawl, relies on his turbine . . .). Flannery, on the other hand, points out in *The Weather Makers* that if one takes a "regional approach" with wind turbines, "it is fairly certain that the wind will be blowing somewhere." He further points out that wind power has been "beset by bad press"—unfairly, he implies.

SOLAR

It makes complete sense to harness the power of that flaming ball in the sky. It's free, it's always there (even if it's hidden), and it's silent. However, as Monbiot, who lives in the UK, points out, sun isn't always a viable alternative for those who live above the forty-ninth parallel. Still, solar power has much going for it. Panels are increasingly affordable and efficient, and technology is consistently improving their capability. My wind-powered friend David also uses solar panels. He loves his off-the-grid system but carefully monitors his energy use on cloudy and windless days. We should all be so vigilant about our power use.

HYDRO

As someone who lives close to Niagara Falls, I learned early in my life about hydroelectric power. (I also learned that wax museums completely freak me out, but that's another story.) Hydroelectric power has a lot going for it: it relies on water and gravity, both of which nature graciously provides free of charge. It thus produces a constant energy supply, with no pollution or waste. Unfortunately, there exist only so many massive waterfalls. Dams cost a lot to build and have a strong impact on the local environment, flooding large areas and affecting water quality and quantity downstream. Many people love hydroelectric power, as long as the plants are not located close to them.

Other Renewables

I don't even pretend to understand the workings of biomass, geothermal, tidal, and other energy options being bandied about. I do know that while the murmurings are getting louder and more insistent, there's still little available for the average homeowner unless she's scientifically inclined or knows someone who is. Flannery puts it best: "If the renewables sector offers one lesson," he writes in *The Weather Makers*, "it is that there is no silver bullet for decarbonising the grid: rather we will see a multiplicity of technologies used wherever favorable conditions prevail." Brace yourselves, folks, for the greening of the grid.

What Can You Do?

Quite a lot, actually—and quite easily. Although there are clearly alternatives to our fossil-fuel-burning power sources, except for an intrepid few, most of us won't adopt them at this point. (Closet anarchists take note: once off the grid, it's sheer delight to thumb your nose at the power companies!) Following the simple steps below, however, can make a big difference in the amount of CO_2 our homes emit.

GREEN YOUR POWER. Take this one simple step: Call your power company and ask about a green power option. If it offers none, log on to www.eere.energy.gov/greenpower/buying/buying_power.shtml and find one in your area. For an extra dollar a day (less than a coffee), our household switched to a provider that will obtain our energy from renewable sources, such as wind or low-impact hydro. We got a fun little sign that we put outside our front door, which could allow us to feel all smug and self-righteous, but since we're not like that (of course not!), it simply lets others know that they too have the option of dramatically decreasing their own household's CO_2 emissions. And, let me tell you, does that feel good!

TAKE A LOAD OFF. Now that you're jacked on virtue and self-sacrifice, reduce your energy consumption. If you want a base point from which to start, conduct an energy audit of your home. You can have someone come in and do this for you—contact the Residential Energy Services Network at www.resnet.us or (760) 806-3448. Or you can do it yourself with this handy little online

The Power of Poop

Imagine if every time you stooped to scoop your dog's poop, you were not only channelling Dr. Seuss, you were helping solve the energy crisis. If all goes as planned, San Francisco could eventually be running on the energy of Rover's roughage. About 4 percent of the city's landfilled waste is puppy poop. Theoretically, it can be diverted to an anaerobic digester—a mixture of dog poop and food scraps—where microorganisms would break it down and produce methane. The methane would in turn be used to produce energy. The world—particularly those cities with a large dog population—are watching this pilot project carefully. And feeding Fido a high-fiber diet.

resource: http://hes.lbl.gov. Check with your local utility to find out if it offers any incentives for a home audit—and any rebates for improvements you make as a result of the findings.

GREENOVATE. If you're planning any major projects, include proper insulation. Eschew fibreglass, which is no fun to inhale and which sometimes contains formaldehyde, in favor of eco-options such as old blue jeans, shredded newspaper and more. Check out this comprehensive chart offered by the Green Home Guide: www.greenhomeguide.com/index.php/knowhow/entry/974/c236. By insulating your walls and ceilings, you can reduce CO_2 emissions by two thousand pounds a year and save about 25 percent in your home heating bills, according to the Environmental Defense Network. For further savings, you may even find that there are tax incentives to any renovation you're planning. Check out this site from Energy Star: www.energystar.gov/index.cfm?c=products.pr_tax_credits.

RENEW YOUR COMMITMENT. If you're not ready to move right off the grid, consider running at least some of your power needs from renewables. Perhaps your garden lights can be solar powered. Or you can install a passive solar hot water system, a good entry-level way to go solar. Think how hot the water in your hose gets on a hot summer day. Now imagine that water making its way into your home each and every day.

TAKE YOUR TEMPERATURE. At my university, there were always people who dressed in shorts and T-shirts all winter long even when the snow was thigh-high outside. Their residence rooms were as warm and humid as a tropical rainforest. Unfortunately,

Plug and Play: Mobile Unit Offers Renewable Energy in a Snap

It's like something out of a James Bond movie—a mobile unit that can be parachuted into hostile territory and can then, in just a few hours, generate enough power from the sun and wind for an emergency operations center, a field kitchen, or a small medical facility, eliminating the need to run long fuel lines over dangerous terrain. Think Afghanistan, Iraq, and New Orleans in the wake of Katrina. In fact, the CIA is. "It's the Tinkertoy solution to energy," says SkyBuilt company president and CEO Dave Muchow, who gleefully reports he played with Tinkertoys as a kid. SkyBuilt's mobile systems, while attractive to the average homeowner, aren't for residential application, at this point anyway. Muchow is careful not to reveal too much about where his systems are being used, noting only that they're in the "world's trouble spots. . . . You can presume that we're involved in places that are in the headlines."

too many of us expect to maintain a tropical clime year round, even if we live in Ohio. The sad irony is that our love of the tropical indoors is taking its toll on the real rainforests, in the form of our excessive CO_2 emissions. Turning your thermostat down by two degrees in winter and up by two degrees in the summer can save about two thousand pounds of CO_2 from being released. Adjust it further when you're sleeping (not literally—program it so that the temperature adjusts when you're sleeping). And, as your mother always told you, wear a sweater if you're cold.

KEEP YOUR COOL. Here's a great site—including nifty pictures—showing you how to maintain your air conditioner in peak energy-efficient form: http://home.howstuffworks.com/how-to-maintain-an-air-conditioner.htm.

BECOME A FOUL-WEATHER FRIEND. Take it from me: we Canadians know a thing or two about cold. I well recall the first winter my husband and I spent in our former home. The windows were decades old (the house itself was 102), and we had rolled towels at the sill of each one to stop the wind from blowing out our dinner candles. We had frost on the inside of our windows! Needless to say, we could have benefited from the advice of our own Natural Resources Canada's guide to window efficiency, which tells readers that "windows can account for up to 25 per cent of total house heat loss." Installing new windows was probably the way to go—though we moved out and left that problem to the next owners. Still, we moved into a new home and did, in fact, replace thirty-two windows with Energy Star windows. If you aren't ready for the financial plunge that new windows entail—or your windows can be repaired or require only minor air-sealing, you can make your windows more efficient with relative ease by taking one of the following steps. And you'll reduce CO_2 emissions by 650 pounds annually simply through caulking and weather-stripping.

DOUBLE-GLAZE. You can create your own double-glazed windows, in a manner of speaking, by applying plastic sheets that fit into your window frames and act as an insulator. These sheets are available at any hardware store. They look a little tacky (depending on how carefully you fit them), but hey, we're trying to save money and the world here. Tacky is immaterial when the stakes are high. If you add some nice drapes (which also act as an insulator), no one will notice.

CAULK. Caulk is goo that you squeeze into the parts of windows that don't move (or that won't be moving over the winter—you can take temporary measures, and remove the caulk when warm weather makes opening windows an appealing option once again).

WEATHER-STRIP. This is a cheap, easy, and effective way to make your home more energy efficient. Weather-stripping is material that you apply to the moving parts of windows and doors (sides, bottom, top). It compresses to form a tight seal when the window or door is shut, then expands when it's open. According to the Department of Energy's Energy Efficiency and Renewable Energy website at www.eere.energy.gov—an incredibly handy site, I might add—you have a number of materials to choose from, forcing me to say it again: Steer clear of vinyl. You have other options.

DON A JACKET. If your water heater is more than five years old and doesn't have internal insulation, buy it a jacket. An insulating jacket can increase efficiency and reduce carbon dioxide emissions by 250 pounds per year. If you're in the market for a new water heater, go for a tankless one that heats water on demand. It'll even reduce costs for hot water by up to 50 percent.

>>> PURCHASE POWER <<<

- Make your home as energy efficient as possible—when building or doing renovations, make choices based on efficiency. New windows, storm doors, and insulation can go a long way toward reducing the costs of heating and cooling—to you and to the planet.

- Buy green power from your energy provider or from an independent company if yours doesn't offer it. You can find out where to purchase green power in your state by going to www. eere.energy.gov/greenpower/buying/buying_power.shtml. If you live in Canada, check out Pollution Probe's Consumer Guide to Green Power in Canada at www.pollutionprobe. org/whatwedo/greenpower/consumerguide/index.htm.

- Go off-grid and purchase the materials necessary to install an alternative power system, or have someone who knows what they're doing do it for you. Plenty of information is out there—and plenty of people are generous with their knowledge of how to get started.

- Check out *The Homeowner's Guide to Renewable Energy: Achieving Energy Independence through Solar, Wind, Biomass and Hydropower* by Dan Chiras, an award-winning author and instructor of alternative energy. Or visit www.homepower.com. Go for it and then let everyone know how awesome it feels.

The Effortless Garden

8

Weeds are flowers too, once you get to know them.   Eeyore in *Winnie the Pooh*

The other day, as I yanked a dandelion from my yard, my five-year-old son gasped. *Why,* asked my bewildered boy, *are you taking out those beautiful yellow flowers?* I looked at the yard and stammered something about "bad flowers."

Stretching out behind our house is a city-owned park. Like many other progressive cities, ours has decided, wisely, to eschew chemical pesticides. The result is a field of yellow—a thing of true beauty to my children, who routinely reward me with fists clutching bouquets of these sunshiny "flowers."

I put down my weeder. Clearly, a beautiful lawn is all a matter of perspective.

Misguided weeding aside, I've never quite seen the beauty in a perfectly manicured lawn. It always looks too clipped, too uptight—like a new haircut or red lacquered nails. I come by my appreciation of the unkempt honestly. My father would far rather toss a baseball than mow the lawn. At our cottage—despite neighbors with luscious green lawns—my parents preferred a yard of sand and scrub grass. More time to watch sunsets over the lake.

In the neighborhood where I live now a well-kept lawn is a source of enormous pride. Yet my husband and I remain steadfastly delinquent, having learned our lesson years ago. I suppose we should have been alarmed when the lawn service workers we hired back then arrived looking as if they worked in Biosafety Level 4 for the Centers for Disease Control and Prevention. Of

Only in America, You Say?

More than 40 percent of the most commonly used lawn and garden pesticides are banned in other countries. American homeowners, however, blithely continue to apply 90 million pounds of these types of pesticides to their lawns and gardens.

course these pesticides were safe, they assured us. And we believed them. Determined to restore the lawn at our hundred-year-old home to its former glory, we overlooked their masks as they doctored our grass.

Then our beloved six-year-old dog, Gunther, was diagnosed with a rare form of cancer. We immediately set about removing anything from his environment that could compromise his challenged immune system. Not far down the list were pesticides.

We're parents of real kids now, not just the furry variety. And these days, we go the organic route—led by our intrepid eco-lawn expert Lee, who shook his head at our misguided pesticide-laden ways. According to Lee, the key to a luxe lawn is aeration, overseeding, and appropriate watering (and, sometimes, an appreciation for the inherent beauty of a bright-yellow dandelion). We haven't looked back, except to admire our gorgeous backyard.

What's the Controversy?

The issue, largely, is synthetic pesticides. The average suburban lawn uses six times the hazardous chemicals per acre as conventional farming. Yep, your kids and golden retriever are romping on a chemical-soaked carpet of green. And those chemicals inevitably make their way into our waterways, wreaking havoc on aquatic ecosystems. And of course they hitch a ride into our homes on the soles of shoes or pet's paws. Pesticides have also been implicated in cancers, lowered fertility, and other reproductive issues in people and wildlife.

But wait, there's more lawn disorder. Per hour of operation, a gas mower emits ten times as much hydrocarbon as a car. And don't get me started on leaf blowers, an auditory blight on civilized society that also billow soot and ozone-depleting chemicals into the air. Just use a damn rake. (Yes, dear husband, I'm referring to you.)

Then, of course, there are the sprinkler systems that go off like clockwork, even when it's raining (drives me *crazy* when I see that!). And no, I'm not referring to my husband this time. At our house we rely on God to water our lawn, though she occasionally forgets. According to the EPA, as much as half of all the fresh water used in urban areas is for watering lawns.

WHAT THE HELL WERE THEY THINKING?

The United States has obtained approval to continue using methyl bromide, an ozone-destroying pesticide. Doesn't matter that an international ozone treaty has banned methyl bromide. Doesn't matter that the United States has heaps of it (11,000 tons!) stockpiled. Doesn't matter that the international community has largely complied with the treaty. Doesn't matter that other countries have proved that safer alternatives are as effective. Treaty partners nonetheless approved the US use of 5,900 tons of the pesticide for 2008. So what does matter? Apparently not our ozone layer.

Meet The Virtuous Consumer Next Door:

Billie Karel, Protector against Spray-and-Pray Pesticides

....

If Billie Karel really did live next door, you can bet she'd have already persuaded you to stop using pesticides on your own lawn. Karel is the program coordinator for Pesticide Education Project (PESTed) and—at only 26 years of age—a passionate advocate of pesticide-free living. At the moment, she's relishing a victory in her state of North Carolina. Thanks to PESTed, the School Children's Health Act requires public schools to reduce the risk of student and staff exposure to pesticides and several other environmental contaminants. Specifically, schools must switch from "spray-and-pray" pest control to a less-toxic alternative called Integrated Pest Management. Schools must also notify parents and staff annually of their pest-management program and seventy-two hours in advance of any high-risk pesticide application at school. As Karel boasts, "It's the first right-to-know legislation ever passed in North Carolina, and boy are we proud."

Parents concerned about a school district's pest-management practices (and frankly, those like me who never really thought about it before might want to take a look) should talk to a teacher or custodian, Karel suggests, and ask about what they see: Are there bugs? Are the pesticides sprayed? Are students and parents warned before the pesticides are applied? Then she recommends speaking with the school system's maintenance director and getting the specifics about the school's pest-management practices. If you don't like what you hear, it's time to get active—start a petition to your school board. You can even download one from PESTed's website: www.pested.org.

Karel believes that people getting involved in their little part of the world is key. "People are at their most powerful when protecting their loved ones or a place that they love," she says.

Not one to rest on her organic laurels, Karel is forging ahead with PESTed plans to bring the same type of pest management to child-care centers. "I feel really strongly about small changes," she says. "Every little bit helps."

What's Up?

People's obsession with their lawns and gardens. According to the thirty-fifth annual National Gardening Association survey, 83 percent of American households participated in gardening in 2005, setting a new record.

This obsession is a good thing, kept in check. People who feel connected to the planet are more likely to take care of it. However, our quest for perfection has a downside. According to Bruce Butterfield, the National Garden Association's research director, American gardeners followed "only three out of twelve recommended environmentally friendly lawn and garden practices. Less than half of all households followed the remaining nine simple environmentally friendly practices." So, while an increasing number of municipalities are voting to go pesticide free in public parks, too many homeowners are still relying on chemicals to give them picture-perfect lawns.

What Can You Do?

It only makes sense that something as natural as grass and flowers are best tended naturally. There's lots you can do.

SOIL YOURSELF. Start by improving your soil, recommends Maria MacRae, manager of Backyard Habitat Programs for the Canadian Wildlife Federation. A quick way to do this is to leave grass clippings on the lawn when you mow. As they decompose, they add nitrogen to the soil, which is what most of us want to add when we use fertilizer. (Leaves do the same thing, so, when fall leaves fall, mulch them with a lawn mower and leave them to decompose.) And leaving grass clippings also stimulates earthworm activity, which is also good for your lawn, according to the folks at *Organic Gardening* magazine. Still not convinced? A University of Connecticut study compared lawns where clippings had been left with those where clippings had been removed. The study revealed that the healthier lawns were those with clippings—specifically they had 45 percent less crabgrass, two-thirds less disease, significantly more earthworms, and a better ability to withstand drought and disease.

CREATE BLACK GOLD. Composting is simple, fun, and strangely satisfying. The transformation of last year's banana peel into this year's peony (in a manner of speaking) makes me feel like Merlin. Maria MacRae points out that compost is a great way to add microorganisms and lots of nutrients to your lawn and garden.

MAKE THE CUT. Another simple way to help your lawn grow healthy and thick is to set your lawn mower so it cuts high. Taller blades of grass absorb more sun, are better at pushing out weeds, and conserve moisture by better shading the soil. Aim for three to four inches. Or chop off only about one-third of the grass height at each mowing. Any more stresses the grass. Cutting a third of the height also leaves clippings that decompose quickly. To give the environment an added boost, use a manual lawn mower, rather than a gas or electric one. The new generation of reel mowers are far less clunky than the mowers of your youth but still give you a workout. Plus, hearing the slicing sound they make as the blades lop the top off your lawn is fun.

GO NATIVE. MacRae points out that adding native plants to your garden is a great way to reduce your own workload—they're adapted to local pests, climate, and soils—and attract wildlife. Native plants provide food and shelter for birds and butterflies. And who doesn't want birds and butterflies in the garden? Be sure, however, that you take height and width at maturity into consideration and choose a plant that won't require a lot of pruning.

DIVERSIFY. Plant a wide variety of plants close together. The pests of one are frequently the dinner of the pests of another, so it's far easier to keep them in check. As MacRae says, "A diversity of plants will allow you to attract in more predators of pest species. This goes for attracting birds, insects, reptiles, and amphibians. They will pay you back for your generosity by eating up all those creatures that are eating your plants." Hmm, I never really thought of all those toads as employees.

PLANT FOR ENERGY EFFICIENCY. Plant deciduous trees—those are the ones that lose their leaves (remember second-grade science? I don't, but my eight-year-old daughter just briefed me)—along the west side of the house, filtering sun in the summer and letting rays through in the winter. Make sure you choose drought-tolerant native species that won't require a lot of water. If there's no room for trees, MacRae says, vines or shrubs planted on the west side will also provide cooling. Add evergreens in cooler climes to absorb the wind and reduce winter heating costs. Evergreens will also attract birds, offering them year-round shelter and protection.

GROW ORGANIC. If your lawn still needs help, go organic. Organic fertilizers decompose and release their nutrients more gradually than synthetics and thus nourish lawns more steadily over a longer period of time. If just 10 percent of us switched to natural lawn care, over half a billion pounds of synthetic fertilizers, pesticides, and herbicides would be prevented from entering the environment—and our kids' bodies. But use organic fertilizers carefully. They can still cause problems if they get into waterways.

>>> PURCHASE POWER <<<

Gardening is big business, so there are plenty of products available to help you achieve your green garden:

- Purchase a compost bin (look for one made of recycled plastic) or create your own. There are plenty of sources for

Forget everything you've ever believed about bats, unless it's good. Bats have suffered from bad PR over the years, being unfairly blamed for everything from hair entanglement to rabies. But with the increased concern about mosquito-borne West Nile virus, bats just might be finally gaining the respect they deserve. Indeed, brown bats can devour up to one thousand mosquitoes an hour, along with gulping down many other annoying bugs. Put out the welcome mat for the bats in your neighborhood by putting up a bat house—either purchased or homemade. You can find them at most hardware stores or garden supply shops. Some local conservation groups even hold bat house–building workshops.

easy-to-follow instructions. I particularly like the information offered at the Environmental Defense site (www.environmentaldefense.org/article.cfm?ContentID=2037).

- Buy aerator sandals—funky (and rather dangerous-looking) contraptions that strap onto shoes and have thick pins at the bottom to poke holes into the ground, allowing water and nutrients to more easily access the roots of grass. They're cheap (less than $15) and easily available at garden stores.
- Purchase plants native to your area, which will likely mean they'll need little water (after the first year, anyway) and maintenance. To find out what works in your area, consult a local nursery. Or check out the website of the National Wildlife Federation (www.enature.com/home) or the Canadian Wildlife Federation (www.wildaboutgardening.org).
- Invest in a push mower. Or a goat.
- If you must water, do so in the evening or early morning, when it won't evaporate so quickly. And use a drip or soaker hose to get water to the roots where it's needed. You might also consider a rain barrel to collect water for gardens. You can find hoses and barrels at most home or garden stores. Get a lid for the rain barrel as it can be a breeding ground for mosquitoes.

Creating Good Car-ma

9

What the virtuous
consumer says about:

Greener options for autos
- *Hybrids*
- *Biofuels*
- *Hydrogen fuel-cell cars*

Reducing pollution
- *Tips on driving green*

Sharing the ride
- *Ride-share and car-share programs*

It wasn't the Exxon Valdez captain's driving that caused the Alaskan oil spill. It was yours. Greenpeace advertisement, *New York Times*, February 25, 1990

I come from a car-loving family. My father has always loved anything fire-engine red that can accelerate like a rocket and sports a dashboard that lights up like a 747. For the most part, he's leaned toward sports cars, though we did spend a regrettable few years in the 1980s with a navy blue Ford Thunderbird with faux leather luggage straps on the trunk. People seemed disappointed to discover it wasn't Huggy Bear behind the wheel.

My brother can forgo the red, as long as the top comes down. My mom just wants something that can plow through three feet of snow without her having to get out and push. And my son, still 11 years away from getting his license, goes into paroxysms of ecstasy at the sight of any souped-up hot-rod or pimped-out monster truck.

So it might come as a surprise to discover that a bicycle has always been my transport of choice. Perhaps it's because I haven't got a clue how a car works—whereas I can easily replace a tube and fix a chain. Perhaps it's because I take life a little slower than the horsepower junkies in my midst. Or perhaps that experience with the embarrassingly hideous Thunderbird made an impression. *Thanks, Dad, but I'll take my bike. . . .*

However, a bicycle might have suited my purposes quite nicely when I was cycling solo. But it just doesn't work when I have three kids and, frequently, two enormous dogs to cart around. So a minivan (oh, how I loathe feeling like a cliché) it is.

Still, I resolved this past spring to leave the van in the driveway as much as possible. My eldest child can now bike quite capably on her own—and my younger two fit (albeit a little snugly—must put them on a diet) into my bike trailer. So we spent much of the warm weather months on two wheels. I lost that final five pounds of post-baby weight that I thought was mine forever, my kids had a blast, and we saved a small fortune when gas peaked at more than $3 a gallon.

But in a climate that features plenty of snow, cycling days have to give way to driving days. And with my minivan coughing and sputtering and showing other signs of decline, it's time to consider our next vehicle. I've discovered that, while there's no such thing as an eco-friendly vehicle (except, of course, a bike), some autos are gentler on the planet than others.

Considering that cars, as we know them, have only been around for slightly more than a century, they've wreaked a lot of havoc. But ironically enough, Henry Ford foresaw a green future for automobiles. His Model T ran on gas, ethanol, or a combination of the two, and he proposed that fuel could be created from fruit, weeds, sawdust, or anything else that could be fermented.

These days, it's hard for a mechanically challenged car-shopper such as me to keep up with the options: hybrids, biodiesel, ethanol, flexible-fuel vehicles, hydrogen fuel-cell cars—the list is growing longer.

What's the Controversy?

Simple. Cars pollute. OK, maybe you need a bit more than that—they pollute a *lot*. The United States alone uses a quarter of the world's oil production. Passenger vehicles suck up 40 percent of that. Then they burn it, releasing four hundred metric tons of greenhouse gas emissions (which cause climate change) and contributing to ground-level ozone pollution—better known as "smog."

But that doesn't deter us from driving more, driving farther, and driving larger. As a result, we're driving this planet's health—and our own—into serious decline.

There's also the political element: By now we're over our incredulity at George Bush's utterly anticlimactic announcement regarding our "addiction to oil." And most of us have discerned that the invasion of Iraq had less to do with the drumbeat of democracy than with drums of oil. Truth is, our love of the automobile has put us in the frightening position of needing a fuel source that exists largely in other countries. Whoops! Indeed, the Natural Resources Defense Council notes that the United States consumes 25 percent of all the oil produced in the world, yet controls only 3 percent of the world's oil reserves. And, of course, much of it comes from the conflict-ridden Middle East, making us vulnerable to the political instability there and creating an increasing threat to American national security.

Canadians (those without dollar signs dancing in their eyes) are getting a wee bit nervous about the vast amounts of oil that lurk beneath Alberta's tar sands. Extracting this oil would require stripping large areas of the Boreal Forest Natural Region, burning tons of natural gas, contaminating groundwater, and belching out greenhouse gases.

It's Not Just the Price That'll Give You a Headache

As the child of folks who always bought their cars secondhand (and paid cash!), I never had my full whiff of "new-car smell" until my husband and I bought our brand-spanking-new minivan. The heady sensation of having a vehicle that no one else had already spilled coffee in soon gave way to headaches. I had to drive—in January—with the windows open. Not surprising, says the Ecology Center, a Michigan-based environmental nonprofit that has studied the issue. "Our research shows that autos are chemical reactors, releasing toxins before we even turn on the ignition," says the center's Clean Car Campaign director, Jeff Gearheart (his real name—how appropriate for a car guy!). These toxins include PBDEs and phthalates, used to soften the PVC so ubiquitous in car interiors, which were found in "dangerous amounts" in dust and windshield film samples and which are linked to birth defects, impaired learning, liver toxicity, and premature births. As usual, the United States lags in protecting its people. Europe has legislation phasing out PBDEs in electronic and electrical equipment, and Japanese automakers have voluntarily agreed to reduce the use of these chemicals. Some states, namely California, Hawaii, Michigan, and New York, among others, have passed laws banning the two worst forms of PBDEs (penta and octa). But there's no legislation at the federal level. In the meantime, certain cars are better than others for their attention to reducing "new car smell." Volvo leads the way, even instituting a "sniff test" where materials must pass muster with the hired noses. Wouldn't you know we'd traded in our Volvo for our stinky minivan? With all those new chemicals wreaking havoc with my brain cells, no wonder I kept getting lost.

For more information and a chart outlining which cars are the most chem free, check out www.ecocenter.org.

What's Up?

Fuel-economy standards are certainly up from the mid-1970s, when the average passenger car got only 14 miles per gallon. Today, passenger cars are required by law to get 27.5 miles per gallon, a standard that hasn't budged since 1990. And the heaviest vehicles—also the biggest offenders, such as the GM Hummer H2 or Ford Excursion—aren't bound by the fuel-economy regulations at all. Clearly, we need—indeed, most consumers want—updated, responsible legislation.

Two bipartisan bills right now aim to require that automakers make vehicles that average 35 mpg by 2018 and save more than 2.5 barrels of oil per day when they are phased in. Indeed, the hope of one of the bills is to encourage debate among Americans and cue up the issue for the 2008 election, explains Dan Becker, director of the Sierra Club's Global Warming Program. In the meantime, consumers have some car choices to make.

The problem for many of us is that each time we open the automobile section of our newspaper, we hear about another hybrid, flexible-fuel vehicle, or "cleaner" diesel on the market that promises to deliver us to greener driving. It's getting hard to separate the news from the noise. Let's look at the options.

HYBRIDS. Toyota sent much of North America into a wild case of Prius envy when it released its revolutionary hybrid in 2004. Waiting lists for the car were months long as the groundbreaking technology quickly proved itself, and a nation of gas guzzlers saw the green light. Dan Becker is a hybrid fan, but he warns consumers to be wary of what he calls "muscle hybrids"—those that are only marginally better in terms of fuel efficiency than their conventional counterparts, which have horrible fuel economy. Consumers also have a number of good resources to help them sift through the hybrid offerings: The Union of Concerned Scientists created www.hybridcenter.org, a site that includes a buyer's guide, a comparison chart, reviews, testimonials, even the Hybrid Watchdog, which helps readers differentiate between a "hollow hybrid" and a full hybrid—indeed, it offers everything but the money to purchase one. Consumer Reports, another reputable objective resource, delivers its Greener Choices site (www.

WHAT THE HELL WERE THEY THINKING?

The province of Alberta's premier, Ralph Klein, went head to head with Al Gore in mid-2006 for comments the former presidential candidate made about Alberta's oil sands and the resulting pollution from tapping the oil-rich tar sands. Klein, who has gone to Washington trying to drum up support for the oil sands (bet that's a tough sell!), has notably rejected scientific data in the past that connects industrial pollution with global warming and has gone on record as saying that global warming trends that occurred millions of years ago may have been caused by "dinosaur farts." Klein has since come around, acknowledging that global warming causes are "manmade."

greenerchoices.org—click "cars") for ratings. The government's own Environmental Protection Agency has the Green Vehicle Guide (www.epa.gov/greenvehicles).

Becker's bottom line? "Look at the combined mileage—55 percent of the city, 45 percent of the highway—the average of the two," he recommends. "There are several good hybrids. . . . Ask yourself, is the fuel economy substantially better than regular technology?" If it is, and you can afford the higher price of a hybrid (money you'll eventually make back due to savings at the gas pumps), go for it.

Automakers are now preparing to meet the demand for hybrid offerings, with more models expected to come on the market within a few years. But most hybrid aficionados note that the plug-in hybrid—think extension cord—is the gold standard. This car takes hybrid technology a step further along the continuum: it can be charged from a standard household outlet (hybrid electric batteries are currently—ha!—charged by the use of the gas engine and the motion of the wheels and brakes), thereby further relegating the gas engine to backup status. With your electric engine always ready to go, you'll rarely need the gas engine for short trips—some say plug-ins can be twice as fuel efficient as other hybrids, which are already generally twice as efficient as traditional cars. Until recently, however, plug-ins were the domain of do-it-yourselfers who jury-rigged their hybrids. There are companies (see Resources), however, that will convert hybrids to plug-ins. And GM, in late 2006, announced plans to unveil a Saturn Vue plug-in hybrid, while Ford promised an Escape plug-in hybrid—though neither company offered production dates. Becker recommends caution with this option, however. "We need to be careful to avoid a situation . . . where we're effectively running cars on coal. We don't want to run a lot of transportation off electricity unless we've first figured out how to clean up the electric grid."

DIESEL. There's been much ado about cleaner-burning diesel fuel—prompting many to consider diesel a viable green alternative. Becker reminds us that it's "cleaner" diesel, as in "cleaner than the dirtier diesel." He points out that roughly a dozen states, including California and New York, won't allow diesel cars to be sold unless they can meet the same air-quality standards as traditional cars, which, because they produce a higher amount of nitrous oxide (a major component of smog), diesels sometimes can't. But diesel die-hards argue that their cars get 20 to 40 percent better mileage than similar gasoline-engine cars, thereby contributing far less greenhouse gas to the atmosphere. Moreover, low-sulfur diesel is becoming increasingly available, and diesel manufacturers are moving toward technology that is expected to cut particulate emissions and nitrous oxide emissions. Diesels account for less than 4 percent of the US market (it's ten times that in the EU, where diesels have long been appreciated for their mileage), but things are looking decidedly diesel.

BIODIESEL. A further argument for diesel-powered cars is their ability to run on biodiesel—fuel created from renewable vegetable sources. Becker cautions that there are "a lot of problems with biodiesel" but admits it can be a good choice as long as you have a reliable source of fuel of reasonable quality. And that's the catch for many who can't or won't make their own biodiesel. Biodiesel fuel isn't widely available—I would have to drive 40 minutes from my home to the nearest station. What's more, Becker says using it in a diesel car can "void the warranty," a pretty big risk to take.

Still, the National Biodiesel Board, the trade association

for the biodiesel industry, has formed the National Biodiesel Accreditation Commission (NBAC) "to audit fuel producers and marketers in order to enforce fuel quality standards in the US. NBAC issues a 'Certified Biodiesel Marketer' seal of approval for biodiesel marketers that have met all requirements of fuel accreditation audits. This seal of approval will provide added assurance to customers, as well as engine manufacturers, that the biodiesel marketed by these companies meets the ASTM standards for biodiesel and that the fuel supplier will stand behind its products." The organization points out that warranties cover only parts and service, anyway, not fuel—and that fuel suppliers must stand behind their product. There are a few keeners who make their own biodiesel, but most rely on the few biodiesel suppliers in the United States. To find one, visit the board's website at www.biodiesel.org.

You can, after a conversion that will run you about $2,000, run your diesel on discarded vegetable oil (you might want to befriend your local Chinese restaurant owners). There's a teensy little issue with legality—the EPA considers cars that run on straight veggie oil a violation of the Clean Air Act and, if caught, you might have to cough up a fine of close to $3,000 (which would pay for a lot of Chinese dinners). However, if living within the law isn't high on your priority list, and you don't mind emitting the odor of pork dumplings (no sulfur emissions, though!), this might be an option for you. There are plenty of veggie-fueled folks out there happy to guide you on your journey.

ELECTRIC CARS. The summer of 2006 put electric cars on people's radar, thanks to a short documentary with the provocative title *Who Killed the Electric Car?* As it turns out, it was General Motors, and I leave it to the film to fill you in on the gory details, not to mention entertain you. Zero emissions make electric cars appealing—though their use is limited because they can go only sixty miles or so between charges. Still, they appeal to many (George Clooney, for example) as commuter cars. They can be plugged into any electrical outlet for recharging, they have only one moving part (as opposed to a gasoline engine's 150 to 250 moving parts), there's no oil to change, the engine is quiet, and they cost little to operate. And, if you get your electricity from a renewable or green power source, these cars are virtually guilt free. The problem? Well, they aren't widely available, most are expensive (like six figures expensive), and they're very small, which is a plus or minus depending on your point of view. There are rumors of mass-produced electrics coming soon—so stay tuned.

Flexible-fuel vehicles (FFVs). While FFVs ostensibly run on E-85, a blend of 15 percent gasoline and 85 percent ethanol, a corn-based fuel, Becker says only a few hundred of the 176,000 fuel stations in the United States even offer E-85. Basically, making FFVs "helps companies evade an environmental law," he explains. Under Corporate Average Fuel Economy (CAFE) standards, which were designed to persuade automakers to create more fuel-efficient vehicles, the companies can average the fuel-efficiency of their entire fleet. Vehicles that theoretically get better gas mileage, like FFVs, give automakers the leeway

The Greener Clean: How to Wash Your Car

Few people consider when they wash their car in their driveways that the water (now contaminated with detergent, gas, oil, and exhaust residue) runs right into storm drains—and into rivers, streams, creeks, and wetlands. Commercial car washes, however, are required by law (in both the United States and Canada) to drain their wastewater into sewer systems, so it gets treated before being discharged into our waterways. And thanks to those high-pressure hoses and nozzles, less water is required for cleaning—up to 60 percent less. Indeed, some car washes recycle water and reuse the rinse water.

Other tips:

- If you use soap at all, pick a biodegradable soap formulated for car parts (Simple Green's Car Wash or Gliptone's Wash N Glow), or something like Dr. Bronner's, which you've likely been using for your own body parts.
- Unfortunately, many car care products are ripe with VOCs and petroleum-based cleaners. Optimum Polymer Technologies promises a greener clean with its products that include biodegradable No Rinse Wash and Shine (two capfuls, the Optimum folks promise, along with just two gallons of water is enough to scrub even the dirtiest car clean), VOC-free tire shine, and a petroleum-free UV car wax. Check them out at www.ecocarcare.net.
- Avoid the driveway. Wash your car on a lawn or over dirt, which will act as a natural filter.
- If you're a frequent washer (that is, if you're in love with your car), start collecting rainwater for just such a purpose. Frankly, I consider my car washed every time it rains. At the least, keep an eye on water usage—use a bucket or a hose nozzle that controls the flow.

Get out of (Eco) Jail Free Card

If guilt about driving is driving you crazy, consider TerraPass. For every pound of gas burned, 28 pounds of carbon dioxide (a greenhouse gas) are pumped into the atmosphere, thereby contributing to climate change. Purchasing a TerraPass (see www.terrapass.com) will offset those emissions by funding clean energy projects that reduce industrial CO_2 emissions. Don't worry, the TerraPass folks will do the math for you—and each purchase they make is third-party verified to be accurate and measurable. For your fee (around $40), you also get a bumper sticker and a window decal, so not only do *you* know you're morally superior to the guy idling in the SUV beside you, but now *he'll* know it too. Hard to put a price tag on that!

to produce less fuel-efficient vehicles (think Hummers) while still holding true to CAFE standards. Another serious problem is that FFVs generally don't run on E-85. In fact, says Becker, some companies, believing that owners would not be using E-85, stopped coating the gas tanks (which they had been doing because ethanol is more corrosive than gasoline). So if E-85 was used—a few people create their own ethanol fuel—the gas tanks got corroded.

HYDROGEN FUEL-CELL CARS. Led by California governor Arnold Schwarzenegger, who has made the hydrogen highway his personal platform, this technology is gaining momentum. A hydrogen fuel cell converts chemical energy into electricity by combining oxygen from the air with hydrogen gas. (Keep in mind I barely get how an escalator works, but I've been told this by smart people.) A fuel cell won't run down like a regular battery or require recharging. As long as hydrogen is available to it, it will continue to produce electricity. And it emits nothing more than a drip of water from its tailpipe. The controversy arises in how the hydrogen is obtained—whether from a renewable source of electricity, such as wind or solar (green hydrogen), or from coal, oil, or nuclear plants (black hydrogen). There are also safety concerns with storing hydrogen, which has a tendency to blow up. However, don't discard this option yet. With Arnold and even George Bush behind it, it's getting plenty of push. In fall 2007, GM will launch a fleet of a hundred SUVs powered by hydrogen fuel cells.

What Can You Do?

One step Becker would love to see is CAFE standards raised, which generally means getting politicians in office that would make this a priority. They aren't there now, but Becker strongly encourages us to ask our members of Congress if they support raising CAFE standards. If they do, he says, thank them. If not, tell them you'll vote for their opponent come election day.

In the meantime, you have plenty of choices in terms of what you drive. You can choose to keep your existing car. This is not a bad option. The manufacture—and transport—of a new vehicle comes with an eco-sticker price. If you do decide it's time for a new vehicle, Becker puts it simply: "Look for the most fuel-efficient vehicle you can afford that meets your needs." It's easier than ever to discern: New vehicles come with a window sticker that reveals how much gas the vehicle consumes and how its mileage compares to that of other vehicles.

BUY A HYBRID. Lift the hood of a hybrid and you'll find an electric engine alongside the gas engine. The electric motor runs the car at low speeds and the gas engine kicks into use when you need more power, say above 20 miles per hour. When the car stops—at a stoplight or in congestion—the engine shuts off. It comes back to life at the press of the accelerator pedal, much like a computer awakens at the touch of the mouse. If you choose to go this route, there are tax credits available—the IRS can fill you in: visit www.irs.gov/newsroom/article/0,,id=157557,00.html.

DO OR DIESEL. If you go with a diesel, run it as cleanly as possible, which generally means using the new low-sulfur fuel, or running it on biodiesel. You can opt for the do-it-yourself approach, or find an accredited supplier by visiting www.biodiesel.org.

NAME THAT TUNE-UP. Whatever vehicle you choose, keeping your car tuned up can go a long way toward improving its fuel-efficiency:

- Keeping tires properly inflated can improve mileage by 3 percent.
- Using the recommended grade of motor oil improves mileage by 1 to 2 percent (look for motor oil with "Energy Conserving" on the API performance symbol—it reduces friction).

- Keep your engine tuned, which can further improve mileage by up to 4 percent.
- Replace air filters regularly, which can improve mileage by as much as 10 percent and keep impurities from damaging your engine.

No Idle Thoughts. Turn off your car if you're stopped for more than 10 seconds. And you don't need to "warm up" an engine. Just drive.

Hitch a ride. While I relied quite effectively on my thumb while an undergrad living in Nice, France, I don't recommend it as an option. Rather, I'm referring to ride-share services—basically a Web-based equivalent to those "ride wanted" or "ride offered" notices thumb-tacked onto a bulletin board at your local coffeeshop. These days ride boards are online—broader in scope and sophistication (see box on opposite page).

Share and share alike. For those who like the idea of sharing but prefer a car to themselves, car sharing is becoming increasingly popular. There are a number of different companies—such as Zipcar, Flexcar, and AutoShare—but the basic concept is the same. You pay a membership fee—Flexcar, which boasts being the "nation's first and largest" car-sharing service, charges $40 annually. You're then given 24-hour security access and a list of leased parking spaces where the cars are kept. You reserve your car, pay an hourly fee (Flexcar charges $7–$10 per hour or $35–$90 daily, which includes gas, maintenance, cleaning, parking, and 24-hour emergency service), and get going. Some companies allow "roaming," which means if you're visiting a city where they are set up, you can use cars in that city. You can also usually reserve a car for a few days, allowing for short trips out of town. Check what's available either in your city or in the city you're visiting. Some are for-profit, others are co-ops. But all seem to be a green option worth considering.

Go public. There are certain cities in which public transit is a pleasure. I never read so much as I did when I lived and worked in a big city with an awesome subway system. I also loved eavesdropping on conversations in pre-MP3 player days.

Muscle power. Walk. Bike. Skateboard. Skate. You'll be healthier. Our planet will be healthier. Win-win.

"Don't make me stop this car . . . "

According to Car Love (www.carlove.org), about one in three parents has uttered this threat. I was surprised, believing this to be a near-universal 1970s experience (just ask your friends!), until I realized that just one in three parents has *admitted* in a survey to uttering this threat.

Going Green

Your options of traveling green are growing. Whether you choose to ride share or rent a hybrid for a weekend escape, you'll be doing your bit to help. To help you find what you're looking for, check out these car-sharing resources:

- Alternet Rides (http://alternetrides.com)
- Autoshare (www.autoshare.com)
- Bio-Beetle (www.bio-beetle.com)
- CarSharing (www.carsharing.net)
- Flexcar (www.flexcar.com)
- Zipcar (www.zipcar.com)

And for those who want their auto assistance program to go green, check out betterworldclub.com. Offering itself up as an alternative to traditional auto clubs (think AAA), Better World Club provides eco-travel services, discounts on rental hybrids, and bicycle roadside assistance among other, greener options.

KEEP THINGS CLOSE. Our suburban lives are in many ways responsible for our reliance on our wheels. Living close to work, amenities (groceries, a medical center), schools, and so on could cut our own addiction to oil.

>>> PURCHASE POWER <<<

Visit the following sites to help you determine which car is the right ride for you.

FUEL ECONOMY. Find the fuel economy of any car you're considering from model years 1985 through now; plus find out more about hybrids, where to find E-85, how to drive any car more efficiently, and more. www.fueleconomy.gov.

SIERRA CLUB. The Sierra Club has a long history of environmental stewardship. This site offers the opportunity to sign a petition to President Bush, get easy-to-understand facts about the impact of vehicles on climate change, and check out the miles-per-gallon calculator. www.sierraclub.org/globalwarming/cleancars.

CLEAN CAR CAMPAIGN. Sign the Clean Car Pledge to persuade the powers that be to deliver greener cars; check out the fuel efficiency of cars from 1978 to date; explore articles, links, and more. Created by Environmental Defense, a highly respected nonprofit. www.cleancarcampaign.org/aboutccc.shtml.

GreenerCars.com. The American Council for an Energy-Efficient Economy offers its ratings of green cars. www.greenercars.com.

Car Talk. A fun site that offers everything from info on alternative fuels to the top gay and lesbian cars of all time. Learn how to change a tire, avoid blowing up your car trying to jump-start it, and other useful tips. www.cartalk.com.

Hybridcenter.org. The Union of Concerned Scientists is noted for being incredibly thorough—and concerned. The result is info you can trust. www.hybridcenter.org.

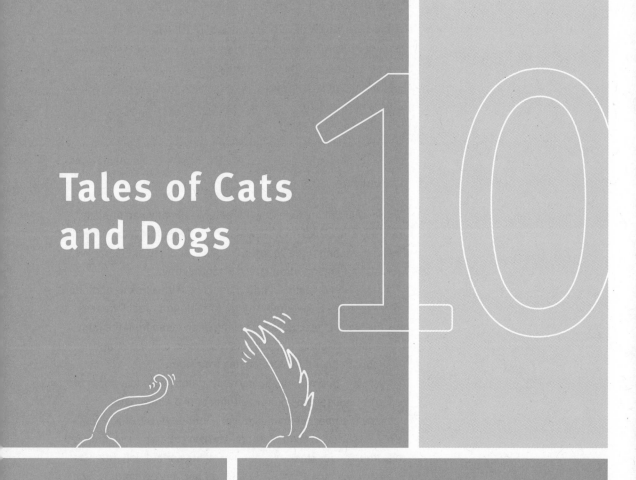

Tales of Cats and Dogs

10

What the virtuous
consumer says about:

Picking the perfect pet
- *How to choose one, where to find it, what to do with it*
- *How to find a secondhand four-legged friend*

Taking care of your pet
- *The front end: A look at holistic, organic, and raw diets*
- *The back end: Disposing of your pet's waste*
- *The pests: Nontoxic pest treatments for your pets and you*
- *The souvenirs: Eliminating stains and odors in an earth-friendly way*

Lots of people talk to animals. . . . Not very many listen, though. . . .
That's the problem.   Benjamin Hoff

We weren't looking for a dog. Indeed, we already had one, and my heart still ached from the loss of another a few years earlier. Besides, we had three young kids, a cat, and a fish. Clearly, we weren't looking for—didn't need—another dog.

Then a friend sent us a photo of a dog, with a link to petfinder.com. Polar was a three-month-old, forty-pound Great Pyrenees mix. He was in "rescue" after having been taken from the farm where he was found, full of parasites, covered in feces, and malnourished. And he was looking for a home.

He found one with us. So my family, along with two-thirds of American households, knows a thing or two about pets.

In my lifetime, I've had eight cats, four dogs, a turtle, a few fish . . . and loved myriad others. My own children have inherited this affection for creatures, and my eight-year-old daughter has been lobbying for a horse, a goat, and her very own puppy. She operates a dog-sitting and pet-grooming company, which is doing a brisk business around the neighborhood.

She's not alone. Animals are big business in North America and around the world. Unfortunately, what's good for business isn't always good for animals or the planet. What we feed them, how we care for them, where we get them—all affect not only our communities but the world.

What's the Controversy?

Animal planet, indeed! The single biggest problem surrounding companion animals is that there are simply too many of them. If there's one thing all pet owners should do, it's spay or neuter their animals. The American Society for the Prevention of Cruelty to Animals (ASPCA) estimates that between eight and twelve million companion animals enter animal shelters nationwide every year. A very small number will be reunited with their families. About a third will find homes. But anywhere from five to nine million will be euthanized (a clinical word for killed). So if you're a dog or cat entering a shelter, chances are it's your last stop.

GONE TO THE DOGS: THE PROBLEM WITH PUPPY MILLS

Despite the overpopulation of dogs, puppy mills do a booming business. Puppy mills are a cuddly term (add *puppy* to anything and it sounds wiggly and warm) that belies the reality of animals being mass produced with little or no regard for their physical or emotional health. The documented problems include overbreeding, inbreeding, little or no veterinary care, poor quality of food and shelter, a lack of human contact, overcrowding, and the killing of unwanted or infertile animals. Those who unwittingly buy puppies raised in such conditions frequently face months or years of veterinary bills to treat health issues, behavioral problems, and the premature death of the dogs from genetically borne diseases.

What's Up?

The amount of money pet lovers lavish on their furry friends, for one. According to stats from the ASPCA, Americans spent an estimated $38.4 billion on their pets in 2006—up from $21 billion just ten years ago.

But not all animals are so lucky. Laws exist to protect animals from cruelty but are frequently unenforced. Puppy mills in particular often get away with treating animals badly. There are consumer protection laws for those who buy puppies that end up with serious health or behavioral problems—or that die shortly after purchase. Referred to as "puppy lemon laws," they are so seldom invoked that they haven't encouraged the improvement in standards they were created to bring about. Still, from three hundred thousand to four hundred thousand puppies are bought at pet stores each year, the Pet Industry Joint Advisory Council estimates. Puppy mills are also successful selling over the Internet and through classified ads.

In the meantime, thousands of unwanted animals languish in shelters or roam the streets.

WHAT THE HELL WERE THEY THINKING?

I get that some of you out there love your little snooky wookums. I get that he's furry and cute and greets you at the door after a tough day at the office as if he's Tom Cruise to your Katie Holmes. I confess I don't get the gift-wrapped chew toys. According to a 2001 CNN poll, 80 percent of people bought gifts for their pets and 67 percent *wrapped them*. That's all I'm gonna say.

What Can You Do?

The place to start is by preventing any more unwanted pets. If you're looking for a new addition to your family, pick a pet from the many cast-offs.

DON'T LITTER. Spay Day USA, February 27, encourages pet owners to spay or neuter their pets. Find out more at the Humane Society's site, www.hsus.org. Not only will spaying or neutering eliminate the chance of unwanted litters of animals, you'll be making your pet healthier. Spaying means no chance of ovarian cancer and a reduced risk of breast cancer (yep, pets can get it too). Neutering means no chance of testicular cancer and a reduced risk of prostate disease. What's more, spaying or neutering generally leads to a less aggressive, more even-tempered, and affectionate animal—in other words, a better pet.

DON'T SUPPORT PUPPY MILLS. The only surefire way to shut them down is to cut off the financial incentive for them in the first place. Ask your local pet store where it obtains its puppies, and insist to see breed registry papers or the interstate health certificate for each puppy. This will include the breeders' and/or wholesalers' names and addresses.

VISIT A SHELTER. Log on to www.petfinder.com and get a sense for how many unwanted animals—mostly beautiful, loving animals—are out there looking for homes. Warning: If you're a total bleeding heart like me, don't take this step until you're prepared to actually get a pet. We both know you're kidding yourself if you tell yourself you're only looking. . . .

BUT DON'T BE IMPULSIVE. Our throwaway attitude applies to pets too—just ask shelter workers in the days following Christmas, Valentine's Day, and Easter how many "presents" are returned to them or, worse, get dumped along highways and backroads to fend for themselves.

CONSIDER OTHER SHELTER OFFERINGS. Pick from rabbits, guinea pigs, hamsters, parakeets, and more.

CONSIDER A MIXED BREED. While they lack the cachet of a purebred, mixed breeds are generally healthier and more even-tempered than many purebreds from lines that have suffered too many years of overbreeding.

CONSIDER A "RESCUE" DOG. If you're looking for a particular breed—or at least a dog that appears to resemble some particular breed—then look into rescue groups that specialize in the breed you're after. Besides, telling people your dog is a "rescue" is a great conversation starter and makes you come across like St. Francis of Assisi. And who can't benefit from feeling like a saint?

THE RECYCLED PET

Hélène Lawler frequently fosters dogs and has worked over the years with various dog-rescue groups. Rescue groups, she says, come in all shapes and sizes, just like the dogs they're devoted to. Some are run by individuals, others by local or national breed clubs, and still others by a rescue network. Most are volunteers who receive private donations. The dogs come into rescue for a variety of reasons. Some are given up when families find themselves unprepared for a breed's particular temperament or when a family member develops allergies. Others are relinquished when an owner becomes too sick or too old to care for a pet. Some are taken because they're abused or neglected. Some are picked up as strays. And some are rescued from shelters because they're not coping well in that environment or because the shelter has a "high kill rate," meaning dogs are euthanized if they're not adopted quickly enough. There are as many stories as there are dogs. Many of them are heart-wrenching.

When we found our dog Polar, I was shocked at the number of available purebred dogs—dogs that would cost a small fortune if they were bought as puppies from breeders. Most, however, were mixed breeds, many were older, plenty were big, and some had issues that made them challenging as a family pet. Too many were simply great dogs that needed a home.

John Wade, a dog behaviorist and syndicated columnist, is an advocate of rescue agencies, noting that they go to greater lengths than shelters and often breeders to ensure a good fit between dog and owner—something he says is key to the success of a union. He thinks people should put more thought into the dog they choose than they put into picking a family car. "Make a list of what you want, what you don't want, and what you'll compromise on," he advises, "before you even look at any dogs. Don't get swayed by a cute face." He admits that he knows most people (like us) won't follow his advice, but he remains

No Day at the Circus

Animals don't live only in people's homes, of course. In fact, if you're a parent you've no doubt been begged to "go see the animals" at some point. Throughout North America, tens of thousands of animals live out their existence in zoos, aquariums, and private menageries, not to mention circuses. Circuses have few supporters in the animal conservation world. The constant travel, tiny transportable cages, and unnatural tricks often learned through beatings and humiliation go against most animals' inherent nature. Many circus animals begin to display repetitive behaviors and other signs of distress—head bobbing, pacing, weaving side to side. Animal behaviorists call it "circus madness." Whatever it's called, it's not exactly family entertainment.

The views on zoos and aquariums, however, diverge. Some activists object to them on principle: they believe that animals should not be caged. Others argue that these facilities perform a valuable service in protecting endangered species and educating the public on the need to protect wildlife and the environment.

You'll feel better if you know how to assess an exhibition and determine whether it has merit.

Zoos run the gamut from well-managed, highly educational, and humane to completely unacceptable. Most of the nearly two hundred major zoos and aquariums in North America are members of national associations—either the American Zoo and Aquarium Association (AZAA) or the Canadian Association of Zoos and Aquariums (CAZA). These zoos are self-regulated and generally hold themselves to high standards. But thousands of so-called roadside zoos and traveling shows are completely unregulated. How to separate the good from the bad and downright ugly?

For starters, the folks at Zoocheck, an international charity to protect wildlife, suggest you ask some questions of any zoo, aquarium, or wildlife exhibit:

- What is the main purpose?
- How many species are on exhibit?
- How many of those are threatened or endangered?
- Does the group participate in any breeding programs for threatened or endangered species?
- How much of the budget is spent on conservation work?
- Have any animals been sold or given away? To whom?
- Were the buyers accredited?
- What happens to "surplus" animals?
- How are animals kept occupied?

If you're dissatisfied with any of the answers, you may want to pass—or visit the exhibit to see for yourself. If you visit, Zoocheck again offers a checklist of what to look for:

convinced plenty of disappointment could be avoided if people would.

According to those who've worked with rescue groups, not all are created equal. While most are run by dog-loving people eager to place dogs in good homes, a few are overzealous and make it easier to adopt a child than get a dog. Still others are too eager to place dogs and skimp on temperament evaluation, health issues, or sterilization. Be prepared to fill out an application form, including references (veterinarians, if you have or had pets) and a waiver that states the dog can be retrieved with no compensation if you're found to not be fulfilling your contractual obligations.

Look for a facility that's clean and a rescuer willing to give references, such as a vet or a previous adopter or two. Rescue dogs should always be spayed or neutered, vaccinated, and at least relatively healthy before purchase. You should be asked questions about your family (kids? other pets?), your home

- Do the animals appear healthy?
- Are the enclosures large enough to allow for behavior typical of the animal?
- Are they appropriate for the weather?
- Can the animals get out of public view, if they choose?
- Are the enclosures clean and in good repair?
- Is fresh water available?
- Are the animals active?
- Do they have any injuries? Runny eyes?

Look particularly for behaviors indicative of stress, boredom, or depression: pacing, circling, swaying, head bobbing, biting or licking cage bars, excessive grooming (look for bald patches), and self-mutilation (leg chewing, tail biting).

Do the animal enclosures contain things to occupy the animal—things that allow for swinging, burrowing, climbing, building? Look also for safety measures for visitors—mesh that keeps people's fingers out of the cages, for example.

Finally, does the exhibit make a concerted effort to educate visitors? Is the information perfunctory or detailed? In other words, is the exhibit meant strictly to entertain or does it hope to inspire education and, possibly, conservation?

Most of us are genuinely drawn to wild animals—the chance to get up close and personal with them is hard to resist. But the experience should leave you feeling a respect for, and an appreciation of, the creatures—not shame for having contributed to their fate.

environment (fenced yard? country? busy city street?), lifestyle (ability to train? time available to spend with dog?), knowledge of the breed, and so on. Beware of requirements that seem to cross the line, such as insisting on unannounced home inspections, maintaining ownership interest in the dog, and so on.

The good news is that most rescue dogs are more than six months old, are housetrained, and are past the chewing stage. Once they get over the initial adjustment, they're usually delighted to be in a loving home. Having experienced some trauma (even if it's just being uprooted), the dog might exhibit behaviors such as fear-based aggression, separation anxiety, or running away. But these can disappear as the dog settles in and learns again to trust. And training any dog is always a good idea.

While success with a rescue dog isn't guaranteed and some adoptions simply don't work out, Wade remains convinced success is more likely if you get a dog from a rescue group than a shelter or even a breeder. "[Rescue groups] are diligent about assessing and following up. They tend to know the dog's strengths and weaknesses," he says. Keep in mind that these are generalizations—there are undoubtedly great shelters, and your local one is probably worth a visit.

To find the pet you might not even know you've been looking for, visit www.petfinder.com. You can key in your city and zip code, specify the breed you're seeking, and get a list of available dogs in your area.

Or try www.pets911.com, which can also put you in touch with a local shelter or rescue group.

>>> PURCHASE POWER <<<

- Buy for the life of the animal—more than twenty years for a cat; ten to twenty years for dogs, depending on the size and breed; up to sixty years for some birds (and around two weeks for every goldfish we've ever owned).
- Buy from reputable establishments—shelters, rescue groups, and breeders should all give you a sense that they have the welfare of the animal in mind. Most won't consider letting you have an animal until they're convinced you have the means—financially and emotionally—to care for it.

How to Avoid Mad Cat Disease

Get ready for this: In the animal abattoir industry, there are cows called "downers." These are cows that are too weak, sick, or disabled to walk to slaughter. Until 1997, it was OK to feed the rendered remains of downers to other cattle, but since then the FDA has banned the practice—which is credited in part for the low incidence of mad cow disease in the United States. However, commercial manufacturers are still allowed to use the meat of downers in their pet food. While dogs can't get mad cow disease, cats can get a version of it, called feline spongiform encephalopathy. Your best bet? Give Fluffy organic cat food.

Taking Care of Your Pet

Once you've brought your furry bundle home, it's time to figure out how to care for it.

THE FRONT END

There's considerable talk these days among environmentalists and health food proponents about raw food diets, which, in pets, translates into BARF (really!). My own foray into raw food for people kinda translated into barf for me, too, but not in a good way. *BARF* for animals stands for "bones and raw food" (or "biologically appropriate raw food," depending on whom you ask) and seems to me like a heck of a lot of work considering my pet store sells really good organic dog food that requires only that I open and pour. However, in the interest of open-mindedness, I'll at least say that my friend Hélène, a wonderful soul who dedicates her life (and much of her home) to rescuing unwanted, neglected, and abused dogs and cats, feeds her own pets a raw food diet and is convinced that it has cleared up health problems and improved behavioral issues. So there you have it. If you're interested, there is plenty of online support for you BARFers. Start at www.barfworld.com (and no it's not an amusement park for bulimics).

One caveat: If you decide to go this route, be careful that you're not introducing parasites into your pet's system. You may want to check out Ian Billinghurst's book, *Give Your Dog a Bone,* which outlines the BARF approach. A number of commercially prepared "raw foods," such as Raw Advantage, are also available.

Those of you who, like me, prefer to go the traditional (read: lazy) route have lots of options, not all of them good for your dog. For example, most of what you find in your grocery store amounts to Twinkies (or worse) for animals. I won't get into the details (beaks, bones, and by-products "unfit for human consumption" and possibly carcasses of sick or diseased animals—'nuff said) of stuff you don't want going into (or out of) your pet. John Wade says that most grocery stores carry pet food that ranges from poor to poorest. The specialty stores boast a wider selection, including a number of foods labeled "organic" (no chemicals, pesticides, hormones, antibiotics, or by-products) and "natural" (no food coloring or additives that have been linked to health concerns). Read the ingredients and pick a food that starts with some type of meat (lamb, chicken, beef). Avoid anything that includes animal by-products. Avoid also ingredients that you can barely pronounce, let alone define. And don't take your pet's diet lightly. Wade insists that diet can play a key role in eliminating or improving a host of health issues.

Our dogs often eat "people food" (long considered a no-no), along with their organic dog food. But when a family eats—as mine does—mostly organic meats, produce, and grains (and your kids leave picked-apart leftovers that cost a small fortune), passing them along to the dogs can be good for them, experts say.

The Back End

What goes in, must come out . . . and we bipeds are generally left dealing with the mess.

Dogs. For the most part, millions (billions!) of puppy poops get picked up in plastic bags and tossed into trash for a trip to the landfill. If your municipal water system can handle pet poop and the attendant pet-borne parasites or diseases (a quick call to your municipal water agency should give you the answer), then by all means scoop and flush. If you stick with the plastic bag method of disposal, you can find any number of biodegradable options on the market. While there's some dissension on the issue of pet waste in a compost, I'm leaning toward "don't," as pet waste from carnivores—like cats and dogs—can have pathogens that make their way into vermin or wildlife (and therefore continue to spread), and can survive in soil for years.

Cats. The concern with cat poop is more about the litter than the waste itself. Clumping cat litter—oh so convenient, I know— is oh so toxic. Lee Bothamley and Mike McKegney from Healthy Paws Pet Food and Supplies note that "cats are clean creatures . . . [and] when they lick their paws and ingest clay-clumping litter, the moisture in the digestive tract can cause the litter to clump in their intestines. Once the litter is in the intestine, it continues to draw moisture out of the cat's body, leading to dehydration and potentially death." The other risk with clay litter (either the clumping or the regular variety) is the dust, which is a known carcinogen. Plenty of biodegradable options are available, including wheat, corn, and recycled newspaper. One such litter is Swheat Scoop (though my dogs responded as though I'd put out a bowl of peanuts, and they simply ate it), another is Yesterday's News, and there are others.

The Pests

Our rescue dog Polar came to us from Arkansas (I wasn't exactly buying local on that one), complete with a tick attached to his back. I, who live so far north that I had never seen a tick, was completely freaked out by this swollen *thing* on my new pet's back. I called Desirée, who operates the rescue group from which we got him, and described it. After determining that I'm a total northern city girl who had never seen a tick engorged with blood, she gave me step-by-step instructions on how to remove it, in between laughing uproariously and saying things like "Y'all need to get out more." Hardy har har.

Still, pests are no laughing matter. And many of the toxic

Growling about Exotic Pets

Wildlife experts put the illegal trade of exotic pets at a $10 billion-a-year business, after drugs and weapons. Despite what many owners and purveyors of exotic pets will have you believe, these animals were not meant to be pets and don't often make very good ones.

Exotics don't make good pets for a number of reasons: They grow—sometimes very big and very strong. They may carry disease—indeed, each year ninety thousand people are treated for salmonella infection contracted from reptiles. They aren't suited to a domestic habitat, and most people lack the knowledge and ability to create one that allows these animals to thrive.

pest-control products for pets aren't either. Fortunately, there are less toxic alternatives.

FLEAS AND TICKS. Many dogs can live a lifetime without being bugged by bugs, but cats aren't so lucky. Indeed, one estimate notes that only 1 percent of fleas are so-called dog fleas, with the vast majority being cat fleas. When dogs get fleas, they're often cat fleas—confused cat fleas, apparently.

Prevention is your best bet. Groom your pets regularly with a flea comb (over white paper so you can see any telltale black specks) and tweezers for ticks. Keep your home well vacuumed. Your vet can provide a once-a-month therapy that prevents flea larvae from maturing.

Natural health expert Annie B. Bond says on her popular Care2 website (www.care2.com) that rose geranium oil is an effective tick repellent. She recommends two or three drops on the dog's collar to repel ticks for a week or so and says you can often find rose geranium in health food stores or online.

THE SOUVENIRS

Pets take their toll on homes. From puppy pee stains to cat furballs, our home can read like a visual diary of our pets' various troubles and transgressions. Soda water ostensibly works on diarrhea and vomit. (We've been diarrhea and vomit free for quite some time, thank goodness, so I haven't given it a test, but it's vet recommended. I can attest to its efficacy on red wine stains, though.) There are some good commercial pet stain removers, such as Out Spot! (recommended by Castor the dog, though I've never met a dog who cared much about stains; see www. castorpolluxpet.com). Or if you're an intrepid natural cleaner, you can make your own with the old staples: baking soda and vinegar. Plenty of recipes are online, including one by Annie B. Bond at www.care2.com/channels/solutions/pets/817.

Celebrations
That Save
the Earth

11

What the virtuous
consumer says about:

Parties for kids
- *Goodies, gifts, and green themes*

Holidays with heart
- *Occasions*
- *Earth-friendly gifts*
- *Wrap it in green*

Saying "I do" to Mother Earth
- *The dress*
- *The reception*
- *The honeymoon*

A final farewell
- *Green your funeral*

There's an alternative. There's always a third way, and it's not a combination of the other two ways. It's a different way.   David Carradine

Parties are personal. They reflect the traditions and values of the party-thrower. But parties have spiraled out of control. Gone are the days when a party meant a few games of Duck, Duck, Goose and a home-baked birthday cake. These days, kids' parties mean a day of medieval jousting astride real horses or a spa adventure worthy of Paris Hilton. Unfortunately, the traditionally modern way of spending many North American holidays involves increasingly lavish celebrations for which we spend more money than we have, buy more gifts than we need, wrap them in more paper than is necessary . . . and basically have an orgy of conspicuous consumption that leaves everyone depressed, deflated, and debt-ridden. Suggest an alternative (Let's forgo gifts! Let's not spend the equivalent of a down payment on a house just to get married!) and you're greeted with shock and a bewildered "But it's tradition . . . "

Well, folks, tradition is tromping all over this planet, so it's clearly time to create some new ones.

What's the Controversy?

Birthday parties, weddings, Halloween, Hanukkah, winter solstice—whatever holidays you celebrate, you surely want them memorable. The problem is that after the relatives are escorted to the door and the decorations tucked away, more than memories are left.

THE TRASH. Almost 25 percent of all retail goods—in 2005, this fraction had a value of $438.6 billion—move out of stores and into people's homes between Thanksgiving and Christmas. And 25 percent more trash—one million extra tons per week—heads to landfills in the same time period. Coincidence? C'mon.

THE WRAPPING. Sure they look pretty—all those wrapped and beribboned boxes. At least for the 30 seconds we look at them before ripping off the paper to get at what's inside. I grew up in a family that took considerable ribbing over the years for our painstaking way of opening presents so as not to rip the paper. We recycled wrapping for as long as I can remember. After I moved away, it struck me as deliciously naughty to rip the wrapping with abandon, but now that I'm aware of the completely unnecessary waste of virgin trees, it just seems naughty. And I don't mean in a good way.

THE CARDS. Here's a question for all you philosophers: If a tree falls in the forest, is it OK to turn it into a generic greeting card to which some ineloquent soul will simply sign his name? According to Robert Lilienfeld and William Rathje, the authors of *Use Less Stuff: Environmental Solutions for Who We Really Are,* 2.65 billion Christmas cards are sold annually in the United States. Why? Most cards come signed only with the sender's name and some lame "best wishes" slop. Just mail mine "c/o The Grinch."

THE GIFTS. I've recently been "outed" as a dedicated regifter. Like everyone else, I am given stuff that I don't want, like, or need but that I think someone else will. I'm all for thoughtful gifts, but if every citizen in the world consumed (indeed gave!) with the abandon of Westerners, we'd need three planets to provide the needed resources. There are so many more options for gift-giving, which I'll get to.

THE DECORATIONS. I giggle to think that what I always interpreted, with a certain shame, as laziness on the part of my family can now be viewed as prescient environmentalism. Take Christmas decorations. It was generally my dad's job to hang the Christmas lights, and they did, eventually, get hung—a pathetic string along the front of our house. How I envied the kids whose dads were on their rooftops arranging brightly lit wooden Santas and reindeer. Or perched atop ladders adjusting twinkly stars on towering trees. Well, it turns out those lights radiate enough energy to power almost two hundred thousand homes for an entire year. My dad wasn't lazy . . . just green.

THE DEBT. Consumers confessed pre-Christmas 2005 that they were "somewhat or very concerned" about paying off that year's anticipated credit card bills. Visa reported that 2005 holiday spending among cardholders was up 17.5 percent from the previous year, to $257 billion. How can a holiday that encourages us to spend money we don't have on things we don't need represent goodwill or good sense? Just asking.

What's Up?

A party revolution, that's what. From "green" weddings to charity birthday parties to gift-free Christmases, celebrations are increasingly about . . . celebrating. Not just, indeed not even, about getting stuff.

As Bill McKibben, the author of *Hundred Dollar Holiday,* pointed out in an online chat with the Center for a New American Dream, "I find very few people in this country who need more stuff. Most of us are looking for more meaning." McKibben believes that the traditions predating the current commercialism of celebrations give us the feelings we're really after—of connection, of joy.

Still, cutting back on gifts makes people uncomfortable. John Perry, our conspicuous un-consumer from chapter 5, admits that his family's gift-free policy has been difficult for others to accept.

Another person I know confided that giving "meaningful" gifts can sometimes backfire. "I gave an acre of wetland to my Republican brother," he said. "He wanted to know if he could develop it—and was really annoyed when he found out he couldn't."

Still, McKibben has said he believes that most of us are willing to give it a try. "Most people are not all that attached to a commercial [holiday]," he said. "Most people are very happy to be given permission to do this in a different way."

What Can You Do?

Start by asking yourself what you want to get out of any particular celebration. What matters most: Time spent together? Doing a particular activity? Continuing a family tradition? Starting a new family tradition? Creating a celebration consistent with your principles of sustainability and social justice? Outline and prioritize your goals; then devise a plan to achieve them. It helps to simply follow your (by now) daily practices of reduce, reuse, recycle—in that order.

REDUCE. Take the emphasis off consumption by working experience into each . . . umm . . . experience. Mark birthdays by planting a tree in the celebrant's honor. Celebrate Christmas with a night hike to look at the stars. Honor anniversaries with a storytelling circle in which everyone shares memories.

REUSE. It's tempting, I know, to go with disposable dishes and cutlery when feeding a crowd. But if dishpan hands have you worried, consider renting reusable dishes—it's surprisingly affordable (I rent dozens of glasses each holiday season for my wine-soaked parties, and I don't have to wash them before returning). And don't buy new decorations for each holiday; instead tuck them away carefully each year so they stay lovely. My family's Christmas tree is covered with decorations from my childhood. What about a tree-trimming party in which everyone brings a decoration they've created out of earth-friendly materials? And, by all means, reuse those plastic eggs from Easter egg hunts. Our birthday parties inevitably include a dragon egg hunt, unicorn egg hunt, or dinosaur egg hunt, depending on the theme.

RECYCLE. Choose materials for cards, wrapping, invitations, and more that can be recycled or, better still, that come from tree-free and recycled sources.

Celebrations

Whatever you're celebrating, ensure that it celebrates our planet, too.

KIDS' PARTIES

In the eight years that I've been a parent, I've entertained the notion of:

- having ponies at my four-year-old's birthday party
- bringing in a carousel to suit a carnival theme
- turning my home into a dinosaur panorama

Fortunately, the look on my husband's face—*Have you completely lost your mind?*—stopped me short of executing any of those ideas. Instead, we've opted for at-home parties, homemade birthday cakes (mostly, except for the year my daughter requested a Spy Kids cake and I just couldn't get the logo right), and fairly reasonable "parting gifts" that I create with the hope that parents won't hate me and kids won't think their friend's mother is robbing them of the requisite booty.

So, with fifteen birthday parties under my belt, I can speak with some authority: Give kids room to run wild, a cake in any shape or form, and some sort of loot bag (parting gift), and you've got the makings of a perfect party, in children's estimation. Let parents drop their kids off for a free few hours (or offer organic martinis or wine on-site), and you'll be crowned the party queen by the grown-ups.

Try these kids' parties on for size:

THE 'TIS-BETTER-TO-GIVE-THAN-RECEIVE PARTY. This idea hasn't really taken root with my own children, though I've worked hard to instill a social conscience in them since they were newborns. (See Mr. Polar Bear? His genitals are getting teensy-weensy, thanks to industrial pollutants . . .) My friend Michelle has had better luck. Her two older girls, aged four and six, decided—with only a wee bit of prodding from Mom—to ask for dog- and cat-related gifts to be donated to the local animal shelter. The invitation noted that the shelter needed blankets (new or used), toys, treats, and food. Guests still had the fun of bringing a gift and the party girls had the fun of taking a whole load of stuff to grateful dogs and cats (and shelter staff!). My kids have also gone to parties for which we've bought mosquito netting (online) for children in Africa and a rabbit for a family in Haiti.

A caveat: One party invitation simply asked for cash donations that would be forwarded to a certain charity. While the intention was no doubt pure, the execution brought with it niggling doubts among parents about whether the money would in fact go to the intended charity. It also removed the chance to make the experience meaningful for children, because they weren't able to choose the gifts.

THE EARTH-FRIENDLY PARTY. It's easy to create a party that celebrates Mother Nature because kids, by nature, love . . . nature. Whether your theme is make your own snowman, plant

a seed, or create a bug lover's paradise, incorporate natural activities into the event.

THE OLD-FASHIONED FUN PARTY. Kids still love the games we played at birthday parties—"I Wrote a Letter to My Love," "Telephone," "Duck, Duck, Goose," and so on. Go online to find the rules, if you can't remember them. Include a cake with waxed-paper-wrapped coins inside, and kids will think they've struck gold.

HALLOWEEN

Treat your little goblins to a celebration that's easy on the planet—and its people.

THE DECORATIONS. According to a website devoted to Halloween, the Chinese celebrate the Feast of the Hungry Ghosts. Ostensibly, the souls of the dead wander the earth in search of affection. They are known as "hungry" ghosts because they seek recognition and care. Surely I'm not the only one who sees the irony in this. Hint: Look where most of our Halloween tchotchkes are made. You got it—the place that has a holiday dedicated to recognition and care. But they aren't getting it in the sweatshops that crank out our dollar-store decorations. Indeed, Halloween is second only to Christmas in the amount of money consumers spend to boost the decorative impact of their homes. If you feel the urge to create your own haunted house, stick to reusable props—create gravestones out of discarded wood or cardboard, use old clothes stuffed with rags to create "dead" people. . . . You get the idea.

THE COSTUMES. Mothers inevitably fall into two camps: those who make their kids' costumes and those who don't. I'm a convert. While we have store-bought costumes in our costume trunk, ghosts of Halloweens past, so to speak, I've learned that it's quite easy to throw together a costume (a bat! a spy! a ladybug!) from the creative use of existing clothes and makeup. And kids, honestly, think you're Martha Stewart even if the other moms can sense that you don't own different varieties of pinking shears or a glue gun. Visit your library for a book of easy-to-make costumes.

THE CANDY. As my eight-year-old daughter explained to her younger siblings as she got made up as Mata Hari for Halloween— "You go door-to-door and ask for candy from strangers. It's the perfect holiday!" Perfect for North American children, perhaps.

Fireworks: An Explosive Situation

It's the very picture of patriotic celebration. Each July 4, we head out to the backyard, where we light off a few fireworks, scare the hell out of the neighborhood dogs, and revel in our children's delight, particularly the forbidden pleasure of burning the tiny schoolhouse. Fun? Sure. Harmless? Well . . .

Fireworks continue to be made the way they've been made for hundreds of years—with gunpowder. According to the folks at *E/The Environmental Magazine,* the ignition of gunpowder releases a variety of toxic pollutants, including the radioactive element barium and carcinogenic copper compounds, along with cadmium, lithium, antimony, lead, and potassium nitrate, all of which can cause respiratory problems and other health issues.

These chemicals and heavy metals can sometimes find their way into the water supply.

As a result of environmental and health concerns, a number of cities and states restrict the use of fireworks. You can find out who has restrictions by going to www.americanpyro.com and clicking on "Directory of State Laws."

On the commercial side, Disney's fireworks recently got an eco-friendly makeover thanks to an innovation from Walt Disney's Imagineering. The new technology uses compressed air to lift fireworks, rather than the traditional black powder and other materials. Not only is this better for the environment, significantly reducing ground-level smoke and noise, but it's also safer for the pyrotechnicians. What's more, Disney is donating the seven patents it holds on this technology to a nonprofit organization that can, in turn, license the invention to other pyrotechnic providers.

Fireworks have also been under fire for being produced by child labor in third-world countries. There are roughly 250 million child laborers in developing and developed countries around the world. We're not talking about kids who pick up a part-time job after school or those who help out on the family farm. These are kids, some as young as four and five years old, who are working instead of going to school, often in hazardous conditions. Many of them have worked long hours in fireworks factories where they mix gunpowder and cut firecracker tubes with machetes, and where they're exposed to chemicals without adequate protection.

According to Jocelyn Sweet, who works with Free the Children, an international nonprofit organization that aims to empower youth, there is no way to know whether backyard fireworks are or are not made with child labor. (She points out that we're referring to backyard, family fireworks, not the large professional pyrotechnical displays we see at commercial venues.)

However, Jack Drewes, the editor of *American Fireworks News,* a publication for those in the fireworks industry, says that fireworks sold in North America are produced either in North America or in China. He points to stringent guidelines in the manufacture and importing of fireworks in North America and says that consumers can be reassured that the fireworks they buy here were not produced by child labor.

And while the Chinese government has a checkered past when it comes to child labor

But not so for the child slaves working on cocoa farms in developing countries to create the chocolate used by Nestlé and M&M/Mars. Or for the earth—what with so many individually wrapped goodies. You can go the fair trade route. If you can't find fair trade Halloween chocolate in your area (I couldn't), you can order it online. Global Exchange (www.globalexchange.org) offers its Fair Trade Trick or Treat Candy and Action Kit, which includes fair trade chocolate, kids' postcards outlining the importance of fair trade chocolate, and a fun door sign. Or consider giving out something other than candy: organic raisins in their little cardboard containers, packets of (fairly) healthy cookies or crackers, or juice boxes. Our childhood neighbor, a dentist, used to hand out toothbrushes. Another gave out tape, which, though useful, was none too eco-friendly.

What about packets of seeds (either harvested from your own wildflowers or purchased)? Grist (www.grist.org), a great source of all things eco, offered up this reduce, reuse, recycle suggestion: Gather all sorts of items you no longer need or want: CDs, toys, trinkets, old jewelry, books, trophies. . . . Create a treasure box and let the pint-sized pirates or goblins choose what they'd like. Of course, you run the risk of being branded the local wacko, but that's OK. Every neighborhood needs one, especially on Halloween.

Valentine's Day
Locally grown flowers or organic roses, fair trade chocolate, soy-based candles, organic personal care products, spa services, vintage or earth-friendly jewelry, eco-conscious sex toys, or a delicious made-by-someone-else meal of local organic food. All

issues—in March 2001, forty-two people, most of them third- and fourth-graders, were killed in an explosion at a Chinese school when they were making fireworks for the government—that country has done a lot to clean up its act. Indeed, the biggest step has been signing, on August 8, 2002, the International Labor Organization's Convention 182, a powerful piece of paperwork that aims to eliminate what the ILO deems one of the most hazardous forms of child labor in the world.

So while child labor, including perhaps in the fireworks industry, continues to be an issue in many countries, it seems fireworks in North America are clean. Still, the eco-cost of burning that little red schoolhouse seems hardly worth it.

good. Tacky petroleum-based lingerie, meaningless card from felled tree, heart-shaped box of non-fair-trade chocolate, pirated porn video of Pamela Lee. All bad. Clip and give to your husband. See? It's simple.

CHRISTMUKKAH

I'm a sucker for the holidays. I love the music, the excitement, the constant supply of home-baked cookies. I love how my social life gets a jump-start and how pretty my normally shabby living room furniture looks in the twinkly glow of our LED-lit tree. But, like so many others, I'm increasingly dismayed at how our holidays have been hijacked by product marketers. It's time to put the hope back in the holidays—hope for a better future and hope for a healthier planet.

THE TREE. If you opt for a live tree, go local and organic. LocalHarvest (www.localharvest.org) should be able to point you in a greener direction. Local farms also often offer wreaths and other decorations. Be sure to recycle your tree. Most cities offer some service—either a drop-off or curbside pickup. There are even rent-a-tree options: check out www.livingchristmastrees.org. If you choose to go with a faux fir, rest easy. Sure they're made of a petroleum product, probably in some far-away place like China. However, they're also a symbol of reuse. My excuse, a valid one at that, is that I have a dog who relieves himself on any live tree—favoring evergreens.

THE DECORATIONS. If you've got kids, you've got all you need for a decorated home. Homemade paper chains, play dough stars on gold string, pine cones decorated with glitter glue—they all add up to homespun charm. Light up with eco-friendly LEDs. Made with light-emitting diodes, these tiny lights are 90 percent more efficient than traditional lights. What's more, they release little heat and they last at least a hundred thousand hours when used indoors.

GIFTS

When buying gifts for any occasion, think outside the mall. Seems daunting at first, but you'll quickly get into the swing of it. Fun, creative, and personal:

BUILD YOUR OWN. My friend Judy Ann, a talented author of many craft books, likes to put together—not surprisingly—craft

E-tail for a Greener Gift

Not only are you likely to find more options for eco-friendly or purpose-driven gifts online, but the practice of shopping online in itself is eco-friendly, according to the nonprofit Center for Energy and Climate Solutions. On their site (www.cool-companies.org) they point out, "Shipping 10 pounds of packages by overnight air—the most energy-intensive delivery mode—uses 40 percent less fuel than driving roundtrip to the mall. Ground shipping by truck uses just one-tenth the energy of driving yourself." And that doesn't even include your own emotional and mental energy required to tackle the mall when it seems the entire free world is circling the parking lot looking for a spot.

Visit these online malls instead:

- EcoMall (www.ecomall.com)
- GreenShopping (www.greenshopping.com)
- Gaiam (www.gaiam.com)
- VivaTerra (www.vivaterra.com)
- Greenloop (www.thegreenloop.com)
- Greenfeet (http://greenfeet.com)
- Global Exchange Online Fair-Trade Store (http://store.gxonlinestore.org)

kits for the people on her list. She can include fabric, buttons, knitting needles, a crochet hook, whatever else is needed, along with instructions on how to proceed. Other ideas for "build your own" kits include art kits, tool kits, and gardening kits. Mix in some of your own favorites—a friend once received his father's beloved hammer along with some new tools when he was just a young teen. He still treasures the hammer that his father's hands held so capably.

GIFT + STORY. Instead of new jewelry, pass along a favorite piece to your teen—along with a story of when you got it, where you wore it, even a photograph of you wearing it.

PEACE. How awesomely appropriate is it that you can really offer the gift of peace. Peace Bonds from Nonviolent Peaceforce, an organization endorsed by no less than the Dalai Lama himself, puts volunteers on the ground in areas of conflict to act as unofficial peacekeepers. They might monitor an election, offer rumor control, protect refugees as they attempt to rebuild their lives, or protect children in areas where they're frequently recruited into armies. Find out more at www.buypeacebonds.org.

ENTERTAINMENT. My friend Bill, a radio personality and town crier (really!), lived in a commune in his younger years and recalls how, rather than gifts, people offered their talent at celebrations: singing, dancing, playing an instrument, reciting a poem or story.

There are so many other alternatives to the standard ties and boxes of chocolate for a birthday, Mother's Day, Father's Day, Christmas, or Staff Appreciation Day. Herewith, some sites to get you started:

- Simplify the Holidays: a great resource for statistics, tips, and ideas (www.newdream.org/holiday/index.php)
- Heifer International (www.heifer.org)
- World Vision (www.worldvision.org)
- Oxfam Unwrapped (www.oxfamunwrapped.ca)
- Carbonfund: offset one metric ton of CO_2 (www.carbon fund.org)
- Changing the Present: allows people to choose from specific gifts, such as preserving an acre of rain forest to paying for an hour of a cancer researcher's time (www.changingthe present.org)
- Help the City of New Orleans: notes which companies have reopened for business and have online stores (www.help thecityofneworleans.com)
- NatureNode (www.naturenode.com/shop/children.html)
- Kate's Caring Gifts (www.katescaringgifts.com/pages/ product/kids/kids.html)
- Green Home Environmental Store (www.greenhome.com/ products/kids/toys)
- A Greater Gift: fair trade handcrafts and foods from around the world (www.agreatergift.org)
- Charity Gifts: while the charities it supports are UK-based, it also offers some good tips and ideas (www.charitygifts.com)

WRAPPING

You no doubt already reuse gift bags. You may even wrap the occasional gift in the Saturday cartoons or your child's artwork. But if you have many gifts to wrap, you might want to visit the local newspaper office. The staff will often give away or sell for a nominal fee the "ends" of newsprint rolls (they're also great to have on hand for kids' coloring projects). Kids can stamp the paper and color it, or you can simply add a small branch of evergreen and a pine cone, tied together with a festive red ribbon. Or reuse scarves passed down from aunts and grannies. What about those scraps of fabric left over from sewing projects (or, if you're like me, left over from sewing projects that never really got sewn)? Give a second life to tourist maps from long-over trips. Die-hards can opt to buy Sellotape on eBay—it's a European brand of tape that uses a more eco-friendly manufacturing process and is made from biodegradable plant cellulose. A novel way to wrap your gifts—and give the additional gift of entertainment—is to use Wrapsacks. Along with fun, whimsical designs, Wrapsacks feature a code that allows you to register your Wrapsack, then subsequent gift givers and receivers can file updates of where the Wrapsack has gone, what gifts have been given in it, and more. Find out more at www.wrapsacks.com.

Sites I Love

All the following sites offer products that are unique but also earth friendly:

NobleWorks, Inc. Funny, subversive greeting cards made from recycled paper. One card I bought that showed Bush responding to Roe Vs. Wade ("I don't care how people get out of New Orleans as long as they get out . . . ") donated 20 percent of its profits to New Orleans Hurricane Relief. www.nobleworksinc.com.

MissionFish. Shop eBay and support charity. www.mission fish.org.

Worldwide Child. Really amazing children's toys that'll make you want to play too. www.worldwidechild.com.

And the Bride Wore . . . Green

Mention an eco-wedding and most people conjure up images of barefoot hippies on a beach wearing daisy necklaces. But these days, more brides and grooms aren't just walking down the aisle, they're walking the eco-talk they live in their day-to-day lives. A wedding should be a reflection of who you are and what you value. Herewith, your guide to a greener "I do."

The diamond. Conflict diamonds—stones that are mined from parts of the world with civil wars, human rights abuses, and environmental disregard, continue to make their way into showcases despite the jewelry industry's hard work to eliminate them. (See chapter 2 for more information.) Canadian diamonds are a clear way to ensure that your rock was mined ethically and with careful environmental consideration. Tiffany is noted for its conflict-free policy. Or consider an antique ring from a dealer, or persuade one of your relatives to part with hers. (I wear my deceased grandmother's engagement ring as my own. My husband and my mother worked something out, probably along the lines of "Take my spinster daughter off my hands, and I'll provide the bling"—and I love that my ring has not only a past but also a future. I plan to pass it along myself.) Or create your own eco-friendly engagement or wedding rings through a company such as Green Karat (www.greenkarat.com) or Touch Wood Rings (www.touchwoodrings.com).

THE DRESS. You might only wear it once, but for that one day you want to look fabulous. Choose a dress based on your own style—but consider also vintage or secondhand (unless the dress belonged to Elizabeth Taylor, it's probably only been worn once), then have it restyled to suit you. Or choose a new gown made from a sustainable fabric—hemp satin is earning a reputation as lovely and luxurious for wedding gowns. I'll never forget my friend Cathy lamenting her choice of un-eco-friendly fabric for her bridesmaids' dresses: "Along with everything else I have to think

Flatulent Friend? Offer the Gift of Guilt-Free Emissions

For those of you (like me!) with a sophomoric sense of humor, consider giving the gift of carbon offsets to your methane-releasing buddies. Truthfully, humans can be blamed for only a half to one and a half quarts of "flatus" per day (compared to the main offender, cows, which release two hundred to four hundred quarts daily) and only one-third of humans release any methane in their anal emissions (nitrogen is the main gas in . . . gas). But for the sake of a giggle and a good cause, let's assume that your friends are in that one-third of methane producers. There are any number of carbon-offsetting programs that will be happy to take your money, no matter how immature the reason. Among them are:

TERRAPASS. www.terrapass.com.

NATIVEENERGY. Invest in wind energy and methane farm projects—ha! www.nativeenergy.com.

e-BLUEHORIZONS. Participate in the capture and destruction of landfill methane, a greenhouse gas with climate change potential 23 times greater than CO_2. www.e-bluehorizons.net.

DRIVENEUTRAL. Neutralize them through large-scale sustainable projects. www.drive neutral.org.

about today," she wailed, "I have to worry about keeping my bridesmaids away from open flame!"

When you're done with your gown, offer it to a group such as Fairy Godmothers (www.fairygodmothersinc.com), which helps outfit high school girls for the prom. Or give it to the I Do Foundation, which will sell it through a partner, donate 20 percent of the proceeds to the charity of your choice, and keep the remainder to support I Do's own work to encourage charitable giving at weddings (www.idofoundation.org).

THE DÉCOR. For my brother's wedding at our family cottage, my mother created earth-friendly table centerpieces out of sand, pebbles, and driftwood. On a glass tray, she simply arranged the materials, then added a small glass bottle tipped on its side, with the date and the newlyweds' names on a slip of paper inserted inside (message in a bottle, get it?). It was simple, elegant, and earth friendly. Other options include the liberal use of soy-based candles or dried flower arrangements. One couple used natural materials that reflected the location and time of year; fallen birch branches, with holes cut in the middle, became candleholders. If you choose fresh flowers, go organic and local. Or choose wildflowers from a local grower (don't just pick your own, unless they're in your garden). Consider asking a guest to make sure the flowers get donated to a shelter, hospital, or nursing home the next day. You can also opt for silk (real silk, not plastic or fabric) flowers or a potted plant that guests can take home.

THE INVITES. Share your green intentions from the get-go with invitations printed on tree-free or recycled paper, or plantable paper impregnated with wildflower seeds. Or consider handmade recycled-paper invitations, such as those from Chicago's Woman-Craft, which are created by homeless women looking to improve their lives (www.womancraft.net).

THE GIFTS. Register at online retailers with products that are easy on the earth: Gaiam (www.gaiam.com) and Greenfeet (www.greenfeet.com) both offer eco-friendly home products and registry options. But, say you already own a toaster, coffeemaker, and all the organic towels you can use. What to register for? Consider having guests donate to a charity that reflects your values—whether environmental, social justice, or humanitarian. The I Do Foundation can help connect you.

Green Guidance:
The Plane Truth about Travel

Flying, while convenient—after all, who wants to take a slow boat to China?—is part of an inconvenient truth. It's one of the biggest contributors to greenhouse gas emissions, which we all know by now is making our planet too hot to handle. While air traffic emits about 4% of greenhouse gases worldwide, these emissions enter the atmosphere at a much higher altitude, thereby increasing its negative impact on the climate. As much as 10% of greenhouse gas emissions today can be attributed to air travel. The solution? Take another mode of transport when possible. Stay longer in one location rather than taking a number of short-haul flights. You can also offset your air travel with carbon offsetting programs (see Resources) and demand that airlines continue to produce increasingly more fuel-efficient planes.

THE FOOD. Ahhh, the food. I'm a confessed food snob, and I've been to far too many weddings where the food was dismal. It's a challenge to feed a large group well and affordably—and harder still when you're aiming to go earth friendly. Still it can be done following the principles of organic, local, sustainable, and seasonal. Again, take your cue from where you're getting married. Is there a particular food that is locally grown and in season? Could a local farmer provide what you need? If you opt for seafood, make sure that it's from sustainable stock. (Check the regional seafood watch card from the Monterey Bay Aquarium at www.mbayaq.org/cr/cr_seafoodwatch/download.asp.)

Consider cutting meat in favor of vegetarian or vegan options, which might also help trim your costs.

THE CAKE. Ask your favorite local baker to substitute organic ingredients (if she doesn't already), though be prepared to pay more. And do you really need a plastic bride (made in China!) atop your wedding cake? Consider chopping the topper from your list of must-haves, or choose a decoration out of edible organic icing that more adequately reflects you as a couple.

THE FAVORS. Go wild . . . literally. Choose saplings, seeds, or herbs that can, sadly, outlive many marriages. My sister-in-law chose jars of local organic blueberry jam for her late summer wedding. My friend Allan and his bride, Mehnaz, gave tiny bamboo shoots. One guest reported his "just won't die," though I'm not sure why he'd want it to. I've also seen organic cookies, maple syrup, honey, and other locally produced foodstuffs. Sweet!

THE TRAVEL. Arrange for guest shuttles from the airport and area hotels, or find a place that rents hybrid cars. Better still, pick a place where you can have the ceremony and reception in the same place or within walking distance. Encourage your guests to carpool. If the bride and groom happen to be getting married in the Big (Green!) Apple, try OZOcar, a luxury limo-type service that offers only hybrids (www.ozocar.com); in L.A., check out EVO Limo (www.evolimo.com). Or consider EV Rental Cars (www.evrental.com), which operates in several western cities. Even some non-eco car rental agencies are keeping a hybrid or two in stock. Ask.

THE HONEYMOON. There are so many eco-tour holidays that you'll have no problem finding something that speaks to your

Resources to Green Your Nuptials

Ecoparti. Biodegradable wedding favors, confetti, and more. www.ecoparti.com.

Just Soap. Consider starting your future as a couple with a clean slate—created by Just Soap wedding favors. What's particularly cool about this company is that the soap is created through a human-powered "bicycle blender," cutting down on energy use. www.justsoap.com.

Green World Project. Give the gift of a seedling to your wedding guests. www.greenworld project.net.

The Bridal Garden. www.bridalgarden.org.

PreOwnedWeddingDresses. The name says it all. www.preownedweddingdresses.com.

Conscious Clothing. Custom-made wedding gowns from earth-friendly fabrics. www. getconscious.com.

Making Memories. Pick a dress from a selection of high-end secondhand designer gowns. Proceeds support granting wishes to women terminally ill with breast cancer. www.making memories.org.

conscience. Ask these questions of any eco-tour company you're considering:

- What is the company's environmental policy? Does the company actively support environmental initiatives? Is the staff trained in these areas?

- Will your visit help with conservation efforts and contribute to the integrity of the area? Are locals affected in a positive way by your visit to further preservation of their environment?

- Are locals benefiting financially from your visit? Does the tour provider support local businesses and service providers by using locally owned services such as hotels and transport companies? Does it rely on community resources whenever possible, such as walking tours, overnight stays, purchases of locally made products?

- Does the tour company respect the local culture? Does it seek out lodging that emphasizes local traditions? Does it offer excursions run by local or indigenous people? Have you been informed about the local environment and customs of the place you'll visit so you may avoid offending the people or harming their environment? For example, it helps to know that Tibetans often greet you by sticking out their tongues. Hmm. My three-year-old must be Tibetan.

- Does the company use hotels that conserve natural resources? Do the hotels use recycled products? Do they use nontoxic cleaning products? Will you use public transportation when possible? Group taxis or vans? Bicycles? Will you be walking?

Dying to be Green: Eco-friendly Burials

If you're anything like my mother, you've given your funeral and burial considerable thought. While some might accuse her of being macabre, let me assure you she isn't. She's just highly organized (and a bit of a control freak—sorry, Mom!). But considering your last act on earth isn't to be taken lightly, you might want to give it some thought. While as my friend Dave, a wilderness survival expert, is so fond of noting, "people are biodegradable," most of us don't anticipate becoming compost after we expire.

The notion of eco-friendly burials has been called a "cottage industry" by those in the business, who note that green options are available but haven't really caught on. I confess I've been caught up in battling a disposable society and have yet to turn my attention to how to dispose of myself. Until now.

Green burial is a simple concept—an unembalmed body is buried in a cotton shroud or biodegradable coffin, often cardboard or wicker, then marked with native vegetation, frequently a tree. If you choose cremation, the ashes will be buried instead of scattered as they can change the ecology of the soil. To find a natural burial ground or look at specific state and provincial regulations, visit www.forestofmemories.org. Or check out www.fullcirclecare.org/endoflife/funeral.htm#gr.

The Ten Commandments of Virtuous Consumption

12

Never doubt that a small group of thoughtful, committed citizens can change the world. Indeed, it is the only thing that ever has.　Margaret Mead

Allow me to indulge my goddess fantasy—no lingerie involved—by sounding omnipotent. By all means, ignore my commandments if you think they're too preachy. I have three kids. I'm accustomed to being ignored. And I do tend to fall into preachiness no matter how hard I try not to. But I really believe all this stuff. Really. I've never been more content. And I'll bet, once you get over the panic and fear that our planet is going to hell and taking a great number of us with it, you'll never have been more content, either, if you follow these principles. Living consciously and in the moment is all we've got. And it beats the hell out of stressing over your latest Visa bill.

1. Reduce, Reuse, and Recycle

This one could be all you need. Reduce the number of things you purchase, and reduce the eco-footprint of whatever you do purchase by ensuring that it's the most planet-friendly option you can afford. Reuse what you have in inventive ways, and reuse other people's stuff by buying secondhand. Recycle what can be recycled, and make sure you know what can be.

2. Create a Community That Feeds Your Soul

You are doing this when you live, work, and shop to support those around you. Try to avoid a long-distance commute to the office—perhaps your boss will consider telecommuting. Eat food grown by nearby farmers. Purchase from local businesses. Get involved in local politics, even if it's just as an informed voter. Embrace the life around you. I don't mean you have to walk around dressed like the Dalai Lama or be doe-eyed with love and compassion. I just mean drink it all in: If we appreciate the natural world, we're more likely to protect it. Plant a tree—or ten. Start an organic garden. Adopt an unwanted animal. Watch TV less and the world around you more.

3. Use Manpower (or Womanpower)

Get around by cycling, walking, inline skating, or taking public transit when possible. Cars are one of the biggest polluters on the planet; heart disease and stroke are one of the biggest killers of us. Using your own body to get you from point A to point B will not only help the planet but also make you healthier.

4. Purchase Green Power

It's so unbelievably simple yet incredibly powerful in terms of offsetting climate change. A call to your utility company can ensure that the equivalent energy required for your home comes from renewable sources. If you can't purchase green energy, ask about green pricing, which means paying a premium on your electricity bill so the company can invest in renewable sources. Or consider purchasing green tags (tradeable renewable-energy credits) or wind certificates, each of which represents a specific amount of clean energy added to the country's power grid in place of electricity generated from fossil fuels. At the very least, remove any lightbulb that Thomas Edison invented (or at least your most frequently used ones) and replace them with compact fluorescents that will last ten times as long and use one-quarter of the energy.

5. Don't Sweat the Really Small Stuff

While I make zillions of suggestions—big and small—in this book, choose those that work for you and your family. And don't pull out the hair shirt every time you slip up. I mean it. Guilt sucks.

6. Consider the Life Cycle of Any Product

Virtuous consumption is, in itself, something of an oxymoron. However, unless we live naked in a cave and subsist on grubs, we pretty much rely on someone else to provide much of what we need. So before you make a purchase, consider the following (this becomes second nature, I promise):

- What materials went into making this product? Were the raw materials virgin or recycled? Plant based or petroleum based?
- How was this product manufactured? (Processing uses energy and water and produces waste and by-products.)
- How was it transported? How far did it travel to get to me?
- How long will the product be used? Once, or often over many years?
- How will it be disposed of? Is it recyclable? Reusable? Biodegradable?

7. Be Generous

Give what you can, whether it's your time, your stuff, or your money. Charities need all three. Sometimes they even need your blood. Go on. Blood is a renewable resource—your body will make more.

8. Be Kind

To yourself, to that person in front of you in the supermarket's express line with twenty-three items, to the person halfway across the world who looks different from you but who also loves his family, his country, his life. Even to the person who idles his SUV in front of your kids' school. Kindness is also a scarce resource these days, and it can transform the world.

9. Be Informed

There are plenty of sources for information on living green and ethically. Indeed, there are more every day. The sustainability landscape has likely changed since I wrote this book, so keep up to date as best you can. And inform yourself about issues that matter to you in particular. Next thing you know, you'll . . .

10. Awaken Your Inner Activist

You wouldn't be reading this book—and you certainly wouldn't have made it this far—if you weren't someone who cares deeply for the future of this planet. And that, my friend, makes you a political force. *Oh no,* you say. *I just want to shop better.* Yes, I firmly believe that every dollar we spend, particularly when we spend it consciously, is a political act. But you can do more than that.

You might start by creating positive change in your home, move on to your kids' school, then your local watershed. Or you might choose a different path. Or be presented with a different path. A defining moment in my life came at eight years of age. My mother, a huge fan of live theater, took me to see *Oliver!,* which takes place, of course, in Victorian England. Afterward I said to her with complete assurance, as only a know-it-all eight-year-old can, "But we don't have poor people today like that." That was all my mother needed to hear. She proceeded to take me on a poverty-and-oppression tour of my hometown. My eyes were opened to neighborhoods I didn't know existed and to social issues I could barely grasp. But I've since lived my life with the understanding that poverty is everyone's problem and we must all participate in the solution. And my volunteer commitments inevitably revolve around that—whether locally or globally.

You might already know what gets your heart beating faster, what particular issue speaks to your soul. If not, start by having a conversation with yourself. *Self,* you might say, *what really matters to you?*

Well, Self might respond, *I like trees. And wildflowers. And the birds in the trees.* Warming to the subject, Self might even say, *and I'm particularly partial to songbirds. I love to hear them chirp outside my window in the morning . . .*

At this point you might want to cut Self off and get back to your point because Self might ramble on forever about the wood thrush or the tufted titmouse, which is all well and good, but this is about activism, not ornithology.

So . . . you might want to point out to Self that she might enjoy participating in a local group that plants trees. Or organizes birding hikes. And helps build nesting boxes. *But,* Self points out, *there are no local groups that plant trees or organize birding hikes or build nesting boxes.*

Aaah, you say to Self. *Then you can create one.*

And that's how it starts.

How it ends is up to you.

Resources

General Resources

CONSUMER REPORTS
The venerable—and trustworthy—Consumer Reports weighs in with its picks for the greenest products on the planet. Consistently updated. Subscribe for free.
www.greenerchoices.org

CO-OP AMERICA
Economic Action for a Just Planet
Responsible Shopper Program
1612 K Street N.W., Suite 600
Washington, DC 20006
Phone: 800.584.7336
www.coopamerica.org

WASHINGTON TOXICS COALITION
4649 Sunnyside N., Suite 540
Seattle, WA 98103
Phone: 206.632.1545
www.watoxics.org

SIERRA CLUB
85 Second Street, 2nd Floor
San Francisco, CA 94105
Phone: 415.977.5500
408 C. Street, N.E.
Washington, DC 20002
Phone: 202.547.1141
www.sierraclub.org

ENVIRONMENTAL DEFENSE
257 Park Avenue South
New York, NY 10010
Phone: 800.684.1322 or
    212.505.2100
Email: members@
    environmentaldefense.org
www.environmentaldefense.org

ENVIRONMENTAL WORKING GROUP
Washington, DC Headquarters
1436 U Street N.W., Suite 100
Washington, DC 20009
Phone: 202.667.6982
Fax: 202.232.2592
California Office
1904 Franklin #703
Oakland, CA 94612
Phone: 510.444.0973
Fax: 510.444.0982
www.ewg.org

E/THE ENVIRONMENTAL MAGAZINE
28 Knight Street
Norwalk, CT 06851
Phone: 203.854.5559
Fax: 203.866.0602
Email: info@emagazine.com
www.emagazine.com

PLENTY MAGAZINE
250 West 49th Street, Suite 403
New York, NY 10019
Phone: 212.757.3447
www.plentymag.com

THE GREEN GUIDE
c/o National Geographic
432 W. 45th St.
New York, NY 10036
Phone: 800.NGS.LINE
www.thegreenguide.com

IDEAL BITE: FREE DAILY TIPS ON GREENER LIVING
www.idealbite.com

GRIST: FREE ENVIRONMENTAL NEWS WITH A SENSE OF HUMOR
www.grist.org

NATURAL RESOURCES DEFENSE COUNCIL
40 West 20th Street
New York, NY 10011
Phone: 212.727.2700
Fax: 212.727.1773
Email: nrdcinfo@nrdc.org
www.nrdc.org

DAVID SUZUKI FOUNDATION
2211 West 4th Ave., Suite 219
Vancouver, BC V6K 4S2
Phone: 604.732.4228
www.davidsuzuki.org

TREEHUGGER
Tips, reviews, blog, and more.
www.treehugger.com
www.hugs.com

UNION OF CONCERNED SCIENTISTS
The nation's leading science-based nonprofit offering info on everything from greener cars to nuclear terrorism, invasive species to the basics of renewable energy.
National Headquarters
2 Brattle Square
Cambridge, MA 02238-9105
Phone: 617.547.5552
www.ucsusa.org

WORLD CHANGING
A site (and book) offering tools, ideas, and articles for building a greener future.
www.worldchanging.com

Great Green Goods
A shopping blog showcasing
eco-friendly products.
www.greatgreengoods.com

Green Drinks
Find a social group in your city that
shares your eco-sensibility.
www.greendrinks.org

1. Speaking Personally . . .

Cosmetics

The Campaign for Safe Cosmetics
Email: info@safecosmetics.org
www.safecosmetics.org

Cosmetic Ingredient Review
1101 17th Street N.W., Suite 412
Washington DC 20036-4702
Phone: 202.331.0651
Fax: 202.331.0088
Email: cirinfo@cir-safety.org
www.cir-safety.org

Women's Environmental Network
4 Pinchin Street
London, E1
P.O. Box 30626
London E1 1TZ
Phone: +44 (0)20.7481.9004
Fax: +44 (0)20.7481.9144
Email: info@wen.org.uk
www.wen.org.uk

Aubrey Organics, Inc.
4419 N. Manhattan Ave.
Tampa, FL 33614
Phone: 800.282.7394 or
    813.877.4186
Fax: 813.876.8166
www.aubrey-organics.com

Avalon Natural Products
1105 Industrial Ave.
Petaluma, CA 94952

Phone: 800.227.5120
Fax: 707.347.1247
www.avalonnaturalproducts.com

Aveda
Parent company: Estée Lauder
Phone: 866.823.1425
www.aveda.com
Storefinder (all countries):
http://www.aveda.com/templates/
    door/locator.tmpl

Burt's Bees
http://www.burtsbees.com

Dr. Bronner's Magic Soaps
P.O. Box 28
Escondido, CA 92033
Phone: 877.786.3649 or
    760.743.2211
Fax: 760.745.6675
Email: customers@drbronner.com
www.drbronner.com/index.html

Dr. Hauschka Skin Care, Inc.
59 North Street
Hatfield, MA 01038
Customer Service: 800.247.9907
www.drhauschka.com

Ecco Bella
50 Church Street, Suite 108
Montclair, NJ 07042
Phone orders: 877.696.2220 ext 19
Customer service: 877.696.2220
    ext 10
Fax: 973.655.9601
Email: service@eccobella.com
www.eccobella.com

Jason Cosmetics
Phone: 1.877.JEVELLE
www.jasoncosmetics.com

Kiss My Face
P.O. Box 224
144 Main Street
Gardiner, NY 12525-0224
Phone: 800.262.KISS

Fax: 845.255.4312
www.kissmyface.com

Lavera Skin Care North America
161 Homer Avenue
Palo Alto, CA 94301
Phone: 877.528.3727
Fax: 877.298.4012
Email: info@lavera-usa.com
www.lavera-usa.com

Peacekeeper
50 Lexington Avenue, #22G
New York, NY 10010
Phone: 866.732.2336
Email: info@iamapeacekeeper.com
www.iamapeacekeeper.com

Suki Pure Skin Care
99 Industrial Drive
Northampton, MA 01060
Phone: 888.858.7854 or
    413.584.7854
Fax: 413.584.1171
Email: info@sukipure.com
www.sukisnaturals.com

Tom's of Maine
302 Lafayette Center
Kennebunk, ME 04043
Phone: 800.367.8667 or
    207-985-2944
Fax: 207.985.2196
http://tomsofmaine.com

Tween Beauty
P.O. Box 688
Fairfax, CA 94978
Phone: 866.489.3367 or
    415.457.3176
Email: info@tweenbeauty.com
www.tweenbeauty.com
Parent site: www.tweenbeauty.
    com/Adult/index.asp
Tween site: www.tweenbeauty.
    com/Youth/index.asp

Feminine Hygiene

GladRags Menstrual Alternatives
P.O. Box 12648
Portland, OR 97212
Phone: 800.799.4523 or
  503.546.5696
Email: info@gladrags.com
www.gladrags.com

Lunapads International Products Ltd.
207 West 6th Avenue
Vancouver BC V5Y 1K7
Canada
Phone: 604.681.9953
Orders: 888.590.2299
Fax: 601.681.9904
Email: info@lunapads.com
www.lunapads.com

Sex Toys

Smitten Kitten
3008 Lyndale Avenue South,
  Suite 202
Minneapolis, MN 55408
Phone: 888.751.0523 or
  612.721.6088
Email: info@smittenkittenonline.
  com
www.smittenkittenonline.com/
  index.cfm

2. Eco-Chic

Clothing

Co-op America Foundation, Inc.
1612 K Street N.W., Suite 600
Washington DC 20006
Phone: 800.584.7336
www.coopamerica.org/programs/rs
www.sweatshops.org

No Sweat Apparel
Phone: 877.99B.STAR
www.nosweatapparel.com

TransFair usa
Audits transactions to ensure fair
trade.
www.transfairusa.org

The Fair Trade Federation
www.fairtradefederation.org

OshKosh B'Gosh, Inc.
112 Otter Avenue
Oshkosh, Wisconsin 54901
Phone: 800.282.4674
Fax: 920.231.8621
Email: consumerbgosh@carters.
  com
www.oshkoshbgosh.com

Hip & Zen
379 Marin Avenue
  Mill Valley, CA 94941
Phone: 888.447.6936 (USA) or
  415.383.2577 (International)
Fax: 415.381.6935
Email customer service:
  customerserv@hipandzen.com
www.hipandzen.com

American Apparel
Phone orders (USA): 888.747.0070
Hours: 11:30am – 8pm ET
Phone orders (Canada):
  866.446.0963
www.americanapparel.net

Patagonia
8550 White Fir Street
P.O. Box 32050
Reno, NV 89523-2050
Phone: 800.638.6464
Fax: 800.543.5522
www.patagonia.com

Timberland
Online catalogue: www.timberland.
  com/ecatalog/index.jsp?
  clickid=mainhome_img
Email: www.timberland.com/help
  desk/index.jsp?display=store&
  subdisplay=contact
www.timberland.com

Levi's® Brand
1155 Battery Street
San Francisco, CA 94111
Phone (USA): 800.872.5384
Phone (Canada): 888.501.5384
www.levistrauss.com

Loomstate
5 Crosby Street, Suite 3E
New York, NY 10013
Phone: 212.219.2300
Fax: 212.219.3555
www.loomstate.org

Giorgio Armani
www.giorgioarmani.com

Edun
www.edun.ie

Mountain Equipment Co-op
Vancouver, B.C.
Phone: 888.847.0770 or
  604.709.6241
www.mec.ca/splash.jsp

Ecoganik
www.ecoganik.com

GreenKnickers
51 St Julians Farm Road
London SE27 0RJ
Email: questions@greenknickers.
  org; sales@greenknickers.org
www.greenknickers.org

Maggie's Functional Organics
306 W. Cross Street
Ypsilanti, MI 48197
Phone: 800.609.8593 or
  734.482.4000
Fax: 734.482.4175
Email: maggies@organicclothes.com
www.organicclothes.com

New Balance
Email: www.newbalance.com/
  talktous/emailus.html
www.newbalance.com

REEBOK
www.reebok.com/useng/default.htm

GREENLOOP
1785 Willamette Falls Drive
West Linn, OR 97068
Phone: 866.898.5483 or
   503.656.5483
Fax: 866.781.8251
www.thegreenloop.com

VY & ELLE
299 South Park Avenue
Tucson, AZ 85719
Phone: 888.285.4367 or
   520.623.9600
Fax: 520.623.5494
www.vyandelle.com

SWAP-O-RAMA-RAMA
Info requests:
   wendy@gaiatreehouse.com
www.swaporamarama.org

ENVIRONMENTAL LABELS

NEW AMERICAN DREAM
www.newdream.org/consumer/
   labels.html

BOYCOTT

ETHICAL CONSUMER
www.ethicalconsumer.org

CONFLICT DIAMONDS

KIMBERLEY PROCESS
www.kimberleyprocess.com

AMNESTY INTERNATIONAL
www.amnestyusa.org/diamonds

OXFAM
www.oxfamamerica.org/art5097.
   html

UNITED NATIONS
www.un.org/peace/africa/
   Diamond.html

3. Food for Thought

ORGANIC CONSUMERS ASSOCIATION
This is one great site—the brain-child of Ronnie Cummins, who's smart, funny, and knows how to mobilize people to action. Log on for information on all things organic and environmental: children's health, factory farming issues, genetic engineering, fair trade, and many more. You can also partici-pate in a number of campaigns that are effective at getting the attention of politicians and policy makers. www.organicconsumers.org.

EATWILD
Site for info on grass-fed meat and dairy.
www.eatwild.com

ENVIRONMENTAL WORKING GROUP'S FOOD SITE
www.foodnews.org

THE FUTURE OF FOOD
Site and DVD on genetically modified food
www.futureoffood.com

Shop online for local food:
www.greenleafmarket.com

Tenets for fish eating:
www.environmentaldefense.
org/article.cfm?contentid=3339

4. Curbing Pint-Sized Consumers

HEALTHY CHILD HEALTHY WORLD
Creating healthy environments for children—food, baby care, nontoxic products, and more.
www.healthychild.org

CENTER FOR HEALTH, ENVIRONMENT AND JUSTICE
Find out about PVC, healthy schools, and more.
www.chej.org

EARTH MAMA GOODS
P. O. Box 493
Williams, Oregon 97544
Email: mail@earthmamagoods.com
www.earthmamagoods.com

WELEDA AG
Dychweg 14
CH-4144 Arlesheim
Switzerland
Tel: +41 61 705 21 21
Fax: +41 61 705 23 10
Email: dialog@weleda.ch
http://www.weleda.ch/
   (Swiss-German)

WHOLE FOODS MARKET, INC.
550 Bowie Street
Austin, TX 78703-4677
Phone: 512.477.4455
Voicemail: 512.477.5566
Fax: 512.482.7000
www.wholefoodsmarket.com

WILD OATS MARKETS, INC.
3375 Mitchell Lane
Boulder, CO 80301
www.wildoats.com

TUSHIES
www.tushies.com

SEVENTH GENERATION, INC.
60 Lake Street
Burlington, VT 05401-5218
Phone: 800.456.1191 or
   802.658.3773
Fax: 802.658.1771
www.seventhgeneration.com

NEW AMERICAN DREAM
Download "Tips for Parenting in a Commercial Culture": www.newdream.org/cnad/user/download.php

ORGANIC CONSUMERS ASSOCIATIONS APPETITE FOR A CHANGE CAMPAIGN

Focuses on children's environmental health, from toxins in toys to pesticides in schools to eliminating junk food to . . . just check it out.
www.organicconsumers.org/afc.cfm

NURSERY DÉCOR

www.greenhomeguide.com/index.php/knowhow/entry/795/C223

GREEN TOYS

www.katescaringgifts.com/pages/product/kids/kids.html
www.worldwidechild.com
www.naturenode.com/shop/children.html
www.greenhome.com/products/kids/toys

GREEN SCHOOL GEAR

A site that sells exclusively eco-friendly stuff: www.greenearthofficesupply.com,

www.containerstore.com

REPORTS ABOUT TOYS

GREENPEACE TOY REPORT CARD

www.greenpeace.org/usa/news/2003-toy-report-card

US PUBLIC INTEREST RESEARCH GROUP'S ANNUAL TROUBLE IN TOYLAND REPORT (NOV. 2005)

http://toysafety.net/toysafety.asp?id2=20594
Send a letter (thanks to PIRG) regarding toxins in toys:
http://toysafety.net/toysafety.asp?id=86&id3=toysafety2002&

MARKETING TO KIDS

www.commercialexploitation.org
www.commercialfreechildhood.org/contactus.htm
www.commercialalert.org
www.media-awareness.ca/english/parents/marketing/issues_kids_marketing.cfm

BABY FURNITURE

Heart of Vermont (catalog)
Phone: 800.639.4123
www.heartofvermont.com
The Natural Bedroom
  Phone: 800.639.4123
www.pristineplanet.com
www.naturepedic.com/research/fiveproblems
www.nontoxic.com

5. Clean Living

CLEANING PRODUCTS

METHOD

Widely available at retail stores such as Lowes, Target, and Longs Drugs.
www.methodhome.com

SEVENTH GENERATION

Available at Whole Foods, Ralph's grocery stores, and other locations.
www.seventhgeneration.com

ECOVER

Available at Whole Foods, Wild Oats, and other natural food stores.
www.ecover.com

MRS. MEYER'S

Find Mrs. Meyer's products at natural food or organic grocery stores.
www.mrsmeyers.com

EARTH FRIENDLY PRODUCTS

www.ecos.com

MOUNTAIN GREEN

www.mtngreen.com

BI-O-KLEEN

www.naturallysafecleaning.com

6. Home, Sweet Home

GENERAL

www.ecochoices.com
www.greenhome.com
www.healthyhome.com
www.gaiam.com

ENVIRONMENTAL HOME CENTER

4121 1st Avenue South
Seattle, WA 98134
Phone: 800.281.9785 or
  206.682.7332
Email: customerservice@environmentalhomecenter.com
www.environmentalhomecenter.com

ENVIRONMENTAL BUILDING NEWS

www.buildinggreen.com

EPA'S RESPONSIBLE APPLIANCE DISPOSAL PROGRAM

www.epa.gov/ozone/snap/emissions/radp.html

GREEN PAINT DIRECTORY

www.greenhomeguide.com/index.php/product/C134

WALLPAPER

www.farrowandball.com

FSC WOOD

www.fscus.org

CARPET AND OTHER FLOORING

INTERFACE INC.

2859 Paces Ferry Road,
Suite 2000
Atlanta, GA 30339
Phone: 770.437.6800
www.interfaceinc.com

FLOR

Recycled modular tiles—the company will even take them back for recycling.
116 N. York Road, Suite 300
Elmhurst, IL 60126
Phone: 866.281.3567
www.florcatalog.com

HABITUS

166 East 108th Street
New York, NY 10029
Phone: 212.426.5500
www.habitusnyc.com

KRONOSWISS OF AMERICA LLC

7811 North Shepherd Road, Suite 115
Houston, TX 77088
Phone: 877.445.7680
www.kronoswissofamerica.com

CARPET AND RUG INSTITUTE'S GREEN LABEL PLUS CARPET TESTING PROGRAM

www.carpet-rug.com/drill_down_
2.cfm?page=8&sub=17

COUNTERTOPS

PAPERSTONE

(KlipTech Composites)
2999 John Stevens Way
Hoquiam, WA 98550
Phone: 360.538.9815
www.kliptech.com/paperstone.htm

ICESTONE

Brooklyn Navy Yard
63 Flushing Ave., Unit 283,
Building 12
Brooklyn, New York 11205
Phone: 718.624.4900
www.icestone.biz

7. Power to the People

HOME ENERGY AUDIT:

A do-it-yourself online home energy audit, the audit is designed to help consumers identify the best ways to conserve energy in their homes. Find resources that will help you implement an energy savings program that is specific to your home and addresses your particular needs. (Sponsored by the US Department of Energy (DOE) as part of the national ENERGY STAR Program. The Home Energy Saver was the first Internet-based tool for calculating energy use in residential buildings.)
http://hes.lbl.gov

Database of State Incentives for Renewable Energy: www.dsireusa.org

Alliance to Save Energy (info on energy-efficient mortgages): www.ase.org/section/_audience/consumers/refinanceremodel/refinancing

Weather stripping chart: www.eere.energy.gov (search for "weather stripping").

8. The Effortless Garden

PESTICIDE EDUCATION PROJECT (PESTed)

206 New Bern Place
Raleigh, NC 27601
Phone: 919.833.5333
Email: info@PESTed.org
www.pested.org

CANADIAN WILDLIFE FEDERATION

www.wildaboutgardening.org

WASHINGTON TOXICS COALITION

4649 Sunnyside N., Suite 540
Seattle, WA 98103
Phone: 206.632.1545
www.watoxics.org/homes-and-gardens/lawn-and-garden

Safe Substitutes for Pesticides in Home and Garden: http://es.epa.gov/techinfo/facts/safe-fs.html

9. Creating Good Car-ma

AMERICAN COUNCIL FOR AN ENERGY-EFFICIENT ECONOMY'S GREEN BOOK

www.greenercars.com/indexplus.html

CO-OP AMERICA

www.coopamerica.org/programs/greenenergy/whattoknow/greentrans/index.cfm

CLEAN CAR CAMPAIGN

A national coalition that includes state and national environmental organizations promoting a clean revolution in the automotive industry.
www.cleancarcampaign.org

SIERRA CLUB

Learn more about hybrids, check out their new mpg calculator, and find out how you can pressure the government to increase fuel efficiency standards.
www.sierraclub.org/global warming/cleancars/

UNION OF CONCERNED SCIENTISTS

www.ucsusa.org/clean_vehicles

ENVIRONMENTAL PROTECTION AGENCY GREEN VEHICLE GUIDE

Certification and Compliance Division
National Vehicle and Fuel-Emissions Laboratory
2000 Traverwood Drive
Ann Arbor, MI 48105
Phone: 734.214.4200
Email: greenvehicles@epamail.epa.gov
www.epa.gov/greenvehicle

THE CALIFORNIA CARS INITIATIVE

A nonprofit startup formed by entrepreneurs, engineers, environmentalists, and consumers to promote plug-in hybrids (PGEVs): www.calcars.org

NATURAL RESOURCES DEFENSE COUNCIL

40 West 20th Street
New York, NY 10011
Phone: 212.727.2700
www.nrdc.org/air/transportation/
   default.asp

Hybrid cars: www.hybridcars.com

Fuel economy/Hybrid tax credits:
   www.fueleconomy.gov

BIODIESEL

NATIONAL BIODIESEL BOARD

3337a Emerald Lane
P.O. Box 104898
Jefferson City, MO 65110-4898
Phone: 800.841.5849
www.biodiesel.org

THE GREASECAR VEGETABLE OIL CONVERSION SYSTEM

Converting your car to run on vegetable oil.
Phone: 413.529.0013
Email: info@greasecar.com
www.greasecar.com

Diesel cars that require no conversion to run on biodiesel: www.
   gotoreviews.com/archives/
   biodiesel/biodiesel-vehicles.
   html

Answers to questions on biodiesel:
   www.biodieselcommunity.org

Consumer Reports' Guide to Stretching Your Fuel Dollars: www.
   consumerreports.org/cro/cars/
   ratings/a-guide-to-stretching-
   your-fuel-dollars/index.htm

Where to fill up—social responsibility rankings for gas stations: www.
   betterworldhandbook.com/
   gasoline.html

10. Tales of Cats and Dogs

PET FINDER

www.petfinder.com

PETS 911

www.pets911.com

THE HUMANE SOCIETY OF THE UNITED STATES

www.hsus.org

PESTS

Great site, but you'll have to navigate the photos of pets in need of rescue to find info (click on "Robin's Tips"): www.paw-rescue.
   org/PAW/dog_tips.php

PET LITTER

SWHEAT SCOOP

Pet Care Systems
1421 Richwood Road
P.O. Box 1529
Detroit Lakes, MN 56502-1529
Phone: 800.SWHEATS or
   218.846.9610
http://swheatscoop.com

YESTERDAY'S NEWS

www.yesterdaysnews.com

11. Celebrations That Save the Earth

NEW AMERICAN DREAM

Simplify the Holidays.
www.newdream.org/holiday/tips.
   php

ONLINE CARBON OFFSETTING CALCULATORS

www.carbonneutral.com/calcula
   tors/index_shop_calculator.asp
www.climatecare.org/guardian/
www.carboncounter.org
www.americanforests.org/
   resources/ccc/
www.betterworldclub.com

Recommended Reading

Brower, Michael and Warren Leon. *The Consumer's Guide to Effective Environmental Choices: Practical Advice from The Union of Concerned Scientists.* New York: Three Rivers Press, 1999.

Editors of *E/The Environmental Magazine. Green Living: The E Magazine Handbook for Living Lightly on the Earth.* New York: Penguin Group, 2005.

Flannery, Tim. *The Weather Makers: How We are Changing the Climate and What It Means for Life on Earth.* Toronto: HarperCollins Publishers, 2005.

Homer-Dixon, Thomas. *The Upside of Down: Catastrophe, Creativity, and the Renewal of Civilization.* Toronto: Alfred A. Knopf Canada, 2006.

Imhoff, Daniel and Roberto Carra. *Paper or Plastic: Searching for Solutions to an Overpackaged World.* San Francisco: Sierra Club Books, 2005.

Kolbert, Elizabeth. *Field Notes from a Catastrophe.* London: Bloomsbury Publishing, 2006.

Monbiot, George. *Heat: How to Stop the Planet from Burning.* Toronto: Doubleday Canada, 2006.

Newman, Nell and Joseph D'Agnese. *The Newman's Own Organics Guide to a Good Life.* New York: Villard, 2003.

Reay, Dave. *Climate Change Begins at Home: Life on the Two-Way Street of Global Warming.* New York: Macmillan, 2005.

We Are What We Do Ltd. *Change the World for Ten Bucks: 50 Ways to Make a Difference.* Gabriola Island, British Columbia: New Society Publishers, 2005.

Wright, Ronald. *A Short History of Progress.* Toronto: House of Anansi Press, 2004.

Index

About the Author

Leslie Garrett is an author, national-award-winning journalist, and mother of three children who frequently send her to the mall in search of snow boots, underwear, or whatever else they've outgrown. Tired of coming home with stress headaches, she began researching how to shop with a social and environmental conscience. Convinced she wasn't alone in her desire to make smarter, more earth-friendly purchases, she developed "The Virtuous Consumer," a syndicated column that appears regularly in newspapers and magazines throughout North America. "The Virtuous Traveler," her column about socially and environmentally responsible travel choices, was a regular feature in the *Globe & Mail* and now appears regularly on the website of Peter Greenberg, NBC's travel editor.

These days you can find Leslie cycling with her kids, walking with her two dogs, or debating the merits of hybrids over biodiesel with her husband Daniel Kelly and searching futilely for a vehicle that will fit her family and her values.

Visit Leslie at www.virtuousconsumer.com to check out her blog and sign up for Virtuous Consumer updates.

 **New World Library**
14 Pamaron Way • Novato, California 94949

NEW WORLD LIBRARY is dedicated to publishing books and other media that inspire and challenge us to improve the quality of our lives and the world. Our products are available in bookstores everywhere. For our catalog, please contact:

New World Library
Phone: 415-884-2100 or 800-972-6657
Catalog requests: Ext. 50
Orders: Ext. 52
Fax: 415-884-2199
Email: escort@newworldlibrary.com

To subscribe to our electronic newsletter, visit
www.newworldlibrary.com